R. C. Shutt
M.C.I.O.B. B.A.

Economics for the construction industry

Second edition

Longman
Scientific &
Technical

Longman Scientific & Technical,
Longman Group UK Limited,
Longman House, Burnt Mill, Harlow,
Essex CM20 2JE, England
and Associated Companies throughout the world.

First published 1982
Second edition 1988
Second impression 1989
Third impression 1990
Fifth impression 1992

British Library Cataloguing in Publication Data

Shutt, R. C.
  Economics for the construction industry –
  2nd ed
  1. Construction industry
  I. Title
  330′.024624   HD9715.A2

ISBN 0-582-01973-7

Set in 10/11 Times Roman

Produced by Longman Singapore Publishers (Pte) Ltd.
Printed in Singapore.

Longman Technician Series

Construction and Civil Engineering

General Editor – Construction and Civil Engineering

C. R. Bassett
Formerly Principal Lecturer in the Department of Building and Surveying, Guildford County College of Technology

Books already published in this sector of the series:

Building organisations and procedures   *G. Forster*
Construction site studies – production, administration and personnel   *G. Forster*
Materials and structures   *R. Whitlow*
Construction technology Volume 1 Second edition   *R. Chudley*
Construction technology Volume 2 Second edition   *R. Chudley*
Construction technology Volume 3 Second edition   *R. Chudley*
Construction technology Volume 4 Second edition   *R. Chudley*
Building services and equipment Volume 1 Second edition   *F. Hall*
Building services and equipment Volume 2 Second edition   *F. Hall*
Building services and equipment Volume 3 Second edition   *F. Hall*
Site surveying and levelling Level 2   *H. Rawlinson*
Building finishes, fittings & domestic services
          Second edition   *R. Chudley*
Building site works, substructure and plant
          Second edition   *R. Chudley*
Building superstructure Second edition   *R. Chudley*

Contents

Chapter 12   The scale of production   **158**

Chapter 13   The location of industry   **166**

Chapter 14   Types of business enterprises and
their financing   **175**

Chapter 15   Government objectives and their
attainment   **191**

Chapter 16   Fiscal control in Britain   **199**

Acknowledgements

The author is grateful to the Controller of Her Majesty's Stationary Office, for permission to reproduce many of the statistics used in this text, from copies of *The Annual Abstract of Statistics, Housing and Construction Statistics 1987*, and *The U.K. National Accounts 1986*.

Thanks are also extended to all those who have in any way helped in the production of this publication.

Cover photograph by Richard Costain Construction Group

Introduction

This book was written to provide an easily read introductory reference work for construction students on economics units of HNC, HND, IQS and CIOB courses. Wherever possible the discussion is put into the context of the construction industry, and certain sections are solely concerned with this industry.

Economics can be said to be the satisfaction of wants by the allocation of scarce factors. It is however very difficult, due to the very nature of the subject, to offer a precise definition. Economics, as will be seen, can be applied to all levels, from an individual, through enterprise and government levels, right through to world economics, covering such aspects as scarce world resource allocation.

On an individual level, economic decisions are often accomplished fairly quickly. When national problems are considered however, the factors to be taken into account are often numerous, complex and inter-related. For these reasons, decisions at this level often come very slowly, and, as has often proved the case, the correct decisions are not made.

The solving of economic problems at the higher levels is not easy; if it was, countries would not face present problems.

A word of advice for the newcomer to the subject. When faced with the various laws and theories, always study the theory on its own first. It should then be applied to a controlled situation, in a similar manner to which a controlled scientific experiment is carried out. Only when it is thoroughly understood, should it be applied to a real situation where other laws may operate simultaneously.

Students should endeavour to increase their knowledge of the subject, by careful reading and application, not only from text books, but also from good daily newspapers and professional journals. The latter should give a feel for the complexity of real dynamic situations existing today.

It should be borne in mind, that economics is not a precise subject, like mathematics or structural engineering. It is a subject where various opinions have to be voiced and where constructive debate should be encouraged, to gain a full understanding of the topics covered.

To
MEAT 3

Chapter 1

The identification of economic resources

Economics is often divided into two parts: **Microeconomics**, which is concerned with the study of the consumer, households and firms; **Macroeconomics**, which is that part of economics concerned with national or international relationships.

Whatever area is studied, it will be seen that economics is concerned with the optimum allocation of scarce factors, to try to satisfy the wants of society, to the best advantage.

What is meant by factors? These are more usually known as factors of production, inputs, or production factors, and are necessary, whether one is producing potatoes, architect's drawings, or office blocks.

The classification of the inputs into the various categories is often very debatable, and economists' views vary in many instances. The following discussion, however, should give the student some idea of what economists mean by the various factors.

There are three factors that all economists agree are necessary for production, these are: Land, Labour and Capital. The fourth category which is regarded by some is the Entrepreneurial function.

Land

These are the natural resources, used in the production processes. Under this heading could be included such examples as:
(a) Land as it is known under the normal definition, e.g. farmland, woodland storage areas etc.

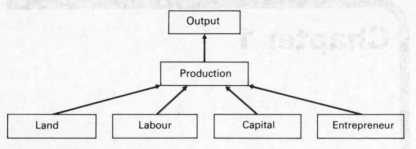

Fig. 1.1 Factors of production

(b) Water and water areas, e.g. river water, the use of the sea, rivers and canals.
(c) The naturally occurring resources, such as minerals, naturally occurring fuels and chemicals. Also organic natural resources, such as fish, timber, pigs, even crocodiles used for handbags, could be included.
(d) Land has also been defined as a gift of nature, and under this definition could be included wind and water power, and even solar power. The machinery used to extract this energy, however, is classed as capital.

It has often been said that land, as a factor of production, has a finite quantity, meaning that there is only a certain fixed amount available. Is this true? Consider three main examples of land:

(a) Land in the form of actual areas of ground or areas of water.
(b) Organic resources.
(c) Inorganic resources.

The first group, one might say, is obviously finite, as areas of land cannot be produced or expanded. Or can they?

There are land reclamation schemes, where areas are being recovered from the sea or fenland, or the filling in of worked out gravel pits, to form farmland. Looking at the other side of the question, there are many coastal regions where erosion of land is taking place, so reducing land areas.

So far, land has been considered as a factor of production, that may be used in the production process as farmland, or for the storing of products during manufacture. If the land is at present completely economically useless, is it still classed as a factor of production? Such an example might be desert land. Here again opinions differ, one could argue that it is useful for defence training, in that bombers must have somewhere to practise. It all depends upon the wants we wish to satisfy. If the requirement is for food then obviously, with present technology, many desert areas would not be economically viable for food production, and should not be regarded as a factor. If, however, by a massive irrigation scheme the desert could be made fertile, then the stock of agricultural land will have been increased.

It can be seen then that the quantity of land areas is not strictly fixed.

The second group, organic resources, is often called renewable resources. These are resources that are possible to replace by biological means, e.g. timber, animals, crops etc. Providing the demand for these resources does not cause extinction, or that pollution does not cause a breakdown in the reproductive cycles, then these resources can be reproduced, so are therefore not finite.

The third group, inorganic resources, also has another name, that of non-renewable resources. This must be qualified by stating that only relatively short-time periods are being considered here. This must be emphasised, for given enough time, say a few hundred million years, many minerals may be formed through geological processes. This does, however, depend upon many factors outside our scope.

The statement concerning the fixed quantity of land is more likely to apply to this third group than the other two.

Law of diminishing returns

A discussion on the properties of land areas is often used as a basis for a discussion on the law of diminishing returns.

This law states that successive application of the other inputs to a given amount of a fixed input, will yield proportionately less output after a certain point. Consider the following example.

A farmer owns a fixed area of land which he wants to make more productive. He does so by adding one extra man at a time, together with additional units of machinery and the necessary supervision. The results are shown in Table 1.1. From this table it can be seen that up to and including the employment of the sixth man the returns are increasing proportionately, and the greatest productivity is when six men are employed. By adding further labour the productivity drops.

Table 1.1 Output showing diminishing returns

Labourers	Total output (Tonnes)	Productivity output/man	
1	3	3	
2	7	3.5	
3	12	4	Increasing returns
4	18	4.5	
5	25	5	
6	31	5.2	
7	36	5.15	
8	40.5	5.1	Diminishing returns
9	45	5.0	
10	48	4.8	

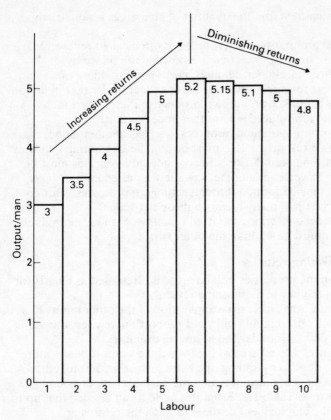

Fig. 1.2 Histogram showing diminishing returns

This is only to be expected, for if it was not the case, a farmer would be able to produce more and more from a given area, by just adding more of the other factors. This is obviously absurd, as the point will eventually be reached where men and machines could not move, due to overcrowding. It is often easier to grasp the situation by showing the productivity of Table 1.1 in the form of a histogram as in Fig. 1.2.

As another example, an owner of a joinery shop wants to increase productivity by putting more men, machines, materials and supervision into the existing premises. The same sort of results would probably occur. The figures would be different but again the situation would give increasing returns initially, followed by diminishing returns.

A nation's land resource

The type of land owned by a country very often dictates, to a certain extent, the type of industry and society that will exist. If the country has very fertile land, then farming may predominate. If it owns vast reserves of minerals, ores and fuels etc. then industry may be the major occupation. Following the argument one stage further, a farming region will have a fairly low population, whereas an industrial region will have a high one.

Labour

This is the easiest factor to define, as it is quite simply the skill and effort expended by manpower. Labour, as a factor of production means not only those people who actually help to produce commodities, such as bricklayers or farmworkers, but also those who help to supply a service, for example architects or teachers.

Different criteria affect labour at different levels of investigation.

Labour at enterprise or industry level

The contribution that labour makes at an enterprise or industry level depends upon two main considerations:

1. The relative mix of other factors: i.e. land, capital and entrepreneurial activities.

In a labour intensive situation, productivity per man will be much lower than in a capital intensive situation, assuming an output of similar products. In other words, many more men will need to be employed in a labour intensive situation, to equal the output of similar products in a capital intensive situation. The mix of labour and land can be discussed along the lines of Fig. 1.2 concerning increasing and decreasing returns. As was seen earlier, only so much labour can be put on a given area of land, before efficiency decreases.

The organisation of labour is a very important aspect of production, generally the better a workforce is organised and supervised, the more efficient it is; without the risk-taking element of production, however, there would be no demand for the labour factor.

2. Working conditions: The psychology of human relations and environment plays a great part these days in the personnel function of any enterprise. A worker in a satisfied frame of mind is more content, works better and is less likely to make mistakes. Hence an employer should consider:
(a) General working environment.
(b) Adequate remuneration.
(c) Job satisfaction.
(d) Sports and social facilities, and other benefits.
(e) Relationships with colleagues.

Labour at a national level

Here different points must be considered to determine labour's contribution to the national output.

The climate of the country: In a temperate zone, workmen may be able to work for long periods without extremes of temperature tiring them unduly. As an example, imagine the probable outputs from construction workers operating:
(a) In Britain.
(b) In Narvik in Norway in the Arctic Circle.
(c) In Kenya on the Equator.

The output from a similar labour force would obviously be different in the three countries, assuming all aspects other than temperature remain constant.

Education and training: These may dictate what type of work a nation's labour force is able to perform. In a nation where there are good educational facilities, the labour force will tend to aim for more complex, skilled jobs, leaving few people to do the more mundane, unskilled work. This tends to be the case in America or Europe. Eventually the situation may arise where the labourers get as much if not more than the foremen, because they are in greater demand.

At the other end of the scale, as was the case in certain less developed countries, labour consisted of virtually a labouring class, through lack of education and training. In these countries it was often necessary to import expert labour in many fields, to help in construction, and many other newly developing industries.

Living conditions and standards: Living conditions and a nation's standard of living are generally decided by the level of national output and growth, in comparison with other countries. Living conditions and standards of living are all relative, but a worker who knows he has a good standard of living feels more content than a worker who knows he hasn't. What benefits are distributed by the nation in the form of health and welfare, can increase output. It could be argued that high state benefits in the form of unemployment or social security sickness payments, may lead to lower output, due to scrounging off the State.

The population: The total population of a country will obviously affect the amount of production that can take place. This in turn affects GDP (gross domestic product) which in turn is likely to affect potential growth rates.

Age distribution: The age distribution of the population together with the total population will show more accurately a country's ability to produce goods. Consider Table 1.2. Countries A and B have the same total population. Country B however has 10 million more workers than country A. Clearly, on purely labour numbers, country B should have a larger output than A.

Table 1.2 Populations

Population/m.	Country A	Country B
Below working age	10	7
Workers	25	35
Retired and non-workers	15	8
Total	50	50

Table 1.3. Populations

	Country A	Country B
Working population	25 m.	35 m.
Total population	50 m.	50 m.
Land areas	Small	Large
Resources	Few	Many
Consumption	Small	Large

Optimum population: The optimum population for a nation is that population which when combined with the country's other factors of production yields the greatest output. This of course has to be related to age distribution of the population. If further information is added to Table 1.2 to give Table 1.3 it could be deduced that country B is underpopulated. By underpopulation is meant that there should be a larger population to obtain the most efficient production. Overpopulation obviously means the opposite.

Types of occupation

The working population of a nation will be distributed over a wide variety of occupations. The types of occupation will show not only the ability to produce certain goods, but also the state of development of the economy of the nation.

Highly developed nations tend to have a greater proportion of their labour force employed in supervisory, clerical and service jobs. An underdeveloped country will have the majority of its workers concerned with the physical production of goods.

Capital

Many words have a completely different meaning when used in economics to that normally understood to be meant in the common language. Capital is one such word, and here will be considered the economic definition as required for the factors of production. Later the accountant's definition will be considered.

Economic capital is often said to be wealth which is used to produce further wealth. A more easily understandable definition may be simply the plant, machinery, raw materials or any other commodity which helps to produce further goods or services. It must be emphasised that in economics it does not mean just money.

Some examples of capital might include: factory premises, sheet steel, plastics, lorries, office furniture, manufacturing plant.

In order to obtain a fixed output of production, it is necessary to maintain the capital items necessary to produce them. A major problem with many capital items is that they wear out or depreciate. Also, certain machines, particularly in the high technology field become obsolete. Even though they may function perfectly well, in the interests of efficiency they should be replaced with the next generation of machine, that works faster, or can produce more or better components. In the late 1970s and early 1980s computers were an ideal example of this last case.

Depreciation is generally fairly easy to understand when talking in terms of a depreciating asset. For instance after 3–5 years it is often cheaper to replace a lorry than to keep it and pay out high maintenance costs. A certain figure must be set aside each year to replace the item, not just to have available the amount of money the item cost initially.

Obsolescence, on the other hand, is often very difficult to allow for. Decisions as to when plant is likely to become obsolete are often just educated guesswork.

To maintain a standard of living it is necessary to set aside certain current production, to allow for depreciation of capital goods. If growth in living standards is aimed for, we need capital growth, not just replacement.

(a) To maintain living standards:

Production must equal **Consumption** + **Depreciation**

(b) To increase living standards:

Production must equal **Consumption** + **Depreciation** + **Capital growth**

This process of adding to capital is known as investment. Again, possibly a conflict of definition. A person might say 'I have just invested £10 000 in the bank'. In economic terms this money has not been invested by the individual. The bank, however, might give a loan of £10 000 to a contractor who uses the money to buy a new tower crane. This act would be understood to be economic investment. In economic theory, money by itself is useless. It cannot be used to produce anything. It is its function as a medium of exchange that enables capital equipment to be purchased, and so aid the production process.

Investment then can be said to be the act of increasing capital.

Consider the following situation.

A country has a fixed amount of production output, this output can be varied between goods which can be classed as investment – e.g. lorries, roads, factories, machine tools and office furniture etc. – or goods which can be classed as consumption, e.g. food, cigarettes, private cars, refrigerators and furniture for the home.

Why can furniture be included in both investment and consumption? The reason is this. An armchair if bought for a home would not aid production. The same chair if put into an office could be said to aid the production process albeit only in a minor way.

This splitting of the above country's production into either consumption or investment can best be seen by a production possibility curve which is also known as a transformation curve. (See Fig. 1.3.)

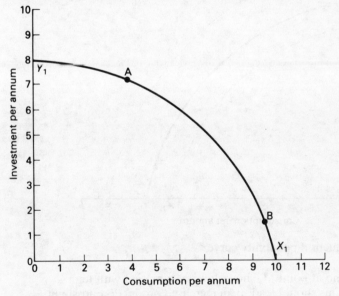

Fig. 1.3 Production possibility curve

A country can, in theory, choose its output to be anywhere on curve $X_1 Y_1$. However, it is more likely to be between points A and B. If the country chooses it to be between A and Y_1, then this would give a production of many investment goods but few consumption goods. If the choice lay between B and X_1, this would give mainly consumption goods, with few investments goods. Remember that for even a static standard of living, some production must be set aside in the form of

10

investment to allow for depreciation and obsolescence.

For a country to be able to increase its net investment, it must either be able to produce more, or consume less, or be given foreign aid with which to build new factories, irrigation schemes or whatever.

Figure 1.4 illustrates the outcome of two levels of consumption. The first, at point L gives high consumption, with low investment, so low in fact, that it probably would not cover depreciation. This being so, the production possibility curve may diminish to $X_2 Y_2$ in the next production period.

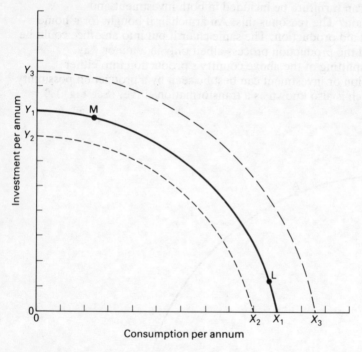

Fig. 1.4 Production possibility curve

The second at point M, shows low consumption with high investment. This should lead to an increased production possibility curve $X_3 Y_3$ in the coming production period.

Remember:

Net investment = Gross investment − Depreciation and obsolescence losses

If net investment is positive, the production possibility curve will expand. If it is negative, it will contract.

Figures 1.3 and 1.4 allow another concept to be examined, that of opportunity cost.

Opportunity cost

There are many ways of classifying costs. Accountants or estimators may talk of fixed or variable costs, or sometimes direct or indirect. costs. Politicians may talk of social costs, but the main concern of economists is opportunity cost.

Opportunity cost may be defined as the cost to the individual, enterprise or whatever, of the alternatives foregone, as a result of a decision to carry out a specific action. Consider the following example. An individual buys a pair of shoes at £40. The opportunity cost to that person, however, may be the new briefcase that he cannot now afford. In this example, the person had £40. He could either buy a pair of shoes, or a briefcase. He chose the shoes, so the cost to him is the briefcase.

Consider another example which is concerned with a time cost rather than a value cost. Imagine it is Saturday morning, and Mr Jones has two jobs that he could do. He could either wash the car, or dig the garden. If he was to wash the car, the opportunity cost to him would be the fact that he could not now dig the garden.

An example of production at national level was used earlier, where a country may decide to increase investment production, at the cost of consumption (Figs. 1.3 and 1.4). Here the opportunity cost of

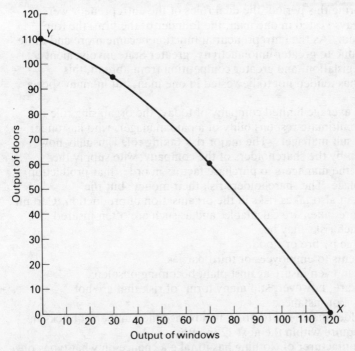

Fig. 1.5 Production possibility curve of joinery manufacture

increasing investment, is the lowering of consumption. A similar argument can be applied at enterprise level. (See Fig. 1.5.)

In this simplified example, a joinery manufacturer combines his factors of production, and can produce with them 110 doors or 120 windows, or a combination anywhere along line *XY*. If the manufacturer chooses to produce all doors, the opportunity cost would be the windows that could not now be produced.

The entrepreneurial function

This is the risk taking or organising element of production, and would include the following:
(a) Discovery, recognition and development of profit-making opportunities.
(b) The providing or acquiring of funds for an enterprise.
(c) The organising of the other factors in the optimum proportions in order to make a profit.
(d) The supervision of production.

In Britain during the late eighteenth to early twentieth century, this was the time for the great entrepreneurs. Men who recognised profit-making opportunities, and who organised the factors to gain that profit. During this period, the dual roles of the entrepreneur were nearly always vested in one man, the founder of the firm, the true entrepreneur. As the entrepreneurial function became more and more complex, due to greater union activity, greater State involvement through legislation, and greater competition from abroad, this dual role has tended not to be vested in one man, but in many specialists.

In the average limited company of today, the organising role is usually the ultimate responsibility of a paid manager, who has under him many sub-managers. The major risk taking role is usually now undertaken by the shareholders of the company, who supply the money for the managers to purchase factors in order that production can take place. The shareholders risk their money, but the management also takes risks in the organisation of production. Certain risks that are taken are calculable, and as such are often insured against. Such risks may be:
(a) Damage by fire or flood.
(b) Accidents to employees or third parties.
(c) One can even insure against plant becoming obsolete.

There are, however, still many forms of risk that are not calculable. For instance:
(a) A builder may need to order in advance the number of bricks he will require within the next 12 months.
(b) A manufacturer of clothing has to take a chance on what types of garment will be in fashion next season.

(c) Mining companies take great risks when deciding upon what areas to concentrate their exploration.

One key problem concerned with risk taking is that of time. A manager may make decisions today on the setting up or altering of a process on which goods may not be made for months, or even years. By the time the process is operational, the demand may have altered or even disappeared.

Profit is the payment for the taking of risks, hence the reason many companies put managers on profit-sharing schemes. It will generally be found, that where greater potential profits exist, greater risks will be taken to try to acquire these profits. Compare the three examples above in the context of their respective risks.

Table 1.4 Potential risks and profits.

	Risk	Potential profit
Builder (brick supplies)	Low	Low
Clothing Manufacturer (styles)	Medium	Medium
Mining company (exploration areas)	High	High

If the decisions made in the examples in Table 1.4 were correct, the potential profit may have been realised. If the wrong decisions were made, the following may happen.
(a) The builder orders too many bricks. He may have to stockpile them until they can be used. His only loss is the interest payable on the money used to buy the stockpiled bricks.
(b) The clothing manufacturer may have to sell off stock cheaply, so that he still gets some income.
(c) The mining company loses its exploration costs, which may be considerable, and gets no income from mineral finds.

Earlier profit was mentioned, but what is normal profit? It can be seen from the above that normal profit would have to take into account the risks involved. Normal profit therefore is that profit required to persuade entrepreneurs to continue in a given enterprise.

Questions

1 Take an average construction company, put down the four inputs, and list five or six items under each that could be used in the construction process.
2 From Fig. 1.3 over a period of several years, a country has had a consumption of 9 units. This has resulted in curve *XY* not fluctuating from the position shown. If due to government measures, consumption was reduced to 8 units, what is likely to happen in future production periods, if the government intervention is removed?

3 A quarry owner decides to increase output per machine. To do this he invests in more excavating machines, labour etc. Using Fig. 1.2 as a guide, determine at what point diminishing returns set in, using the figures below.

Number of machines	2	3	4	5	6	7
Total output/day in tonnes	70	110	155	195	220	237

4 From Fig. 1.5, what would be the opportunity cost of producing 60 doors and 70 windows.

5 As a construction student, why do you think it is necessary to study economics? Write a few brief paragraphs expressing your thoughts at this stage.

Chapter 2

The allocation of resources

So far we have considered the various inputs necessary for production. In this chapter we will see how these inputs are distributed according to the many requirements of society.

Why do they need to be distributed, one may ask, surely there are enough resources to go round?

In normal situations, all things are scarce, which in economics means supply is limited relative to demand. Most people would like to own a large house, a fast car or fine clothes etc. but cannot have them at the price they are willing to pay.

Scales of preference

Society, faced with this problem of scarcity, tries to satisfy rationally as many wants as it can within its means. Again, this idea can be interpreted at all levels of society, be it individual, family, business enterprise or nation.

For example, a consumer may have a list of wants such as the following:

(a) Television set.
(b) Replacement car.
(c) Lawn mower.
(d) Greenhouse.

If these items were in preference order, the consumer would gain the greatest satisfaction from the television. The next greatest satisfaction from exchanging his car for a new one, and so on. This list is particular to the person concerned, as another person's choices may be totally different. These lists are known as scales of preference, and it is the study of such lists which aids the formulation of demand statistics required by entrepreneurs.

Society in general then tries to distribute its resources in such a manner as to give the greatest degree of satisfaction within that society. This may be said to give the greatest standard of living within the prevailing circumstances.

Utility

The ability of a good to satisfy wants is known as its utility. It must be emphasised that in economics, utility does not mean how useful a good is. It was stated earlier that each person has his or her own scale of preference at any one time, therefore a television, for instance, is likely to have a different utility for different people.

From everyday situations it can be deduced, that the more a consumer has of a certain good, the slower will be the rate of increase of the total utility the good will give to the consumer. For example, the more ice creams a child eats in an afternoon, the less will be the satisfaction derived from eating the next.

Economists tend to use not total utility as a measure of satisfaction, but marginal utility. Marginal utility may be defined as the amount of satisfaction to be derived from the possession of an extra unit of the good.

Utility is best described with the aid of an example. Consider the following.

A contractor has tendered for several jobs, requiring many loads of bricks. He decides that because there is a brick shortage, that is expected to last for several months, he will buy up all the bricks he can. From the first load he buys he will derive a high satisfaction. The next load will give slightly less satisfaction and so on, as his worries, concerning the supply of bricks for the contracts, are reduced.

Finally the contractor may reach the point where he has no room left to stack any more bricks. At this point, the last load may have given him no extra satisfaction at all. (See Table 2.1.) There are no units of satisfaction therefore notional units have to be allocated when considering utility.

Table 2.1 can be graphically represented as Fig. 2.1.

From the above, we can see that the more we have of a particular good, the less satisfaction we get from owning more of it. To show the effect of marginal utility in the above example, the number of loads of bricks can be plotted against the marginal utility as in Fig. 2.2.

Table 2.1 Utility of loads of bricks.

Loads of bricks	Total utility	Marginal utility
0	0	0
1	50	50
2	90	40
3	120	30
4	140	20
5	140	0

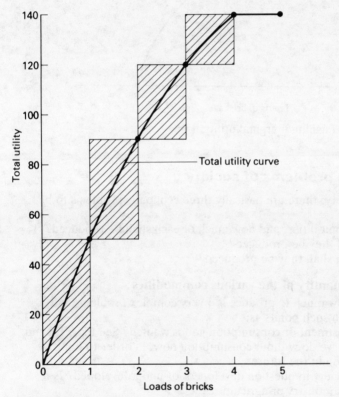

Fig. 2.1 Total utility

The effect of the law of diminishing marginal utility shows up clearly in Fig. 2.2. This law states: The more a single commodity is consumed during any period of time, the less satisfaction will be given from the consumption of additional units of it.

This law of diminishing marginal utility applies to all goods in all situations with very few exceptions.

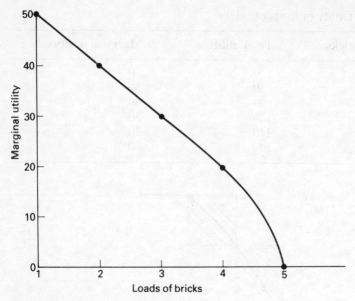

Fig. 2.2 Diminishing marginal utility

Economic problems of society

For any society, there are basically three economic problems to be
resolved:
1. What commodities, and how much of each shall be produced?
2. How shall they be produced?
3. For whom shall they be produced?

Type and quantity of the various commodities

What and how much to produce is a very complex problem, and
depends upon such points as:
(a) Are investment or consumption goods wanted? See Figs. 1.3 and
1.4. Can we do without consumption now, in order to improve
production in the future?
(b) Is the society in question developed, or underdeveloped? Is it
based on industry or agriculture?
(c) Is production for 'home' consumption, or are the goods to be
exported?
(d) What input factors are available? This point is closely linked with
point (b).
(e) What forms of goods should be produced? Should we produce
arms for defence, or food for consumption in the home market?
Food will satisfy individual wants. Defence will satisfy only a
collective want of society.

19

(f) Is there competition from abroad?
(g) What goverment policies are likely to affect the production of the goods considered?

How are the goods to be produced?

Here again, many questions have to be answered before a final decision can be arrived at. Such questions might be:
(a) Are labour intensive or capital intensive methods to be employed? This point brings into focus many ideas raised earlier under labour inputs.
(b) What are the levels of unemployment in an area?
(c) Is it worth investing heavily in plant for the production process? This is governed by whether the demand is large and stable.
(d) Is it to be large of small-scale production?
(e) What types of resources other than labour are available?
(f) What government policies are likely to affect production methods? For instance, what form of energy should be chosen for furnaces, heating, etc., should it be gas, electricity, oil or coal? We will see in later chapters, that all forms of energy are affected by some form of government control.

For whom are the goods to be produced?

Before goods can be produced, there have to be customers who may be persuaded to buy them.

The type of customer often has an influence on production decisions, particularly with relation to the size of likely demand, and whether or not the demand is stable. Such questions relating to this problem may be:
(a) Is demand from within a country, or from other countries?
(b) How are export markets likely to be affected by government decisions?
(c) Are the goods to be produced for government, business enterprise or individuals?
(d) How are the goods to be distributed amongst the consumers?
Many of the above points will be discussed in later sections.

Entrepreneurs battle over such decisions daily, and these decisions may be reached on any of the three problems in different ways.

In certain industries, entrepreneurs may become so skilled in forecasting the likely demand for a particular good, that they may take chances on decisions, being guided purely by instinct. The world of female fashions is based on the whims of fashionable ladies. No one knows for certain what style will be in or out of demand. Trends may suggest a certain direction, but no one is sure, and decisions on the styles to be produced often have to be based on intuition.

Types of economy

The three problems detailed above can all be affected by government action. In communist countries there is a great deal of State intervention in industry. There tends to be very little free enterprise, with most branches of industry being under State control. In such economies, a government can virtually dictate the type and quantity of goods to be produced, and also the methods of production to be used. The State also has a much greater say in who will consume the final goods.

This form of economy, controlled by central government planning is known as a command economy or planned economy.

An economy which is directly opposite in nature to the planned economy would be a free economy. A country operating a free economy would be following the *laissez-faire* policy of having no State interference in production or trading, and would allow the normal free enterprise system to work unhindered.

Most countries in the world today operate a mixed economy, that is, an economy that falls somewhere between the two extremes of planned and free economies. Britain today has a certain amount of government intervention in trade, which takes the form of taxes, control of interest rates, the issuing of grants and subsidies etc. One major area of government activity however is in international trade, as will be seen in later chapters. Trade in Britain still operates mainly along the lines of free enterprise, however.

It's doubtful whether a true free economy exists in a developed society, but it is in the context of just such a theoretical free economy that the **Price Mechanism** operates, to allocate the various resources available.

The price mechanism

In a free economy, there is by definition great freedom of choice. The owners of the factors of production are free to choose at what price and how much of their factors they will supply to production. The entrepreneur on the other hand, is free to choose what type and quantity of factors are needed to supply goods at a certain price. Meanwhile the consumers decide what type and quantity of goods they want at the prices they can pay. Consumers, however are also the owners of the factors of production, so the whole system tends to create a circular flow, as in Fig. 2.3.

Figure 2.3 can be divided into two interacting areas, the left side which is concerned with the supply and demand of factors, and the right side which is concerned with the supply and demand of produced goods.

Take for example a factory worker, who is an owner of the labour

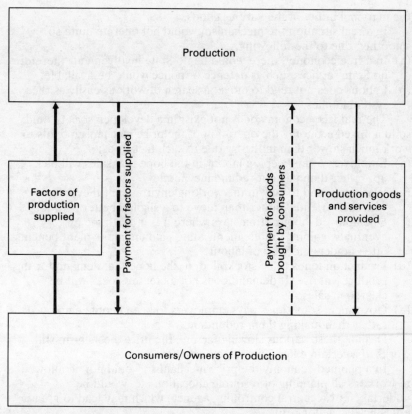

Fig. 2.3 The price mechanism in a free economy

factor. He obviously wants the greatest reward he can obtain for
supplying his labour, and so he finds a highly paid job. The high wages
paid would also attract many other workers, and so, to attract just the
right amount of labour, the entrepreneur may drop wages, as it would
be wasteful to be paying too high a wage. If he does not drop wages,
which would in practice be difficult to accomplish, he may decide to
increase output. Society may buy the increased production, if it is
wanted. If the increased supply of goods is not wanted, then the
entrepreneur will cut back on production, and the workforce will have
to find employment at other factories where goods are produced that
are wanted by society.

It can be seen then, that the price mechanism tends to allocate the
factors to the areas where they are most wanted, and where they will
give the most satisfaction to society.

The system tends to act as a delicate balance, weighing up the
needs of society against the requirements of production. These needs,
as was discussed earlier, are related to preference scales, and

the marginal utility of the various goods.

In a real situation the mechanism would not operate quite so smoothly, due to the following:

(a) In a free economy, there would be no State involvement, therefore no State services such as defence or police would be available.

(b) Labour does not tend to move in search of work as easily as the system implies.

The real free economy does not exist in a developed society, and so in a mixed economy the operation of the price mechanism tends to work much slower than in theory due to such factors as:

(a) Employers often keep on labour in the hope that sales will pick up, rather than pay out redundancy money.

(b) Workmen tend to stay in the working environment they know, with their friends, rather than move to a slightly better paid job.

(c) Unemployed labour often stays where it is in the hope of eventually gaining employment. State paid unemployment benefits often hinders mobility of labour.

(d) Production tends to be stockpiled, in the hope that demand for the product will rise. If demand does not increase, stocks will be cleared in sales.

(e) Goverment sometimes pays employers to keep people employed, rather than making them redundant.

Despite these various slowing factors, the price mechanism still works to a certain extent in a mixed economy.

In a planned economy the price mechanism would not be allowed to work, as all planning of resource allocation etc. would be undertaken by a central controlling agency, which may lead to greater efficiency in the long run.

The question must arise: what does society want? Does it want freedom of choice and a reasonably efficient economy. Or, does it want a dictatorial system where resources are allocated possibly more beneficially and goods distributed more fairly, but at the cost of society's freedom of choice.

Questions

1 Produce a scale of preference list, that government may draw up on behalf of the nation. (It will be interesting to compare your list with the discussion on government in later chapters.)

2 Discuss two situations where marginal utility might be a negative figure.

3 (a) A bottle of fresh water may have different utility to two different men travelling across the desert, why?

(b) Discuss why a candle may have different utility to the same person in different situations.

4 Would a society based on a command economy, or a free economy, tend to have a better army?

5 Why are there so few true entrepreneurs today?

Chapter 3

Cost benefit analysis

In the previous chapter, the allocation of resources was discussed. In a planned economy, decisions concerning problems of both industry and society are made purely by a central planning authority. In a mixed economy, however, government has to take a great deal more notice of what society wants. Decisions concerning commercial problems are settled by the entrepreneur and the price mechanism. Where society is affected by far reaching proposals, for example the siting of an airport, or the positioning of a new industrial estate, a means of scheme evaluation now gaining popularity is that of cost benefit analysis.

Educated society of today insists that much more thought is given to all possible alternative schemes before arriving at the best solution obtainable. It is only by evaluating all alternatives, that society in general can be best satisfied by choosing the proposal most suited to their needs.

In order to use cost benefit analysis there must be several alternative schemes to be considered. They need not all be new schemes, for instance it may be possible to evaluate an existing shopping area, and compare it with an evaluation of the same area modified to allow the inclusion of offices and dwelling units.

Why is cost benefit analysis needed? Surely the good old price mechanism can cope with all problems? It may be able to cope with the majority of situations, but what sort of society would it be, where everything was governed purely by profit. Students may feel that society is concerned purely with profit. Certainly it plays a large part, but without safeguards of many sorts, how could society cope with the following:

(a) Noise, dust and atmospheric pollution generally.
(b) Health.
(c) Ecological conservation.
(d) Parks and open spaces within urban areas.

It is by constant vigilance by the public, and in particular certain pressure groups, that the environment in which we live is preserved.

Industry provides many benefits; it provides employment for workers, who spend their money within the local community, thus benefiting many others. Industry also benefits the community by satisfying their wants with the goods produced. However, it should be remembered that a benefit to one part of society need not necessarily be a benefit to all of society, indeed by giving to some sectors of the community, other sectors must often incur costs. A factory may provide employment, but this factory may also cause pollution, and a devaluing of local house prices, due to noise, increased road transport, etc. Cost benefit analysis then, is concerned with evaluating schemes for the whole of society, not just for isolated sectors, and for it to be valid it is essential to evaluate the effects on all affected parties. In an analysis studying two or three alternatives, the researchers may initially be looking for the scheme giving the best net gain to society in general. However, a particular scheme giving the highest net gain may not be the one chosen, as the sectors of society who gain, and those who loose, may not be distributed fairly. Consider the following:

	Scheme A	Scheme B
Cost to wealthy	—	—
Benefit to wealthy	£1 m.	£0.4 m.
Cost to poor	£0.1 m.	—
Benefit to poor		£0.4 m.
Total benefit of	£0.9 m.	£0.8 m.

It is unlikely that society would allow scheme A to be adopted. Scheme B, although not quite so financially beneficial to society, is more evenly weighted to the affected sectors, and so is more likely to be carried out.

When carrying out evaluations, it may be that everyone is made better off by a particular scheme. Should this be the case, this is known as a pareto improvement as in scheme B.

In the majority of schemes, however, a potential pareto improvement is looked for. Here, certain sectors of the community benefit, and others lose. If the benefits are greater than the losses, then there is an overall social benefit, but not everyone gains personally.

A potential pareto improvement can be converted into a pareto improvement, providing costless transfers of goods and/or money can take place among the various sectors of society. Transfer payments are those made, other than in exchange for productive services. They may be gifts, but the most common form of transfer payments are those operated by government. Here payments are taken from certain sectors of the community in the form of income taxes etc., and are given to the poorer sectors in the form of grants, subsidies, supplementary benefit payments etc.

It can be seen then that when first looking at scheme A, it seems very unfair. If transfer payments operated, the final outcome may be as follows:

original benefit to wealthy £1 m. transfer via taxes   − £0.5
original cost to poor   £0.1 m. transfer via State aid +£0.5

final benefit to wealthy   £0.5 m.
                                            } pareto improvement
final benefit to poor   £0.4 m.

By the operation of transfer payments, a grossly unfair situation becomes workable.

Method of carrying out cost benefit analysis

1. Identification of the problem, and alternative solutions

This sometimes is more difficult than may first be imagined. It is necessary to evaluate not only any proposals put forward to date, including the existing scheme, but it may be necessary to question exactly what is trying to be accomplished, and are there any other methods which may fulfil the basic objective?

2. Identification of the sectors affected

The extent of detail to which an analysis goes, will depend upon the problem and what one hopes to prove with the analysis. In theory whatever project is carried out, it could be argued that every person in the country is affected indirectly, e.g.

(a) Government taxes which are paid by the majority of people are needed to pay for roadworks, schools, reservoirs etc., therefore these projects are a cost to all people. Conversely they are also benefits to all people.

(b) Industrial pollution is not selective about whom it affects. Dust or noxious gases may give coughs or sore eyes to whole areas of population depending upon the direction of the wind.

When carrying out cost benefit analysis, it is better to concentrate on the sectors directly involved with the scheme. Remember, it is necessary to try and keep the evaluation as accurate as possible, the further the investigation delves into the fringe areas, the more inaccuracies are likely to be included.

3. Identification of the costs and benefits

The different sectors of the community may each have different types of costs or benefits allocated to them. Some benefits may be easily spotted, others may be much more difficult to determine. Two simple examples follow.

Example 1: The building of a dam, and flooding of a Welsh valley to provide water for a Midlands town.

Benefits:
- To local residents, in the form of employment during construction of the dam.
- To the Midlands town, in the form of security of water supply.
- To sportsmen, in establishing a watersports facility possibly with fishing.

Costs:
- The obvious loss of livelihood and heritage of the farmers, whose land is flooded.
- Possible ecological losses due to the flooding of swamps in which nested rare birds etc.
- Financial cost of the scheme.

Example 2: The construction of a by-pass road around a narrowly streeted village.

Benefits:
- Safer, less congested travel for road users.
- Less noise and smoke for residents of the village.
- Possible increase in house values in the village.
- Safety, health and welfare of shoppers increased.

Costs:
- Financial cost of the scheme.
- Possible loss of existing homes by people in the path of the new road.
- Noise and pollution transferred from village to outer housing areas.
- Reduction in house values close to the new road.

The first example, that of flooding a valley, gives a good idea of one major difficulty in these evaluations. When do the costs and benefits accrue to the various sectors, and for how long do they operate? Employment would only be available to local labour while the dam was being constructed, so it is a very short-lived benefit. The providing of water for the Midlands may begin soon after the dam starts filling, and presumably will continue for many years. Fishing stocks may take many years to build up to a level that enables angling to be carried out.

4. Quantification of the costs and benefits

After identification of the relevant costs and benefits, the next stage is how to value them.

Financial costs or benefits are often fairly easy to calculate, but the correct costs or benefits must be used. For example, it may be stated that one benefit of a scheme is to reduce unemployment in an area. The benefit to the unemployed individual may be thought to be the value of the income he might now receive, or is it? Before gaining employment, the individual may have been receiving £50 per week unemployment benefit. If, when he obtains work, he now receives £80 per week, the benefit to him is £30 per week. Conversely if, as in Example 1 above, the by-pass has reduced the value of a house from £40 000 to £35 000 the cost to the houseowner is £5 000.

The benefit of £30 and the cost of £5 000 are known as compensating variations and it is on such variations that evaluation should be based.

A compensating variation may be defined as the sum of money which, if received or paid after the scheme has been put into operation, would make the individual no better, or worse off, than before the change. It is then the opportunity cost, or opportunity benefit of carrying out the scheme to the individual.

Government intervention in industry through subsidies, grants, taxes etc. makes it much more difficult to ascertain the true opportunity cost of factors or products. For example, a farmer may be encouraged to produce butter, and sell it cheaply, by giving him a government subsidy. If the cost of this butter entered into a cost benefit analysis, it would be difficult to set a price on the butter, as the costs are not related to a free market situation in which the price mechanism sets prices. The butter cost included in an evaluation may be the shop price, plus the subsidy paid to the farmer. This 'correcting' of prices to put them in line with the true opportunity cost of a free market situation is known as the setting of shadow prices.

The idea of shadow prices can be best demonstrated concerning a command economy. Imagine that a cost benefit analysis is to be carried out concerning a production or service industry in such an economy. Because no free market situation exists to automatically set prices of factors and products, how can such an analysis be valued, as the prices charged for products or services may bear no resemblance to the true production costs. It is in such situations that prices will have to be 'corrected' to try to acquire a realistic figure.

With costs or benefits other than financial, these are often much

more difficult to assess; indeed in some instances a quantitative
analysis is impossible and a qualitative approach has to be adopted.
Some examples of such problems are:

Example 3: A new road shortens the travelling time of 10 000
commuters, to and from their place of work. How is this measured? As
travelling time to and from work is not generally carried out in the
'company's time' it would not be right to charge the time saved at
the hourly work rate. So what rate is chosen? It is necessary to try to
determine a valuation of an individual's leisure time.
     Consider the following, which may be one solution:
The travelling habits of a large sample of a commuting community
travelling a similar distance, is analysed into the following:

	Time (hrs)	Cost (£)
By taxi	1	5
By train	1½	2
By bus	2	1.50

A particular individual may decide to travel by train, thus, to save ½
hour in leisure time he pays an extra 50p. From this it may be deduced
that he values his leisure time at £1 per hour. Alternatively, an
individual in a higher income bracket who may have very little leisure
time, might travel by taxi. Here, he is willing to pay an additonal £3
above the train fare to save ½ hour. His leisure time is then valued at
£6 per hour. Often, this degree of detail is not needed, and a time
saving can be shown as a benefit by using the term $(t+)$ or $(t+++)$.
Conversely a time cost would be shown as $(t-)$ or $(t--)$ etc.

Example 4: The new road in Example 3 may create a great deal of
localised traffic noise and pollution in the form of fumes, dust etc.
How is this cost to the individual houseowner valued? One method
often used, is to consider a similar scheme to that proposed, that has
already been carried out in a similar environment. The effect on
property values before and after the scheme is compared and this will
give a ratio that can be applied to property values in the present
scheme under consideration.

Example 5: This same new road may have to traverse a local beauty
spot. How is the loss to the community, of a pleasing natural landscape
that is now spoilt, to be valued? It is almost impossible to put a
monetary value to this cost. It is most important, however, that such
costs and or benefits are included in a cost benefit analysis, for the
main reason for carrying out such evaluations is to take into account

the effects on society in general. It was stated earlier that when a cost benefit analysis is undertaken it must compare alternative schemes. If the alternative to the road cutting through the middle of the beauty spot, is having the road skirt around the edge, then this second alternative is less of a cost when considering the landscape. It may be shown as an immeasurable, or intangible cost as follows:

Road A (through beauty spot) $(i---)$
Road B (around beauty spot) $(i-)$

Should this appear in a table, it can be seen at once that road A has a higher social cost than road B. This, however, is about as much as can be deduced, if accuracy is to be maintained. With this last example it is always necessary to sample public opinion, to arrive at some measure of value, in the form of numbers of pluses or minuses.

5. Summary and conclusions

When carrying out an analysis, it may take dozens of people many months to complete, including many meetings with thousands of people. The results may run into hundreds or thousands of pages. One extreme example is of a report concerning the path of an oil pipeline across Alaska. The report took two years to complete and resulted in 4 600 pages of script. It can be seen that it is essential to have the results summarised, so that the alternative schemes can be easily compared.

When the summary has been completed, conclusions can be drawn. The final decision may not always be the obvious one to the majority of people. When all the facts are presented, it is still often settled by the groups with the loudest voices, or those with the greatest influence. During a cost benefit analysis, and especially when decision time arrives, it is essential that the whole of society makes its views known, and helps to form a decision. If left purely to pressure groups, why bother with cost benefit analysis?

An example of a simple analysis followed through

The problem

Five years ago, an extensive site, including a large warehouse, came up for sale near a town centre. The local authority decided to buy it, as it was proposed at the time to redevelop that particular area and construct an area of open space. Since then, the open space proposal has been dropped, and the planning officer has been asked to prepare suggestions as to what should be done with the area, in order that the interests of the local community can be best served. As the position of the site is on the border of light industrial, and residential zoned areas, the uses of the area would be concentrated on these alternatives.

The present warehouse is rented out to a firm (XYZ Ltd) who employ 40 men on the site as storemen and drivers of delivery vehicles based at the warehouse. Only half of the floor area is at present utilised however.

The proposals
One of the proposals, Scheme A, is to leave the warehouse as it is. The main objection to this is that all the rest of the similar older buildings in this area have been demolished, and this particular warehouse, which is of brick, and five storeys in height is rather obtrusive.

Scheme B involves the demolition of the existing warehouse, and the erection of several smaller self-contained warehouse/factory units spread over the whole site.

Scheme C again involves the demolition of the existing warehouse, but in this case it is replaced with 80 maisonettes.

The sectors involved
(a) The local authority.
(b) The occupiers of the existing warehouse.
(c) The local inhabitants of the area.
(d) The ratepayers of the town and surrounding area.
(e) New occupiers of housing in the area.
(f) New occupiers of warehouse/factory units in the area.

There may very well be other sectors affected, for instance, there may be existing stocks of unlet or unsold warehouse/factory units and dwelling units in the town. The effect of more units being offered for rent may lead to a lowering of rents in an attempt to attract occupiers to the properties. It is necessary to restrict the evaluation to areas that are relevant, and to areas where a definite benefit or loss can be deduced.

The costs and benefits

1. The local authority
The local authority, here has a dual role; that of developer, and that of caretaker of the local environment.

As a developer, the local authority will have the normal construction and development costs, together with the benefits in the form of rents, rates, and because it is a local authority, any subsidies or grants paid by the government.

As the local authority has to answer to public opinion, two points should be borne in mind:
(a) Schemes should wherever possible be self-financing, as any deficit is ultimately made good by the ratepayers, or taxpayers.
(b) Many complaints have been received concerning the obtrusive

nature of the existing structure, and it would clearly give a much better impression of the town centre if Scheme B or C was carried out, as this would remove an unsightly building from an otherwise pleasant modern centre.

2. *The occupiers of the existing warehouse*

The local authority has made it clear that should they require it, XYZ Ltd can have an equivalent floor area of new warehousing space allocated to them, if Scheme B went ahead. At present, the firm's management is not committing itself as there is a rumour of rationalisation of the distribution network of the firm. It is therefore very difficult to know what costs or benefits may be allocated to XYZ Ltd as they are not sure of their future plans themselves.

3. *The local inhabitants of the area*

The existing site is clearly visible from many dwellings on a large housing site some little distance away. It would obviously be to their advantage to have the site tidied up.

A problem which has been increasing in the last nine months is that the site is not adequately fenced at present, and unlawful tipping has been taking place on the site. This not only adds to the unsightly appearance, but has led to occasional camping by tinkers, who sift through the deposited rubbish. The council is at present reluctant to erect a satisfactory fence, as the site is rather extensive, and they are awaiting the outcome of this investigation.

Other problems created by the state of the existing site are:
(a) Increase in vermin.
(b) Considerable risk of accidents to children playing on the site.

The local inhabitants would see a large benefit if Scheme B or C was adopted, there would still be a small benefit if Scheme A was adopted, as the council would carry out adequate fencing.

There are no direct costs to this sector.

4. *The ratepayers of the town and surrounding area*

For this sector strictly the financial aspects are considered; whether each scheme is financially viable or not will determine whether it is a cost or a benefit to the ratepayer.

5. *New occupiers of housing in the area*

If scheme C was carried out, this would provide an area of accommodation, closer to the town centre than any other. Many people would state that living in a town centre is a cost, however there are still many people requesting such accommodation, and there should be no problem in finding people who would willingly occupy such properties. It can be assumed that these people are only willing to occupy these dwellings because they see town centre accommodation as a benefit. A major benefit to the occupiers may be less travelling time to work.

The costs to the people in the maisonettes of Scheme C, are the costs of rent and rates, over and above similar properties in the more suburban areas.

6. *New occupiers of warehouse/factory units in the area*

This analysis does not go into enough detail concerning the exact amount of industrial accommodation already vacant in the area. It is known however, by the number of enquiries received by the local authority that there is a shortage of the type of accommodation under consideration in Scheme B. There will therefore be a benefit to this sector, should this scheme go ahead.

Quantification of the costs and benefits

1. *The local authority*

From Table 3.1 it can be seen that Scheme A has the least annual cost, of £66 993. The income, from rents, rates and subsidies is also the least, at £34 000. Scheme B shows the greatest annual cost at £216 591, but also the highest income at £217 000. Scheme C however, shows the greatest financial loss to the local authority. On strictly financial grounds, it would not be justified to use the site for housing. To achieve a break even situation with the housing scheme would require a yearly rental per dwelling of £1 590 against that estimated in the table of £1 092. It would not be practical to try to obtain such a high rental, as rentals for similar suburban properties are in the region of £900. From Table 3.1 it seems that Scheme B would be the most advantageous, especially as this gives a financial benefit to the local authority. It would also relieve the local authority of the problem of the unsightly warehouse, which would persist if Scheme A was adopted.

2. *The occupiers of the existing warehouse*

As was stated earlier, XYZ Ltd is unsure of its future needs regarding warehouse premises in this area. However if it is assumed that its business must continue as at present, then with Scheme B, the company would be moving into new modern premises in the existing location. This could be beneficial in many ways, such as a better working environment, a better image for the company, less problems with tinkers etc. These benefits are difficult to measure and may be classified as intangibles; this is shown as $(i+)$ in the tables. If Scheme C was carried out, and XYZ Ltd still needed premises, there would be a financial cost involved in moving the business to new premises to be found by the local authority. Intangibles may be a benefit or a cost, depending upon the premises found.

The annual cost in Table 3.1 is based on the annual repayments on a 60-year mortgage which is a normal loan period on local authority schemes.

The annual figure is found using the following formula:

$$A = \frac{PR^n(R-1)}{R^n - 1}$$

Table 3.1 Financial considerations

	Existing	**Scheme A**	**Scheme B**	**Scheme C**
Costs				
Site:				
(a) original site cost	500 000	500 000	500 000	500 000
(b) roadworks etc.	—	15 000	40 000	45 000
(c) demolition	—	—	25 000	25 000
Total land costs	£500 000	£515 000	£565 000	£570 000
Construction:				
(a) industrial units	—	—	1 100 000	—
(b) dwellings	—	—	—	800 000
Total construction costs	—	—	£1 100 000	£800 000
Total capital cost	£500 000	£515 000	£1 665 000	£1 370 000
Annual cost (p. 35)	£65 042	£66 993	£216 591	£178 216
Revenue				
Rent:				
(a) existing warehouse	30 000	30 000	—	—
(b) new industrial site	—	—	180 000	—
(c) new housing	—	—	—	87 360
Total rent income	£30 000	£30 000	£180 000	£87 360
Rates:				
Rate income	4 000	4 000	22 000	16 000
Central government subsidies	—	—	15 000	35 000
Total revenue p.a.	£34 000	£34 000	£217 000	£138 360
Local authority overall position p.a.	£−31 042	£−32 993	£+409	£−39 856

where A = annual repayment required to pay off capital and interest

$$R = 1 + \frac{r}{100}$$

r = rate per cent interest per annum (taken as 13%)
n = number of years

Scheme A: $\dfrac{515 \times 10^3 \times 1.13^{60} \times 0.13}{1.13^{60} - 1}$ = $\dfrac{515 \times 10^3 \times 1\,535 \times 0.13}{1\,535 - 1}$

$$= £66\,993$$

Scheme B: $\dfrac{1\,665 \times 10^3 \times 1\,535 \times 0.13}{1\,535 - 1}$ = £216\,591

Scheme C: $\dfrac{1370 \times 10^3 \times 1\,535 \times 0.13}{1\,535 - 1}$ = £178\,216

Existing scheme: $\dfrac{500 \times 10^3 \times 1\,535 \times 0.13}{1\,535 - 1}$ = £65\,042

---

3. The local inhabitants of the area

From an environment viewpoint, Scheme A clearly gives little benefit, except that the fencing will be carried out, and hopefully this will remove the problem of tipping, and tinkers. It is expected however that within the next few years the structure will deteriorate, unless major renovation work is carried out. The operation of Scheme A is therefore not likely to be a benefit or cost to the local inhabitants, considering the present situation. Scheme B obviously improves the area, but will still give an impression of an industrial environment. Scheme C then would give a small environment benefit $(i+)$.

In this study it was thought that road transport would stay about the same, whichever scheme was adopted, also, as there is only light industrial activity in the industrial schemes, little pollution would result. These and similar factors have therefore not been considered.

4. The ratepayers of the town and surrounding area

From Table 3.1, the most financially beneficial scheme is Scheme B. Should Scheme A or C be carried out, then the local authority would have to subsidise the scheme by increasing rates. Detailed calculations concerning the effect of the subsidies on existing rate demands have not been carried out at present, but can be indicated as follows:

Scheme A = $(m-)$
Scheme B = $(m+)$
Scheme C = $(m--)$

5. *The new occupiers of housing in the area*

Should Scheme A or B be carried out, then this would give no real
benefit or cost to occupiers of housing in the area. It could be
argued that there is an opportunity cost, in that the land is being
used for industry, at the cost of housing. It must be remembered,
however, that the schemes under consideration should be compared
throughout with the existing situation, to make this particular
analysis valid.

Should Scheme C be carried out then several benefits and costs
come to light. Financially, the cost is that of extra rent and rates
paid for town centre accommodation, compared to those paid for
suburban accommodation. There could be a benefit in the form of a
saving in travelling time, as people might live nearer their work; this
could be shown as $(t+)$.

It is assumed that people taking town centre accommodation,
do so because they feel it a benefit to live there, rather than in a
suburb; this could be shown as $(i+)$.

6. *New occupiers of warehouse/factory units in the area*

This sector would derive a benefit from Scheme B, as the new firms
concerned could be expected to show increased profits in the long
term. Again, detailed figures would be difficult to calculate and
could be highly inaccurate. This is classed as a benefit in general, as
it might cover financial aspects, time, and intangible factors.

Scheme C, when compared to the existing situation clearly
shows an opportunity cost, as there is a loss of industrial area should
houses be constructed on the site. This is shown as a general cost, as
again many factors might be considered.

Scheme A does not affect this sector one way or the other, as
the accommodation stays as existing.

Conclusion

The student should bear in mind that this study is only intended to
give an introduction to the methods used during cost benefit
analysis. This particular simplified example is only one way of
carrying out an evaluation. Other people might have chosen slightly
different affected sectors, and costs and benefits, but their final
conclusions would probably have been the same.

In cost benefit analysis, where a definite cost or benefit can be
recognised, but where it is impossible to allocate a value in the form
of an actual figure, the following abbreviations are often used.

M indicates Money
P indicates Physical
T indicates Time   Used where there is a once and
I indicates Intangibles   for all, cost or benefit.
N indicates Number

m indicates Money
p indicates Physical
t indicates Time
i indicates Intangibles
n indicates Number

} Used where there is an annual flow of cost or benefit.

To determine whether each factor is a cost or benefit, a plus (+) or a minus (–) is put after the indicating letter. The greater the number of pluses, the greater the benefit. The greater the number of minuses, the greater the cost.

In a real situation, costs would have been investigated much more deeply, but it is doubtful whether it would have changed the order of preference for each sector. It is the final allocation of weightings to the various sectors that causes the most heated discussions in public debates, when conclusions are trying to be formed by the various parties concerned. Is it right to say that the ratepayers should have a bigger say than the local authority, or *vice versa*? Tables 3.2, 3.3, and 3.4 set out the benefits and costs for Schemes A, B, and C, respectively. Table 3.5 summarises the costs and benefits to give an overall picture on one sheet. From the summary it would seem that the first choice would be Scheme B, the second choice Scheme A, and the third choice Scheme C.

Table 3.2 Scheme A, compared to existing.

	Costs	Benefits	Balance
Local authority	interest charges on £15 000 = £2 000 p.a.	$(i+)$ due to fencing	$(i+)$ – £2 000
Existing occupiers	—	$(i+)$ due to fencing	$(i+)$
Local inhabitants	—	—	—
Ratepayers	Financial cost (m –)	—	(m–)
Occupiers of housing	—	—	—
Occupiers of warehouses	—	—	—
Nation	—	—	—

Table 3.3 Scheme B, compared to existing.

	Costs	Benefits	Balance
Local authority	—	Financial improvement on existing £31 451 p.a. environment $(i+)$	+£31 451 $(i+)$
Existing occupiers	—	environment $(i+)$	$(i+)$
Local inhabitants	—	environment $(i+)$	$(i+)$
Ratepayers	—	Financial gain $(m+)$	$(m+)$
Occupiers of housing	—	—	—
Occupiers of warehousing	—	Benefit	Benefit
Nation	Subsidies £15 000	—	– £15 000

Table 3.4 Scheme C, Compared to existing

	Costs	Benefits	Balance
Local authority	Financial cost £8 856 p.a.	Environmental $(i+)$	– £8 856 $(i+)$
Existing occupiers	Cost	—	Cost
Local inhabitants	—	Environment $(i++)$	$(i++)$
Ratepayers	Financial cost $(m--)$	—	$(m--)$
Occupiers of housing	Financial cost $(m-)$	Time $(t+)$ Environment $(i+)$	$(t+)$ $(i+)$ $(m-)$
Occupiers of warehouses	Cost	—	Cost
Nation	Subsidies £35 000	—	– £35 000

Table 3.5 Summary

	Scheme A	Scheme B	Scheme C	Order of preference		
				A	B	C
Local authority	− £1 951 p.a. (*i*+)	+£31 451 p.a. (*i*+)	− £8 814 p.a. (*i*+)	2	1	3
Existing occupiers	(*i*+)	(*i*+)	Cost	1	1	3
Local inhabitants	—	(*i*+)	(*i*++)	3	2	1
Ratepayers	(*m*−)	(*m*+)	(*m*−−)	2	1	3
Occupiers of housing	—	—	(*t*+) (*i*+) (*m*−)	2	2	1
Occupiers of warehouses	—	Benefit	Cost	2	1	3
Nation	—	−£15 000	35 000	1	2	3
Totals, allowing equal weighting to each sector				13	10	17
Taking the lowest total to be the first choice, this gives an overall order of preference of				2	1	3

Questions

For this exercise, students should work in two's or three's, in order that there should be some difference of opinion on values etc. This tends to give a more realistic impression of a practical situation.

The problem

The town of Hightown has for some years had a problem of increasing heavy traffic, going from a growing industrial complex north of the town down to the docks in the south. The main traffic flow travels along North Street (see Fig 3.1) and has been causing many problems of noise, fumes, congestion and accidents. It is believed, that as a result of a fatal accident, greater pressure is being brought to bear on the authorities to construct a by-pass around the town.

40

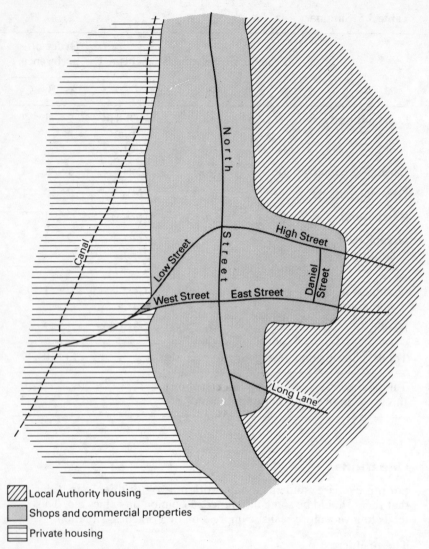

Local Authority housing
Shops and commercial properties
Private housing

Fig. 3.1 Hightown as existing

Scheme A (see Fig. 3.2): proposes a by-pass to the east and
incorporates a new roundabout at point (X), sweeping round and
along the line of the existing Daniel Street, before continuing on to
a new roundabout at point (Y). It will be necessary to demolish 135
local authority dwellings, and 30 shops, on the east side of Daniel
Street. A new flyover will also have to be constructed over Long
Lane.

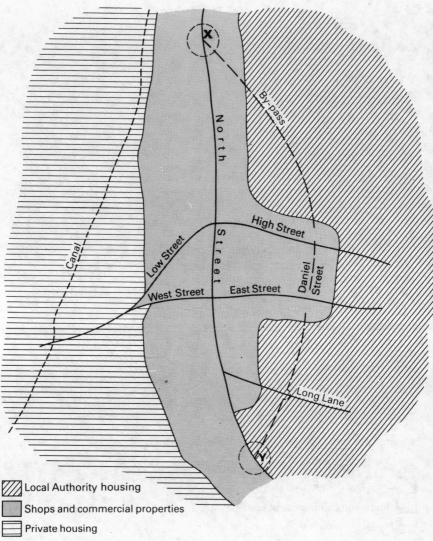

Fig. 3.2 Hightown scheme A

Scheme B (see Fig. 3.3): if carried out will take the by-pass to the west. It will again require a new roundabout at (X), will sweep round to a new roundabout at (Z), on West Street, and on to roundabout (Y). Due to a canal, it will be necessary to elevate a half mile section of roadway at point (Q). This scheme will involve the demolition of 110 private dwellings.

Prepare a cost benefit analysis, comparing the two schemes with

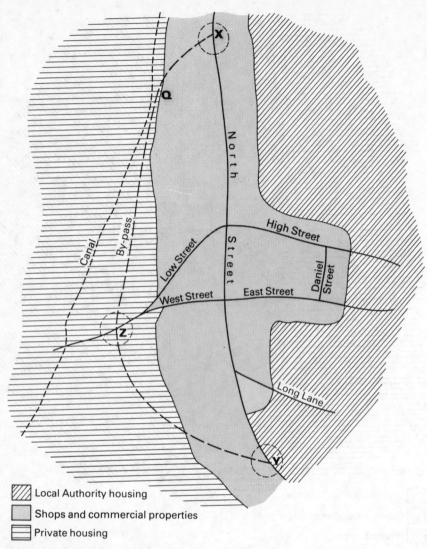

Local Authority housing

Shops and commercial properties

Private housing

Fig. 3.3 Hightown scheme B

the existing situation. Remember, when deciding upon the
weightings, if this method is used, that the schemes are proposed to
improve the safety, health and well-being of the community of
Hightown; financial cost may be of secondary importance.

Chapter 4

Economic growth

What is meant by economic growth? Economists may talk of increases in Gross Domestic Product (GDP), or of the increase in consumption per head, but both these indicators may imply one thing, the increase in the standard of living of the population as a whole.

It should be remembered, that economic growth and increased living standards are not exactly synonymous. If one sector of society, say the entrepreneurs, increased their wealth, then there may be economic growth, but this does not necessarily ensure that the whole of society has a better standard of living.

How then can economic growth come about?

If societies are studied from primitive to modern times, there can be seen distinct stages or 'stepping stones' along the way, which aid growth:

(a) Primitive self-contained villages eventually exchange goods, which tends to lead to specialisation.
(b) Exchange leads to better communication and transport systems.
(c) Exchange of goods also tends to lead to a system of barter and eventually necessitates a medium of exchange.
(d) Gradual growth of towns and population causes greater demand for goods.
(e) Further specialisation and division of labour, sets the scene for mechanisation.
(f) Growth of industry under the capital intensive system.
(g) Large industrial production units seek more outlets abroad, to reap the benefits of large-scale production.

44

The development of society plays a large part in economic growth, but so also do other factors:

Capital investment: In Chapter 1, the argument was put forward of increasing capital investment at the expense of consumption goods. A country which has a relatively high standard of living and a well-developed industrial and commercial structure is better able to gear up for higher investment in capital, than a less developed, mainly agrarian society. Unless aid is given to the less developed countries, the gap between the living standards of the two types of society will widen.

A country's population: Its age range, size and education, plays a large part in determining the rate of economic growth, as discussed in Chapter 1.

Scientific and technical progress: This may bring about discoveries leading to new, more efficient manufacturing processes, innovations to machines or faster communication systems. The developments in micro-electronics in the late 1970s are even now continuing to revolutionise many aspects of society.

Demand for products: To establish an environment in which growth can take place, there should be a reasonable demand expected, for the products produced. This demand needs to be at a high enough level to encourage entrepreneurs to invest in new capital equipment.

The fluctuations of the demand are often thought to be more important. A steady, relatively low demand may give more incentive for investment than a highly fluctuating demand with a higher average figure especially when large items of specialised plant are likely to be idle for long periods.

Division of labour: This results in greater efficiency within an enterprise, and may eventually lead to greater economic growth. Division of labour is the splitting up of a complex process into many simple stages. Thus instead of highly skilled craftsmen being required to produce a commodity, semi-skilled persons, who are nevertheless skilled in their own particular task, can produce the goods, often with the aid of machines which can carry out many of the simple, but laborious actions.

Advantages of division of labour:
(a) It utilises a person's aptitude for a particular job, to the best advantage.
(b) It promotes skill and dexterity in performing a few simple tasks, thus giving a saving of time.
(c) It enables the increased use of machinery, which leads to

standardisation and interchangeability of parts of the commodity being produced. The use of machinery also relieves the worker of laborious manual effort.
(d) There is more chance of finding a semi-skilled person to carry out the work, who will need the minimum of training for the job.
(e) As division of labour makes possible the use of machines, there is a stimulus for research to develop even better and faster production methods, which would be impossible under a system where division of labour did not operate.
(f) Higher wages are possible due to greater output.

Disadvantages of division of labour:
(a) Simplification of tasks, tends to cause monotony.
(b) There is no possibility of the worker showing his artistic ability in the production of the article, as all products from the same production line will turn out the same. This leads to a decline in craftsmanship.
(c) There is a greater risk of unemployment, as there is more interdependence of workers on one another for a continuing operation. A disruption on one machine can stop a production line. Similarly in the car industry today, a disruption at a tyre producing factory could prevent cars from leaving the car production plant, which ultimately may lead to lay offs at other component plants.
(d) With division of labour, there tends to be greater transportation of materials and components, whether it is within a factory, or whether the materials have to be transported from one plant to another.

In Britain the Industrial Revolution of the eighteenth and nineteenth centuries was the period in which division of labour flourished. It was of course carried out before that time, and has been since, but it was during that period that it had the greatest effect on the economic growth of this country.

Factors of production: The availability of the various factors of production obviously affects economic growth. In a labour intensive economy, a lack of labour would obviously prevent growth, unless mechanisation could be introduced. The lack of money for investment in mechanisation or other large-scale schemes is a major problem in less developed countries. Expertise often has to be induced to come into the country to enable the development of new, or improvement of old, industries.

In the previous section, the various prerequisites and contributing factors concerning growth were listed. The student should constantly be trying to relate the points made earlier with the reality of British economic history, and, in particular during its heyday, the Industrial Revolution.

Brief economic history of Britain

The Roman occupation of Britain

The Roman invasion of Britain led by Julius Caesar began in 55 BC.
The Romans were interested in Britain for two main reasons:
(1) Its young men could serve in the Roman army.
(2) The mining of minerals and the exploitation of other commodities
such as wool, cloth and metalwork would be of great advantage to
them.

At this time, there was specialisation taking place, people that
worked in wood or metal; weavers of cloth, and potters. The various
goods produced were exchanged within communities, or were
transported by rough roads, or rivers, to ports, where trading was
carried out with the Phoenicians and Greeks. Small coins were being
used for currency, but much trade was carried out by exchange.

After the Roman invasion, many new Roman towns were built,
especially in the South. Forts, too, were built all over the country but
more especially in the North and West, where the main opposition
occurred to the occupation. Between the forts and towns were
constructed the famous straight Roman roads, the major ones radiating
from London, which even then was the main port in the country. The
building of these roads greatly encouraged communication and road
transport from one centre to the next.

The Romans also brought with them their own form of buildings,
the most well known being the villa which was built to incorporate
underfloor heating. The villa was a country home, which formed the
centre of commerce for the district. The main occupation of these
communities was based on the land, but the other needs of the people,
in the form of pottery, weaving, woodwork and metalwork were also
carried out at the villa. If coal or other minerals were available locally,
mining would also be undertaken. Each of these communities was
headed by a wealthy Roman, or in some cases a Briton who had slaves
working for him. The villas operated a system of self-sufficiency, with
most of their needs coming from within the community.

Overall, the Roman occupation of Britain caused the development
of quite a sophisticated economic system with much of the trade of the
urban centres depending upon the demand of the numerous officials
and soldiers.

The period AD 410–1066

The last of the Romans left Britain in about 410 to defend their own
country. This left Britain completely open to the attacks of the Saxons.

The Saxons had simpler tastes than the Romans, tending to settle
in agricultural communities whilst totally ignoring the towns which
developed under the Romans. With the disappearance of the demand
for much of the commerce of the towns, the urban way of life had to
be abandoned by many. In some areas, it is possible that a Saxon lord

stepped into the shoes of a Roman, and took over the villa, running it on much the same lines as before. In general, however, the Saxons constructed dwellings and halls of a much less lavish nature.

It is thought probable, that feudalism developed during this period. Feudalism is the system whereby each class is subservient to the one above. The system of agriculture was based on a three field system, for example, one field grew oats, one barley, and the other lay fallow. The next year the crops would have been rotated.

After the Saxon invasion and occupation, there were frequent attacks by the warlike Danes, who initially came to attack and plunder coastal villages rather than to find new areas for settlement. Eventually, however, the Danes did settle in Britain and this led to the splitting of the country into two, the North East under the Danish rule, and the South West under Saxon rule headed by King Alfred. Alfred introduced various forms of taxation, as did the church, during this period. Alfred required the money to maintain defence and to placate the Danes by paying 'Danegold'. The Danish King Canute made laws, laying down the responsibilities and rights of each class of citizen. This helped to consolidate feudalism so that each person knew precisely his rights and position on the ladder of society. Towards the end of this period, towns were again growing in size and importance due to increasing trade and commerce.

The Middle Ages 1066–1300

William the Conqueror led the Norman invasion of Britain in 1066, and with it continued an era of expansion of the manorial system that had developed earlier.

The manor resembled, in some economic respects, the Roman villa, the manor itself being owned, or held on payment of allegiance to the king, by a lord, and occupied by dependent cultivators, the whole community being based on feudal lines.

The labouring class was granted the use of several strips of land by the lord, the payment for this being that the labourer worked so many days per week for the lord; the actual number of days depending upon the time of year and the manor to which they belonged.

Each manor sought to be self-sufficient, the main occupation still being based on agriculture, but most other requirements were also satisfied by specialists within the manor. Very few commodities had to be imported, only such things as metals, salt and tar, the latter being used to prevent sheep diseases. Due to the small-scale craft activities operating within the manors, there was little scope for manufacture or commercial activity, outside that of normal village life.

Foreign trade was stimulated by the close relations between Britain and Normandy, and merchants and moneylenders started to arrive from overseas to encourage growth in commerce.

The crusaders also fostered trade with the East, and encouraged woollen cloth manufacture. The knights and lords who went to the

Holy Land often found this exceedingly expensive, and many had to sell their lands to the newly emerging merchant class. This led to the undermining of the power of the Barons, and proved to be the first step towards the decay of the feudal system.

Throughout this period Christianity flourished, and with it there was a strong feeling to despise wealth or extravagance. To many people, this acted as a deterrent to commencing any form of commercial activity that would have profited the individual. This outlook was one reason why foreigners were tempted to step in and carry out much of the trading at this time. Another reason for this Norman involvement was that they were much better organisers, both in the governing of commerce, and the country.

Towns continued to grow throughout this period, although they were not very numerous, or very large. The Doomsday survey of 1086 recorded only 41 towns of any significance, London, of course, was the trading centre of the nation, and as such was the largest urban area. Towards the end of the Middle Ages, many towns were able to buy the right of self-government from the lords who originally owned the land; this was known as the purchasing of a Charter. The towns then had the privilege of levying local taxes, the power to conduct their own courts, and often the power to hold local markets. These markets or fairs were generally held weekly, and were of considerable importance, as this was where the majority of trading took place.

The period 1300–1750

The operation of the manorial system began slowly to break down during this period.

The lowest working class, the serfs, objected to having to work for the lord, and consequently the lords found it was more beneficial to both sides to pay wages for work carried out by the serfs. The serfs in return paid rent for their land holdings.

The unplanned growth of towns often resulted in many epidemics of plague and typhoid, due to the filth and rubbish left in the streets, which often polluted the water supply. Remember, at this time, there were only wells for water and the effluent from crude toilets sometimes seeped into these water supplies. The worst of these plagues was the Black Death which occurred in 1348/9. It effectively halved the population of Britain, and made the old manorial system very difficult to manage, due to the competition for the available labour. Because of the limited labour supply, wage rates rose, and this resulted in the 'Statute of Labourers' being passed in 1351. This tried to limit the wages to the old rates, but was very unpopular, and was in many instances ignored. General unrest amongst the working classes resulted in 1381 in the 'Peasants' Revolt', led by Jack Straw and Wat Tyler. The revolt did not accomplish a great deal, as the lords were determined to try to maintain the status quo, to enable manor life to continue as before. Eventually however changes did occur, and many lords let out their lands, freeing serfs who were still operating the old system.

In the manorial system, the available land was of four types:

(a) That owned and used by the lord, but worked by serfs.
(b) That used by serfs.
(c) Common land, on which the serfs had the right to graze cattle.
(d) Waste land, from which firewood was collected by all.

With the difficulty concerning labour, much of the agricultural land which initially consisted of many strips, was converted into large fields, and vast areas of common land were also 'Enclosed' to graze sheep on. Sheep rearing was far less labour intensive, and also there was a great demand for wool, both for export, and for the manufacture of cloth, which was often carried out in village cottages.'

In the sixteenth century, Henry VIII destroyed many monasteries, and their lands and buildings were often used in the woollen industry.

The decline of the manorial system tended to create a drift of population from the country to the towns. With the increase in sheep farming, the land was not now available for the serfs to work, neither were their services required. In the towns, many found work in the developing crafts and industries, many however did not, and these added to the ranks of the many paupers already existing in urban life.

During the seventeenth century, there was a considerable growth in industry, which has become known as the Minor Industrial Revolution. Coal mining was one of the first forms of large-scale capital enterprise, needing many people to put up money to enable funds to be available for the sinking of shafts. With deep shaft mining, it was many months from the sinking of the shafts to the actual mining of the coal, hence the need for large sums over long periods. Iron ore mining and foreign trade were also financed by a joint stock method. As early as the sixteenth century, the merchant adventurers had established trading links in the far corners of the world, and this resulted in trading companies being set up:

Muscovy Company in	1555
Levant Company in	1581
East India Company in	1600
Hudson's Bay Company in	1670

The Agrarian Revolution

During the seventeenth century, many improvements were made to agricultural methods. Much of the unused wasteland was being converted to agricultural land, by clearing woodlands or draining marshes and fens.

Another great advance was a change in the method of farming the available land. The open field system, which was the one used by the manorial system, was wasteful in time and effort, as it necessitated the working of scattered strips of land. It was also wasteful as one field was always left fallow. By enclosure, and by rotating certain crops, greater returns could be obtained from the land.

It was Lord Townshend who first used the root crops of turnip, mangel-wurzel or swede in rotation with grain or clover crops.

Up to this time, many beasts had to be killed off in the autumn as there was very little winter fodder to keep them through the winter. Turnips proved to be an ideal cattle food, and helped keep large stocks of cattle for breeding the following year.

In 1701, Jethro Tull invented a seed drill, which improved enormously the return obtained over broadcast sowing. Horses proved to be 50 per cent faster than oxen, which was the traditional motive power, and in 1714 Tull invented a horse drawn hoe.

During the seventeenth and eighteenth centuries, scientific breeding and cultivation methods started to result in better strains of animals and crops, which enabled higher yields to be obtained.

With these various improvements, there was now a better chance of feeding the growing population of urban dwellers, who could no longer grow their own food.

The Industrial Revolution

This is generally understood to cover the period from about 1760 to 1850. During this time there was considerable economic growth, which affected not only industry, but social and political life as well.

No single factor was responsible for the Industrial Revolution, but more likely it was due to the culmination of many factors which arose and developed in previous centuries. A list of such factors might include:
(a) Politically strong and united, with no internal strife at this time.
(b) Merchant contacts in many parts of the world, ensuring an expanding export market.
(c) Climate suitable for processing wool and cotton, which were the main exports.
(d) Banking and credit facilities well developed.
(e) Large resources of iron and coal ready for exploitation, in close proximity to one another.
(f) Capital had been built up by foreign trade.

At this time, there was considerable profit to be made in the trading of cotton and slaves, between Britain, West Africa and America. Britain also imported many raw materials, and re-exported finished goods, particularly textiles and metalwork.

There was a great deal of discontent among the working classes for many had been forced into the town by enclosure, and entrepreneurs, quick to realise that labour was plentiful, succeeded in suppressing wages for many years. The workers had to live in tiny slums, and were often forced to buy from company shops on credit, and so they never effectively got out of debt. The labourers had very few rights, and working conditions were harsh. Children were often sent out to work at the age of five, to oil unguarded machinery in the factories, or to carry out other simple tasks. In many factories, the workers were fined for petty offences, whilst having to work long hours for poor pay. The lack of a piped water supply and proper drainage, still caused much disease in the overcrowded towns. It is not surprising that the working class got very frustrated with its situation, but could do very little, as the entrepreneurs were well represented in parliament, whereas the workers were not.

Population

Table 4.1 Population of England and wales.

Date	Total (m.)	Percentage increase on previous figure
1700	5½ estimated	—
1750	6½ estimated	18
1801	9 census	39
1851	18 census	100
1901	33 census	83
1951	44 census	33
1977	49 census	11

Source: Annual Abstract of Statistics 1980.

The first population census was not carried out until 1801, figures up to that date are therefore based on estimates. In the centuries preceding 1700, the population is thought to be fairly static, perhaps growing only slightly. So why in the eighteenth century does the population suddenly start to increase so fast? Several reasons have been put forward for this:
(a) There may have been an increasing birth rate, but more importantly, there was thought to be a marked decline in the death rate.
(b) The improvements in agriculture were producing more food, which led to less starvation and better diets.
(c) Many workers were no longer tied to craft apprenticeships which meant that they were free to marry earlier in life.
(d) Interest in medicine and hygiene started to develop.
(e) Large families produced a greater income, as the children often worked from an early age.
   Whatever the reasons for its growth, the larger population added fuel to an increasing consumer demand, giving industry greater incentive to increase output.

Technical and scientific growth
Since the time man first started to use tools, innovation and discovery

have led to improvements in his standard of living. Through the centuries, this improvement was initially very slow, but with better communications, and greater demands from both manufacturers and agriculture, invention continued, and still does so today, at an almost exponential rate.

Below are listed just a few of the important discoveries concerning industry. Remember however that the advances made in agriculture are just as important to the growth of this era.

(a) In 1733 John Kay invented the flying shuttle, which greatly increased both the speed of weaving, and the width of cloth that could be produced.

(b) James Hargreaves produced in 1767 the first successful spinning machine, the spinning jenny. This invention is often thought by many to mark the beginning of the Industrial Revolution.

(c) Coal mines during the late seventeenth century were getting deeper, due to the surface deposits having been worked out. Deeper shafts encountered problems of flooding, but this was overcome, for in 1705 Newcomen patented a steam pump for pumping out shafts.

(d) Several people tried to improve on the steam pump, without great success, but in 1781, Boulton and Watt developed a viable steam engine. Their factory turned out many of these engines, for use in mills, potteries and breweries.

(e) One problem when the steam engine was first developed was that of accurately boring the cylinders. Jack Wilkinson of Broseley overcame this problem, making the steam engine a great deal more reliable and durable.

(f) In the 1790s, Joseph Bramah invented a wheel cutting machine, a machine for making locks, and also the hydraulic press. At this time, a colleague of Bramah, a Henry Maudsley devised a screw cutting lathe.

The Industrial Revolution gave great encouragement and impetus to engineers and inventors, as the faster scientific discoveries were made, so technologists had to devise practical ways of making the discovery usable in industry.

From the early 1800s the growth of many large industries has continued, which were often based on simple discoveries or inventions.

(a) From the 1830s the railway industries grew.

(b) Shipbuilding started to grow during the 1850s.

(c) The start of the motor car industry was in the 1890s.

(d) Aircraft and radio engineering grew from 1900.

(e) From the 1940s grew the electronics and nuclear industries.

Development in transport

Roads

Up to the end of the seventeenth century, much transport was carried out by coastal and river vessels, due to the fact that roads were very poorly developed, and ill maintained since the Romans left.

There was considerable pressure to improve transport and communication facilities, for military reasons and to enable goods from industry and agriculture to be more widely distributed.

Between 1750 and 1800 there were many turnpike roads. People were granted the right to charge a toll for the use of the road, in exchange for maintaining it. These gradually disappeared towards the end of the nineteenth century due mainly to competition from the railways. The last tolls were abolished in 1895, the responsibility being transferred to Highway District Boards. In 1909 the Road Improvement Board was formed to administer the funds raised solely for roads by the imposition of a road fund tax. As roads developed it became obvious that a national plan for road transport was needed. This led eventually to the construction of the motorway systems of the 1960s and 1970s.

Canals

Due to the rapid growth in the mid-eighteenth century, there was a great demand on the poor transport facilities available.

In 1761 the first canal, the Bridgewater canal was constructed to link Manchester with a colliery at Worsley. This proved a great success, and was extended from Manchester to Runcorn. Following this, other canals were constructed, the Trent and Mersey in 1777, the Leeds and Liverpool in 1777 and many others, until construction peaked in about 1792. Finance for their construction tended to dry up, but they still managed to find backers and continue building into the nineteenth century.

The development of the railways in the 1830s marked the start of the decline of the canals.

Initially, canals were financed and owned privately, like the turnpike roads. The Transport Act of 1947 however brought the majority of inland waterways into public ownership. For several decades after this, the canals' traffic continued to decline, until a recent interest for leisure activities caused a revival in the 1960s.

Railways

Railways, or as they were known initially plateways, had existed at coal mines from the seventeenth century. Plateways were similar to railways, except that the rails were of wood, and the motive power was horses or men. Various experiments were tried with steam power, but it was not really until 1825 when George Stephenson improved his locomotive design and the Stockton and Darlington railway was opened, that the era really began.

In 1830 the Liverpool to Manchester railway was opened, and the Rocket started its service.

The heyday for railway construction was 1830–50, and by the end of 1850, 9 600 km of track had been constructed.

The railways had many advantages for society:

(a) Cheap rapid transport for people and freight to many parts of the country.
(b) Faster communication, particularly for newspapers and mail.
(c) It encouraged time to be standardised at Greenwich mean time. Up until 1852, when the telegraph lines were completed, it was impossible to verify time accurately in different parts of the country.

Railways again like the early roads and canals were privately financed and in the early days large fortunes were made or lost on transactions involving railway companies. Track continued to be laid up until 1900, and by 1914 there were 32 000 km of track.

Since then there has been a steady decline in the length of track in use, due mainly to increased motor transport.

From 1830 onwards the Railways have been subjected to a great deal of legislation covering many aspects, under such topics as safety, maximum fares, accounting methods, and hours and wages of employees.

The Railways Act of 1921 led to the amalgamation of 121 separate railway companies into four. The London, Midland and Scottish Railway; the Great Western Railway; the London and North Eastern Railway; and the Southern Railway; it was hoped that this would bring economies, and lead to a better cheaper service for the customers. The railways however still continued to lose money, due not only to competition from road transport, but also because of labour troubles, and a general decline in trade particularly between 1914–39. Up until 1939, the railway companies had to apply to the Railway Rates Tribunal before any increase in fares was allowed. In 1939 the Transport Advisory Council suggested that the companies should be allowed to charge whatever fares they thought fit. The government took over the organisation of the railways in 1939 with the outbreak of war. After the war, the great deterioration that had taken place had made it almost inevitable that nationalisation in some form would occur. This happened with the advent of the 1947 Transport Act. As a result, on 1 January 1948, the four main railway companies were taken over by the British Transport Commission. At the same time, the commission also obtained control of harbours, inland waterways and road haulage. From 1948 to the present day, there has been massive investment in the railways. Even so, today they have great problems in breaking even, despite the cutting of uneconomical rural services, and further mechanisation. In the 1970s, the track being used measured about 18 000 km compared with 32 000 km in 1914. Staff in the 1970s numbered about 250 000 against 700 000 in 1948.

Perhaps with problems of road congestion and the soaring cost of oil, the economics of rail transport may cause it once again to be the main means of transport in the years ahead.

Social problems and attitudes throughout the ages

In the sixteenth century, pauperism rose to such proportions that in 1601 a poor law was passed, putting the parish in charge of administering relief to this ever growing sector of the community. This relief was financed by the levying of a poor rate on households.

In 1722 the Workhouse Act was passed, and under it, unemployed people were required to work at these houses which were often contracted out to industrialists. If the unemployed refused to work, then they received no benefit. The object of this Act was to relieve the householders of the burden of the poor tax. In practice it did not have much effect on the level of tax, as pauperism still continued to increase. In the 1790s under threat of possible revolution, the Speenhamland system developed. This consisted of parishes supplementing low wages, thus preventing starvation conditions. The amount paid was related to the price of bread, and the size of a person's family. The result of this was that employers tended to keep wages low, knowing that the workers would receive a supplement. Again this threw a heavy burden on the poor rate.

At the beginning of the nineteenth century there was a change of direction concerning social ideas. There were three main reasons for this:

(a) T. R. Malthus published his various essays on population, which attracted a large following. Basically his theory was that unless parents decided voluntarily to restrict the size of family, then population would continue to rise, which would result in no increase in the standard of living.

(b) There was in 1830 a labourers' revolt mainly in areas where existing supplementary payments were highest. This indicated the necessity of reform.

(c) The ever increasing burden of the poor rate on the rest of society.

The Poor Law Amendment Act of 1834 was the result. It tended to cut relief to a minimum, thus making it more financially beneficial for people to seek employment, rather than rely on supplements. In general it aimed at making workers, rather than the parishes, responsible for supporting themselves and their families.

Throughout the nineteenth century, following this attitude of *laissez-faire*, there was considerable economic growth. The wealth, however was by no means equally distributed, with the entrepreneurs becoming richer to the cost of the workers. One major problem was that most workers were employed as casual labour, and due to political problems in the overseas markets, they often found themselves out of work. In 1909 the first Labour Exchanges were set up, their name being changed in 1916 to Employment Exchanges, when the Ministry of Labour was formed. Following Lloyd George's National Insurance Act of 1911, National Insurance Benefit was paid within selected industries, and the Old Age Pension Act of 1908 had provided a pension to all over the age of 70, subject to certain conditions.

The depression of the interwar years led to further benefits (dole money) being paid in addition to the minimal poor law relief which still continued to be administered by poor law unions.

In 1934 the Unemployment Assistance Board took over the relief of all those who were now entitled to benefit; also the administration of the poor law was put in the hands of a national agency.

In the 1930s and early 1940s, there was much pressure for reform, which resulted in the Beveridge Report of 1942. These proposals outlined State involvement to give aid, 'From cradle to grave', and included unemployment benefits and measures for re-employment, besides a health service and family allowance.

During 1945–46 the Labour government embodied these ideas into several acts:

(a) The Family Allowance Act of 1945, where allowances would be paid from general taxation revenue.

(b) The National Health Service Act 1946 which gave care to all, financed from the National Insurance fund, rates, and from taxation.

(c) The National Insurance Act 1946 set out payments for sickness, retirement, unemployment, maternity, family allowances and death. These were paid for out of funds collected from employer, employee and the State.

(d) The National Assistance Act of 1948 led to the formation of the National Assistance Board to administer benefits along the lines of the old poor law, to anyone whose needs were not met by the previous Acts of 1945 and 1946.

It was hoped that these supplements would ease as wages increased. Many people however still experienced hardship, and this continues even today.

Since the 1934 Special Areas Act, government has tried to relieve unemployment in areas of declining industry, by grants and loans to new industries, in an attempt to create employment. Other Acts followed in 1936 and 1937 and some areas which were particularly depressed were designated Special Areas. These included South Wales, much of the North East, and the central lowlands of Scotland.

In 1945 the Distribution of Industry Act renamed the Special Areas as Development Areas, and in 1947 it became necessary to obtain an IDC (industrial development certificate), before a factory could be constructed above a certain size. By using the granting of these IDCs as an incentive, much industry was persuaded to move into development areas.

In 1960 the method of designation was changed, the Development Areas being replaced with Development Districts, and defined as any Employment Exchange District where unemployment was over 4½ per cent.

The 1966 Industrial Development Act replaced Development Districts by the present Development Areas. These now include larger areas than previously, and include the whole of Northern England, the majority of Scotland, and most of Wales, Cornwall and North Devon.

In the 1970s the government granted much money to many

industries in an attempt to preserve or create jobs. Many other measures, besides grants, were carried out in the late 1970s including:

(a) From 1977 firms in Special Development Areas with fewer than 50 employees received £20 per week subsidy for each additional worker employed.

(b) Various other payments and subsidies which tended to aid new employment possibilities, especially for school leavers and people needing retraining.

With Britain's entry into the EEC there is a common policy to improve employment opportunities by increasing the mobility of labour. The following actions were taken by the Council of Ministers in 1974:

(a) Equal pay for men and women.

(b) Standard 40 hour week, and four weeks annual holiday.

(c) Procedures were suggested for mass dismissal and for the rights of workers when transferred between different firms.

The development of banking

During the Middle Ages, it was thought wrong, both by the Church and by the State, to charge interest for the loan of money. This view, not unnaturally, led to most people having to finance their commercial activities from their own funds, or with the help of friends and relatives. With the developing of industry and commerce there was a change of mood, which eventually led to Acts during the late sixteenth and early seventeenth centuries legalising the charging of interest. The way was now clear for the commencement of the modern banking system.

In spite of the feelings of society, money lending had taken place from early times. During the early fourteenth century the Lombards who were wealthy Italian merchants, settled in London and were granted an area of land which became known as Lombard Street. They carried on trading mainly as goldsmiths, but also as pawnbrokers and bankers. As finance for trading became necessary banking activities expanded considerably although throughout the seventeenth century it was carried out side by side with pawnbroking and goldsmithing.

At the end of the seventeenth century the receipts that private bankers gave to their customers for the deposit of bullion came to be widely accepted as currency, and a banker by the name of Francis Childs was reputed to be the first to produce printed banknotes. Many banks followed Childs' example, and printed their own notes.

With the increasing expansion of trade, the small private banks found it difficult to cope with the large-scale activities which were now requiring finance. The Bank of England resulted, and was founded by Royal Charter in 1694, its capital coming from public subscription.

The activities of the Bank of England at this time consisted of:

(a) Accepting deposits and making loans.

(b) The issue of banknotes. Between 1708 and 1826 it had the monopoly of banknote issue, in banks with over six partners.

(c) Discounting bills of exchange.

The Bank initially made a loan to government of £1 200 000 which was another major reason for the allowing of its formation. From the outset, the bank maintained very close links with the government, and in 1751 it took over the majority of the national debt. Further loans were made to government from time to time and eventually, it was thought necessary in the nation's interest to nationalise the Bank in 1946.

The Bank of England certainly helped trade in London, it also helped government, it did not however solve the need for large-scale banking in the provinces. The Bank had no intention of setting up branch offices, until it was threatened in the 1820s by bankers wishing to set up joint stock banks.

The smaller private banks, i.e. those controlled and financed by one owner, had to cater for these areas, particularly up until 1826 when the Bank of England's note issue monopoly was lifted in all areas except London. Before 1826 the private banks experienced two main problems:

(a) Lack of capital.

(b) Frequent runs on the banks, which led to a general lack of confidence in small banks.

The obvious answer was to have joint stock banks, i.e. those controlled and financed by several people, as the facility then existed for obtaining more capital should it be required. After 1826, joint stock banks were allowed to issue notes, which was regarded as an essential part of banking, and after this date joint stock banking increased.

In the 1830s and 1840s these newly formed joint stock banks had to struggle for survival as they were often suppressed by legislation. The Companies Act of 1862 detailed the law with regard to joint stock banks, and classed them the same as other forms of trading companies, particularly with regard to limited liability. It should be noted that other forms of trading had enjoyed limited liability since 1855. The 1862 Act gave security to the banks. During the next 100 years, mergers took place which eventually reduced the number to six main banks:

Barclays, Coutts, Lloyds, Midland, Natwest, and Williams and Glyn's.

Gilds

During the Middle Ages, trade between towns and within individual towns were carried out by merchants. For mutual protection these merchants started to form their own associations or gilds. Eventually the gild merchants had monopoly of trade within their own town, and outsiders were only permitted to trade with members of the gild.

The gilds not only protected the merchants, but also the townspeople, as the gilds fixed fair prices, and checked weights and measures. They were administered by a council with an alderman at the head. There were also wardens whose duty it was to enforce the rules, and offenders would suffer fines, or expulsion from the gild.

The welfare of its members was another activity undertaken, as the gild looked after the sick, and the widows and children of its members.

From the twelfth century, groups of craftsmen also formed gilds, often for maintaining good standards and self-protection. In many instances the merchant gilds insisted on craft gilds being formed, to enable better control of that particular activity. These craft gilds were separated by craft, so that many could exist in one town. This was unlike merchant gilds where only one generally existed in a particular town. They were organised along similar lines to the merchant's, with standards being assured by the use of warders.

Within the craft gilds were three levels of workman, the mastercraftsman, the journeyman and the apprentice. Initially, many boys were taken on as apprentices, who were bound to their master for the duration of the apprenticeship, usually seven years.

Journeymen were those who had completed their apprenticeship and who worked for the master for wages. The journeyman was considered the halfway stage between apprentice and master, and he could in theory leave the master at any time, to set up his own workshop. In practice this often had to be sanctioned by the gild. As gilds developed they became more exclusive, and eventually only the sons of craftsmen were taken on as apprentices, and even then a premium had to be paid.

The mastercraftsmen were the owners of the business, and it was these people who were responsible for ensuring that apprentices were properly trained and that standards were obeyed in each business.

Like the merchant gilds, there existed a welfare system, and some gilds ran their own schools. Religion played a large part in their activities, and each mystery or craft often performed mystery plays. These were plays portraying a scene from the Bible concerning the particular craft in question.

In the fourteenth century, as the craft gilds became stronger, the merchant gilds found that they could no longer supervise the various trades, and consequently lost much of their powers with regard to the crafts.

As trade expanded, the mastercraftsmen developed further their role as employers of labour and so prospered, and evolved into a middle class society which laid the foundation of Britain's expanding trade in the centuries to come. The journeymen at this time became aware that there was little chance of ever becoming masters, and in order to divorce themselves from the same controlling gild as the masters, they set up journeymen associations, or yeomen's gilds. It has been argued that these were the earliest form of trade union, as they were trying to secure reasonable working conditions, hours of work and wages for the working classes.

As industry developed still further in larger workshops, and ultimately into factory systems, the craft gilds found that they no longer had a monopoly hold over the supply of a specialised craft labour. Due to the division of labour it was not often required by the new production methods. The gilds also had no hold over the quantity or quality of products being produced, and there followed a gradual decline in the craft gilds. The yeomen's gild did not last long, due to lack of finance, and the fact that they constantly had to battle against very influential people.

Trade unionism

In the Middle Ages, craft gilds contained both the masters and the workers, both often living in the same house, and together they worked in an harmonious atmosphere. As society developed more and more the idea of profit making, there came a rift between the employers and the employees which continues to grow ever wider to this day, according to some points of view. The Industrial Revolution saw employers fighting with the aid of parliament, to quell the demonstrations of the overworked, underpaid workers.

Until the Industrial Revolution, much work was done on a domestic level, particularly in the woollen industry. Here middlemen would take raw wool to the peasants' cottages for the family to turn into cloth. The worker in this environment could to a large extent, please himself how hard, and what hours he worked. With the advent of larger, powered machinery, it was often only financially feasible to set up the large-scale production in factories. These new factories could be managed more efficiently than the old outworker system, and soon undercut the price of domestically produced products. This inevitably drew many workers to the new factories. These workers had to adjust to much more discipline, working set hours for low wages in conditions they could not improve themselves. Add to this the squalor that many townsfolk had to live in, and one can start to understand the environment in which worker unrest flourished. Workers began to combine together to try to improve wages, but when this came to the ears of government there was grave concern. It was felt that any type of reform might lead to revolution, as had just taken place in France in 1789. The result was the passing of several Acts from 1796 to 1801, all of which were generally referred to as the Combination Acts. These prevented the combination of workers, for the purpose of trying to raise wages. The arguments put forward against combination were:
(a) That this tended to restrain trade.
(b) Should higher wages be paid, British goods could no longer match up to the competition of cheaper foreign goods in our overseas markets.

These Acts stayed in force until they were repealed in 1824, thanks to the efforts of Francis Place. After 1824, many trade unions flourished, but after the middle of the century, violence erupted again which resulted in the passing of the Trade Union Acts of 1871, 1875, and 1876. These clarified precisely the legal position of the unions, giving them the right of peaceful picketing, without the participating members being accused of conspiracy.

Throughout the 1830s and 1840s, workers tried to strengthen their position by forming first national unions of particular trades, and eventually general unions which were composed of all trades. During this period, Robert Owen with his ideals of co-operative ownership founded the Grand National Consolidated Trade Union (GNCTU) in 1834. The union was formed by the amalgamation of several large trade unions, the idea being that a single large national union could wield a 'bigger stick' than several smaller unions. However, instead of unified action, the individual unions tended to look after their own members, rather than the wider aspects of the national union. This resulted in many small local disputes which destroyed the GNCTU before national strikes could be arranged.

In 1851 the 'New Model' trade union came into being with the Amalgamated Society of Engineers. This union had a centralised expert administration and a back up of large funds, most of which were used for welfare in the form of sick pay, unemployment pay, and pensions. There was still the possibility of strikes, but peaceful picketing and negotiation was generally preferred. Other unions followed the example of the ASE, and it was largely their efforts that brought about the legislation of 1871–75. One of the major union successes of this period was in 1889 when the London dockers won their 'Dockers' tanner' per hour.

By the close of the century, many unions and employers had agreed on negotiating and grievance procedure, and many wages boards and committees were in existence.

In the 1890s workers were content to have orderly pay negotiations, but by 1910 their attitudes had changed. In 1906 the Labour Party was formed, and by 1908 there were 50 Members of Parliament sympathetic to the workers' problems. Union membership at this time was 2½ million, which rose to 4½ million by 1914. In 1919 unions again grew militant and in 1926 much disagreement, particularly in the mining industry, resulted in the general strike of 1926. It lasted only 9 days before the men reluctantly returned to work.

In the 1930s and 1940s membership continued to grow, and began to encompass clerical and professional workers, besides the trades already catered for. Today, total union membership stands at over 12 million and, as such a large proportion of the working population belongs to a union, industry and government must take heed of their requests. Many people argue that the balance has swung too far. In the seventeenth and eighteenth centuries the employers held the upper hand, and large profits were made at the expense of the workers' wages and conditions. Today, unions can be said to be a very strong body, demanding ever increasing wages, at the cost of employers' profit. But, if profits fall too low, there will be no investment and possibly the closing of factories, leading to mass unemployment.

Has the balance swung too far?

Comment

In this chapter are laid out very briefly some of the facts and ideas leading through a continuous period of economic growth. There have been many books written on economic history, and one of the main problems in writing such books is whether or not the author has correctly interpreted the facts. Several historians may be presented with identical facts from identical source material. Their theories and ideas concerning the particular period however may be completely different from one another. The student should realise that when reading such a work, it is often only the author's interpretation of the evidence before him. It is necessary to develop an analytical approach, sorting out the relevant facts, and coming to one's own conclusions. In the following questions, it will be necessary to do just that with the material of this chapter.

Questions

1 In your opinion, which was the major step forward in economic growth, in Britain's history, and why?
2 Discuss the main reasons for the appearance and disappearance of the gilds.
3 Was enclosure a good or bad thing for Britain?
4 Why did the agrarian revolution come about. Suggest the likely outcome for Britain, if it had happened 100 years later.

Chapter 5

Supply and demand analysis

The first four chapters have tried to give a general impression of the subject matter of economics. In these earlier chapters certain facts have been assumed to be known in general knowledge. One such fact is basic supply and demand behaviour. Most people realise that if a shop suddenly reduces its prices, more goods will be sold. Conversely if the same shop doubles its original prices, it is likely to sell fewer goods under normal circumstances.

This chapter will delve more deeply into the workings of supply and demand analysis, and will show its uses in the economy of today.

Demand

Demand can be defined as the amount of a good or service that a person or society will buy at a particular price at a particular time.

A typical demand curve is shown in Fig. 5.1. When investigating demand curves, it is best if one can relate oneself to the consumer who may buy the goods. In Fig. 5.1 it can be seen that if the price was relatively high, at y_1, then demand would be relatively low, at x_1. If on the other hand the price was to drop to y_2 then the quantity demanded would rise to x_2. This movement which can occur along a single curve is known as contraction or extension, as indicated on Fig. 5.1.

The market demand for any good can be found by adding together the demand of all the separate consumers. For example, consider the number of people who would buy a new washing machine, if the prices of new machines were as shown below:

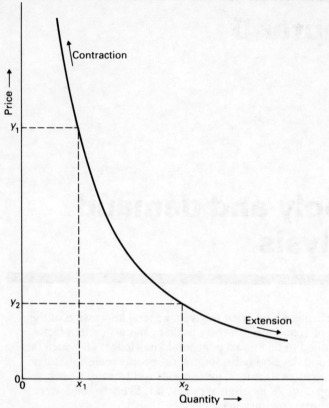

Fig. 5.1 Movements along a demand curve

Price of m/c's (£)	260	250	230	200	180	170	159
Number sold (1000's)	1.35	1.35	1.6	2.5	3.85	5.0	8.0

These values are shown in graphical form in Fig. 5.2.

The workings of a single curve as in Fig. 5.1 assume that all external forces remain unchanged, and that only the price of the particular good in question, changes. If certain outside influences are altered, then this could result in a 'shift' of the curve to the left or right of the original position, as in Fig 5.2. This would indicate a decrease or increase in demand.

Explained below are several influences that could bring about these 'shifts':

The price of other goods

Two types of relationships between goods exist, which can cause this movement. They are complementary goods, and competing or

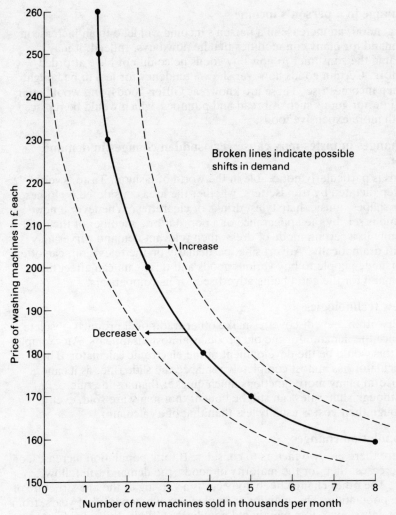

Fig. 5.2 The market demands for washing machines

substitute goods. In the building industry, a good example of complements would be that of undercoat and gloss paint. Generally one is not bought or used without the other, and if for some reason the price of gloss paint suddenly doubled, people may not redecorate quite so often, hence the demand for undercoat would drop, although its price had not changed.

Wallpaper on the other hand could be classed as a substitute for emulsioned walls. If a revolutionary printing process suddenly halved existing wallpaper prices, then the demand for emulsion paint might drop, as more people would choose to wallpaper their rooms.

Change in a person's income

In general, an increase in a person's income will lead to an increase in demand for many commodities that he now buys. Indeed, it may enable the consumer to now buy goods he could not have afforded before. Certain goods however show a tendency for less to be bought when incomes rise. These are known as Giffen goods, and would refer to inferior goods such as bread and potatoes, which would be replaced with more expensive foods.

Changes in tastes may cause very sudden changes in demand curves

This is particularly noticeable in the world of fashion. Taste is very often dictated by trendsetters, whether the area considered is clothes, car shapes, music, hairstyles, drinks or cigarettes. Whenever a new trend is set, by the appearance of a pop star or a member of the royal family in a certain mode of dress, then relevant demand curves may shift dramatically. Advertising, particularly on the television, can often persuade people to buy various goods and this again can affect the demand for the good being advertised, or its competitors.

New technologies

Very often, new discoveries make other traditional products obsolete, hence the demand for the old products almost disappears. An example of this would be the development of the electronic calculator. The calculator has almost completely replaced the slide rule, as it can perform many more functions much quicker than a slide rule. Although slide rules can still be bought, not many are sold, even though their cost is usually less than that of a calculator.

Population changes

Here there are two factors to consider. If total population increases, or decreases, then for the majority of goods, the demand will follow.

The other change likely to occur is a varying of the age structure of the population. This may for example vary over a period of years, from a mainly young, to a mainly old population. Whilst this would not affect some goods, such as foods, it would affect demand for types of clothes and toys.

Taxation, and the distribution of income

Taxation, as will be discussed later, is imposed by government either to raise revenue, or to try and cut back demand. There may be times when it is thought to be in the nation's interest to reduce sales for example on imported goods.

Taxation can also be used to try to correct inequalities of income distribution. The object is to level out the incomes of the very rich, and very poor, by taxing the rich heavily, and giving subsidies to the lower income groups. Consequently, the poor now have more money to spend, and so demand for the goods that they buy should increase.

67

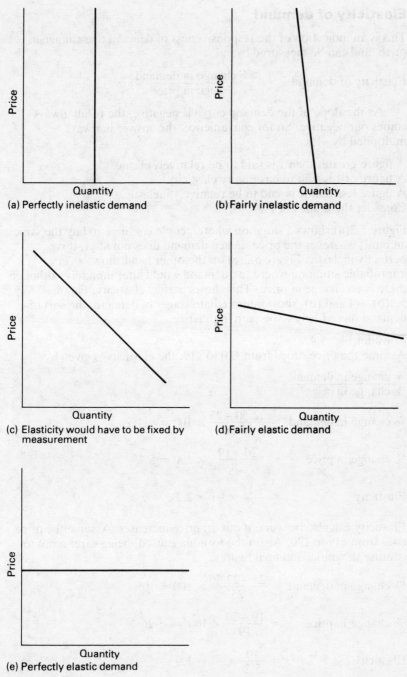

(a) Perfectly inelastic demand

(b) Fairly inelastic demand

(c) Elasticity would have to be fixed by measurement

(d) Fairly elastic demand

(e) Perfectly elastic demand

Fig. 5.3

Elasticity of demand

This is an indication of the responsiveness of demand to a change in price, and can be measured by:

$$\text{Elasticity of demand} = \frac{\%\ \text{change in demand}}{\%\ \text{change in price}}$$

As the slope of the demand curve is negative, the result always comes out negative. So for convenience, the answer is always multiplied by –1.

A figure greater than 1 is said to be relatively elastic.
A figure of 1 is said to have unity elasticity.
A figure less than 1 is said to be relatively inelastic.
Consider the graphs of Fig. 5.3.

Figure 5.3(a) shows a situation where people continue to buy the same amount, whatever the price, hence demand does not alter, it is perfectly inelastic. Figure 5.3(e) on the other hand shows a very improbable situation where the demand would alter infinitely, although there is no change in price. This shows perfect elasticity. Figures 5.3(b), (c) and (d), show intermediate stages of demand, the sort of demand more likely to be seen in practice.

Consider Fig. 5.4.
Assume the price drops from £20 to £19, the elasticity is given by:

$$\frac{\%\ \text{change in demand}}{\%\ \text{change in price}}$$

$$\%\ \text{change in demand} = \frac{22.50 - 25}{22.50} \times 100 = -11\%$$

$$\%\ \text{change in price} = \frac{20 - 19}{20} \times 100 = 5\%$$

$$\text{Elasticity} = \frac{-11}{5} \times -1 = 2.2$$

Elasticity can also be worked out on price increases. Assume the price rises from £19 to £20. Again the formula is used, being careful not to confuse the initial and final figures.

$$\%\ \text{change in demand} = \frac{25 - 22.50}{25} \times 100 = 10\%$$

$$\%\ \text{change in price} = \frac{19 - 20}{19} \times 100 = -5.26\%$$

$$\text{Elasticity} = \frac{10}{-5.26} \times -1 = 1.9$$

Note, there is a difference between the two figures. If elasticity is

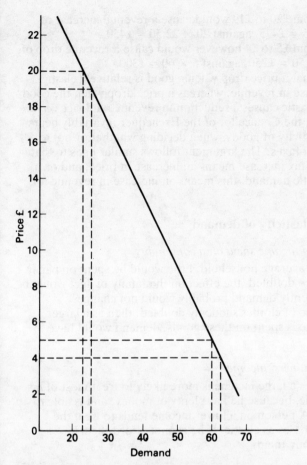

Fig. 5.4 Determining elasticity of demand

calculated for a price drop from £5 to £4 the figure for elasticity is about 0.21.

From the wide variations of these figures it can be seen that to determine accurately the elasticity of demand of a good, the exact range over which we are interested must be specified together with the direction of movement. Most demand lines are curves, not straight lines, and a curve such as in Fig. 5.2 would tend to have a more constant elasticity than the straight line of Fig. 5.4. For the majority of situations, it is only necessary to know that a good is either relatively elastic, or relatively inelastic, precise figures are not needed.

It has been shown how elasticity can be calculated, but to what purpose can it be put?

(a) A producer can determine whether his total revenue is likely to increase, or decrease, following a change in price. Consider Fig. 5.4.

A price drop from £20 to £19 would cause a revenue increase of £25, i.e. 19 × 25 = £475, against 20 × 22.50 = £450.
A price drop from £5 to £4 however would cause a revenue drop of £50, i.e. 4 × 62.50 = £250, against 5 × 60 = £300.
It can be seen that a price drop when a good is relatively elastic causes an increase in revenue, whereas a price drop when the good is relatively inelastic causes a reduction in revenue, and *vice versa*.

(b) At budget time, the Chancellor of the Exchequer invariably bears in mind the elasticity of goods, when deciding whether or not to increase indirect taxes. The argument follows similar lines to that in (a) above. A tax increase means an increase in price, and on a relatively inelastic demand, this means an increase in revenue for the government.

Factors affecting elasticity of demand

1. The proportion of income spent on a commodity

For example, in the average household, little would be spent on paper tissues, so if the price doubled, the effect on the family budget would be negligible. Consequently demand probably would not change.
However, if the price of clothes suddenly doubled, then as a larger proportion of income is spent on these goods, demand would have to be cut back.

2. The level of consumers' income

A person who enjoys a large income is more likely to treat most of his purchases as inelastic, because he has plenty of money, and is able to easily afford them. A person on a lower income tends to treat the majority of his purchases as elastic. If he cannot afford them he obviously does not buy them.

3. Does the good have any substitutes?

Goods which have no substitutes will tend to be inelastic in demand. An example of this is glass, which has no cheap substitute; people have to buy glass if they want windows in their buildings. Goods which have many substitutes however, will tend to be elastic in demand, for if the price of this type of good increases, the consumers will buy a substitute.

4. Is the good a luxury or a necessity?

In general, goods which are neccessities such as food have to be purchased, and so are inelastic. Luxury goods, such as caravans, boats, freezers etc. can be done without, so that if the funds are not available they will not be bought. Luxury goods then are elastic in demand.

5. Is the good a single use or durable use commodity

In other words, is the good used once only, like food, paint or fuel, or is it used many times like tools. When a single use good has been used, then it has to be replaced, its demand is inelastic. With durable use goods, because they can still be used even when well worn they can if necessary be replaced less often; this gives them an elastic demand.

6. Is the good linked with a trend or habit?

Many young people feel compelled to buy certain clothes, because they are in fashion. Therefore, over a relatively short period of time, the demand for green wigs, should they be in fashion, would be inelastic.

Certain goods are linked with habits, particularly alcoholic drinks, and tobacco. If people find it difficult to give up smoking or drinking, then these goods will tend to be inelastic.

Income elasticity of demand

This can be defined as an indication of the responsiveness of demand for a particular change in income.

$$\text{Income elasticity of demand} = \frac{\% \text{ change in demand}}{\% \text{ change in income}}$$

The demand for luxury goods, i.e. cars, boats, caravans etc. would obviously rise with an increase in income. They would tend to have an elastic income demand. Basic foods such as potatoes and bread would be required whatever a person's income, so would be relatively inelastic.

Cross elasticity of demand

This is often used by manufacturers, to determine how complementary or competitive two goods are.

$$\text{Cross elasticity of demand} = \frac{\% \text{ change in demand of commodity X}}{\% \text{ change in price of commodity Y}}$$

Consider the following examples.

Example (a): There are two commodities, A and B. The price of A doubles, which results in demand for B being halved. Are the goods complements or substitutes?

$$\text{The cross elasticity of demand} = \frac{-50}{+100} = -0.5.$$

(Negative figures always indicate complements.)

Example (b): The doubling of the price of commodity X causes a doubling in demand of commodity Y. Again, are the goods complements or substitutes?

$$\text{The cross elasticity of demand} = \frac{100}{100} = +1.$$

72

(Positive figures always indicate substitutes.)

Example (c): The price of good M is doubled, this makes no difference to demand for commodity N. What is the relationship between the two goods?

Cross elasticity of demand = $\dfrac{0}{100}$ = 0.

(Zero figure indicates that the goods are totally unrelated, as one would expect.)

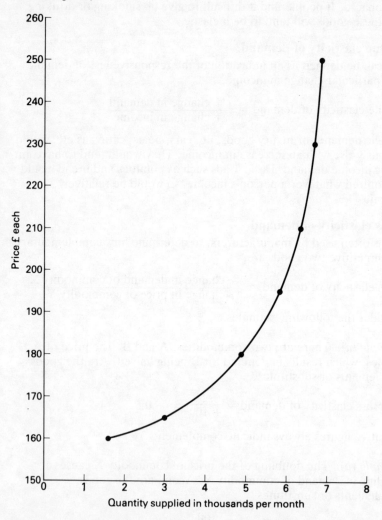

Fig. 5.5 Typical supply curve for washing machines

Supply

This can be defined as the amount of a good, or service, that producers will put onto the market at any particular price.

When analysing supply curves, one must think in terms of the producer, whereas with demand curves, one has to think in terms of consumers. A typical supply curve is shown in Fig. 5.5. From this graph it can be seen that the higher the price, the more will be supplied. There are two explanations for this:

(a) If a higher price can be realised for a product, then more profit can be made, therefore manufacturers want to turn out more products.

(b) As the selling price of a good rises, more firms are now able to produce the goods at this higher figure, whereas at a lower price they could not compete and so would not produce the goods.

With supply curves, as with demand curves, they can extend or contract, or they can increase or decrease, as in Fig. 5.6. An extension or contraction would be determined by the price charged for a commodity, whereas a decrease or increase would be brought about by changes in the conditions of supply. These may be due to the following cause.

1. A change in the prices of factors of production
An increase in the prices of materials or labour, means that less

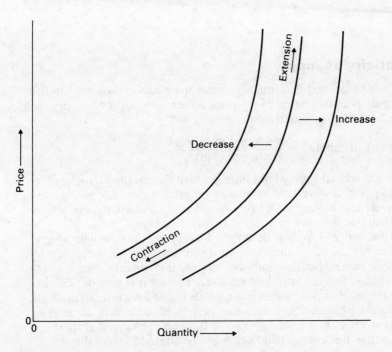

Fig. 5.6 Movement of supply curves

manufacturers would be able to supply the good, whilst maintaining prices. This would result in the supply line shifting to the left. A decrease in factor prices would cause a shift to the right.

2. Farm products being affected by weather

Bad weather may result in farmers requiring greater prices per unit, to compensate for a smaller crop. In this instance, bad weather would result in a shift to the left. A good harvest, on the other hand, would result in a shift to the right as vast stocks of crops are sold off at low prices.

3. Advances in technology altering production methods

Very often, in industry, a new production process results in faster and cheaper production. This will lead to an increase in supply, as goods can now be produced more cheaply than before, so that manufacturers make more profit than previously, at any particular price.

4. Taxes or subsidies

Should the government impose a tax on a product, the tax will often be paid initially by the producer, so that this in effect works the same as an increase in the factor costs, and results in a supply decrease.

A subsidy paid to the producer however will result in a supply increase.

Elasticity of supply

This can be defined in a similar manner to demand elasticity. Elasticity of supply is an indication of the responsiveness of supply to a change in price, and can be written as:

$$\text{Elasticity of supply} = \frac{\% \text{ change in supply}}{\% \text{ change in price}}$$

As nearly all supply lines have positive slopes, the elasticity of most lines is positive, and again a figure greater than one would show a relatively elastic supply. A figure of one is unity elasticity, and a figure less than one denotes an inelastic supply. See Fig. 5.7.

Elasticity of supply is determined largely by the ease with which producers can change their level of operations. Certain industries, for example the shipbuilding industry, require investment months, or even years ahead of actual production. Consequently it is very difficult to alter the level of production when goods take a long time to produce. Products with such long production periods have inelastic supplies, whereas when the production can be stopped or changed at short notice then the level of production can be altered to meet the prevailing circumstances quickly.

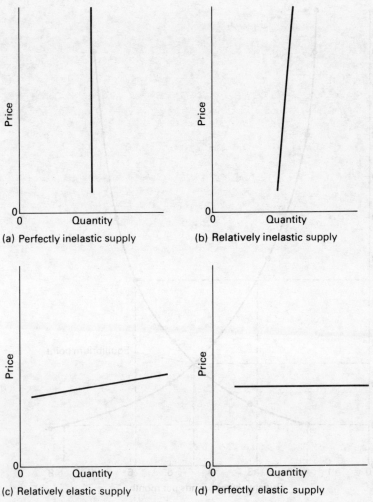

Fig. 5.7 Elasticities of supply

Equilibrium price

Equilibrium price comes about, as a result of the interaction of supply and demand. If Fig. 5.2, the demand curve for washing machines, and Fig. 5.5, the supply curve for washing machines, are combined, this gives Fig. 5.8. On this diagram, there is one point at which both sellers and buyers are satisfied. At the price of £175 the demand equals supply at 4 400 machines per month. This point of intersection of the curves is known as the equilibrium point.

Over a period of time, the market situation adjusts automatically

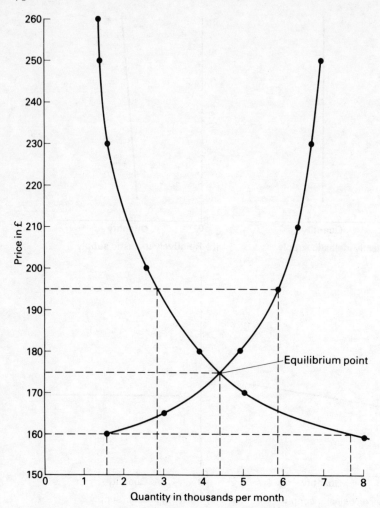

Fig. 5.8 Equilibrium price of washing machines

to an equilibrium price, given that certain conditions of perfect market competition exist. The idea of a perfect market assumes the following:

(a) The commodity produced is exactly the same as all other products of that type: Thus if a manufacturer produced kettles, then it is assumed that they are exactly the same as all other kettles produced. This cuts out any possibility of choice based on brand, colour or gimmicks.

(b) There are a large number of buyers and sellers: If this situation exists, then no one buyer or seller can influence the demand or supply of a particular product. If there was only one buyer, then he could dictate what price he will pay, or how many he will buy.

Similarly if there was only one supplier, then he could fix the amount of goods produced, or the price at which he will sell.

(c) There is perfect market knowledge: By this is meant that all buyers and sellers have immediate knowledge of price movements, and supply movements. Thus, if, due to a surplus of stock, the price of a good was reduced, then the market as a whole is assumed to know this immediately, and there would be a sudden increase in sales.

(d) All commodities produced are perfectly mobile: This ensures that the previous assumption could be achieved, and that in a particular market only one price existed. The majority of commodities are mobile, in the construction industry however it is just the opposite. At the present time in certain areas there is a shortage of dwellings, in other areas there is a glut. This is the main reason for the vastly different house prices in different parts of the country.

(e) Firms are free to enter or leave an industry: If a firm is making particularly good profits, then other firms will be attracted into the industry. If on the other hand a firm is making a loss, then it is free to cease operations in that industry, and seek a more profitable alternative.

(f) All factors of production are perfectly mobile.

Now that the assumed environment has been studied, it should be easier to understand the self-adjusting mechanism of the market. In Fig. 5.8, if it is assumed that the price of washing machines was fixed at £195 then the demand would be 2 800 machines per month, but supply would be 5 850 machines per month. Because there is an excess of the goods, the price would fall, there would be an extension in demand, and a contraction in supply, until the equilibrium point was reached. In practice, the speed with which the equilibrium point is reached is dictated mainly by assumption (c) above, the degree of perfection of market knowledge.

If it is now assumed that the price was initially set too low, say at £160, then the demand of 7 650 machines would far exceed the supply of 1 550. As demand was so much higher than supply, then the price would rise. As this happens however, the demand will contract whilst the supply extends, until the equilibrium point is reached.

The effect of changes in demand on the equilibrium point

In Fig. 5.9, there exists a steady market demand of 150 cast iron spiral staircases per month, at £500 each. As a result of a new television series in which such a staircase is often shown, a new trend has been set and demand has increased which is now shown by demand line 2. As the same conditions of supply are still in existence, the supply line is unaltered. A new equilibrium point is eventually reached at a price of £700 for a quantity of 250 per month.

Conversely a decrease in demand might come about due to an

78

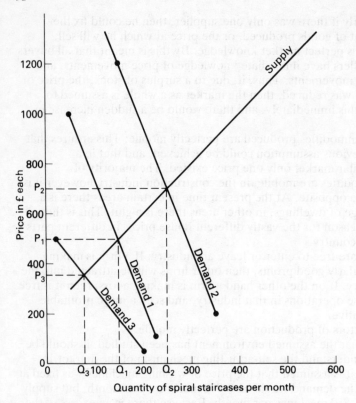

Fig. 5.9 The effect on price of a change in demand

amendment of the Building Regulations making such staircases illegal
for new works, in certain situations. This demand drop is represented
by demand line 3 on Fig. 5.9, and shows that with such a situation,
there is a drop in price coupled with a drop in demand.

The effect of changes in supply on the equilibrium point

In Fig. 5.10 the supply and demand situation for cast iron spiral
staircases is again represented. Supply line 1 indicates the initial
situation resulting in the sale of 150 staircases per month at £500 each.

Due to technological breakthrough in the casting process,
manufacturers are now able to supply more units at any particular
price. This causes the supply to increase to supply line 2 resulting in
more sales, but at a lower price. Note that demand conditions have not
altered.

Alternatively, a decrease in supply could be brought about by a
massive wage settlement of say 50 per cent being paid to the foundry
workers. This results in less manufacturers being efficient enough to
offer the units at a particular price. Supply line 3 demonstrates this,

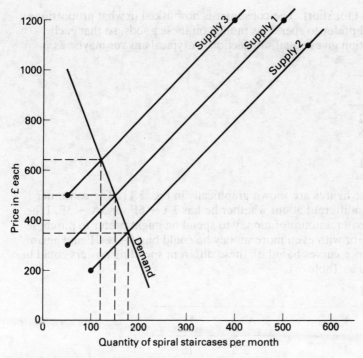

Fig. 5.10 The effect on price of a change in supply

and shows that a drop in supply, coupled with an increase in price, would result.

Normal price and market price

The normal price is often termed the long-period equilibrium price, for it is that price at which demand will equal supply, in the long term.

Market price is the short-period equilibrium price and this price will indicate short-term fluctuations in the market conditions. For example, there are occasionally scares that sugar will be in short supply. Imagine that as a result of political or climatic problems a possible shortage has been announced. The result may be panic buying, which in turn may result in a doubling of price. This high price would only be a short-term market price, for people would not, under normal circumstances tolerate such a price.

Demand and indifference curve analysis

An indifference curve in its simplest form, considers a consumer's choice of different combinations of two commodities. Assume that a consumer can buy only two commodities, say accommodation and food

(A and F) for short. The consumer is now asked in what proportions he would prefer to spend his money on these goods, so that each combination gives equal satisfaction. A typical answer maybe as follows:

A	F
2	12
3	6
5	3
12	1

These figures are shown graphically in Fig. 5.11. The consumer then, is indifferent about whether he has 3A + 6F, or 5A + 3F. If he had a greater amount of money to spend he might prefer to purchase 5A + 5F or with even more money he could buy 5A + 7F and again indifference curves based on these different spending powers could be compiled as Table 5.1.

Table 5.1

A	F	A	F
2	15	2½	16
3	9	3	12
5	5	5	7
12	3	12	5

Figure 5.12 combines the figures in Table 5.1 and Fig. 5.11 to show the pattern created by a series of three indifference curves. Remember that the consumer is indifferent about the exact position he occupies on any single curve, but he cannot jump from one to the other, unless the amount of money he can spend changes, or the cost of the goods changes. The consumer would much prefer to be on curve N rather than either of the other two, because he would be buying more units. Thus the further out the line is from the origin, the greater the satisfaction. He could of course only get to curve N, if he had more to spend. We will now look into increases in income, and see how they affect the consumer's demand.

If the consumer spent all his income he could either buy 10 units of food, or 10 units of accommodation. This can be shown as a consumption possibility line as in Fig. 5.13. The consumer could buy either 10F + 0A or 0F + 10A; or 8F + 2A or 3F + 7A or any combination, so long as it remained on the line. These positions do not however give equal satisfaction, only the various positions on a single indifference curve can do that. To find the consumer's optimal choice, Figs. 5.12 and 5.13 are combined to give Fig. 5.14 from which can be

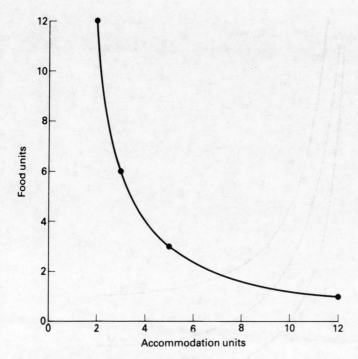

Fig. 5.11 An indifference curve

determined the consumer's choice that would give maximum satisfaction. Remember that the further the curve is from the origin, the greater the satisfaction. The consumer's best buying combination is the position on the outermost curve that just touches the consumption possibility line, in this case curve M.

Indifference curves are useful for studying a consumer's change in demand for certain goods, relative to his income, and to other goods that he buys. In Fig. 5.15 the positions are shown for both an increase and a decrease in income.

The initial assumed income has an optimal demand of 5.5F + 4.5A.

The increased income has an optimal demand of 7.25F + 4.75A.

The decreased income has an optimal demand of 3.75F + 4.25A.

From analysis of the increase, it can be seen that this consumer would prefer to spend a greater proportion of his increase on food, rather than accommodation.

His demand for food has gone up from 5.5F to 7.25F, whereas his demand for accommodation has increased only from 4.5A to 4.75A. A similar trend is shown with a decrease in income, with a drop in demand for accommodation units of 0.25A and a much larger drop in food units of 1.75F.

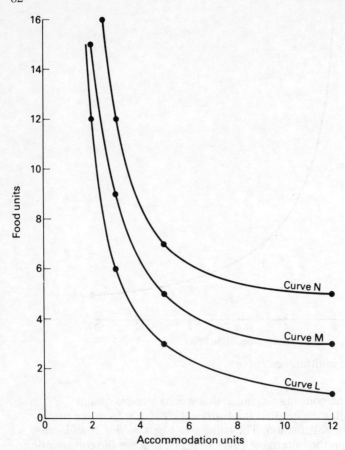

Fig. 5.12 An indifference curve series

The result of a change in the price of one of the goods under observation, can also be studied with indifference curves. Consider Fig. 5.16. With the original situation, the consumption possibility line was fixed with the consumer being able to buy either 10F + 0A, or 0F + 10A units. Assume now an increase in the price of accommodation, whilst food prices remain unchanged. This may now result in the consumer being able to buy only 6.5A, if all his money was spent on accommodation, instead of 10A as previously. This fixes the new consumption possibility line at 10F + 0A to 0F + 6.5A and this will effectively reduce the optimal demand of 4.25F + 3.75A on curve L. Thus his demand for food has reduced, even though the price remains constant.

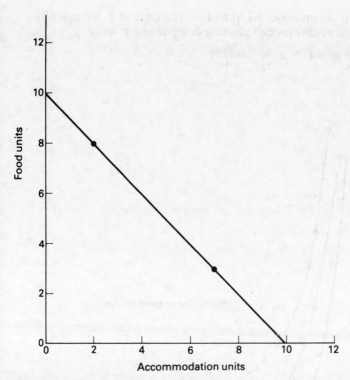

Fig. 5.13 Consumption possibility line

Questions

1 Suggest two commodities that would fit approximately the demand
   curves for Figs. 5.3(b), (c) and (d), and give reasons for your choice.
2 (a) From Fig. 5.4 determine the elasticity of demand for a price
       change from £12 down to £10.
   (b) At this point, is it elastic or inelastic.
3 (a) Determine graphically the equilibrium point from the figures
       given over the page.
   (b) A change in conditions causes a shift in demand which can be
       shown by including the following figures, on the graph.
       (i) Determine the new equilibrium point.
       (ii) Suggest reasons for the shift in demand.
4 From the following figures:
   (a) Determine which commodities are complements, substitutes,
       unrelated.
   (b) Suggest commodities that would fit approximately the figures as
       shown, explaining your choices.

84

There are four commodities KLM and N. The price of K increases by 20 per cent and results in the following demand movements:

K   −10%   M   −12%
L   0   N   +7%

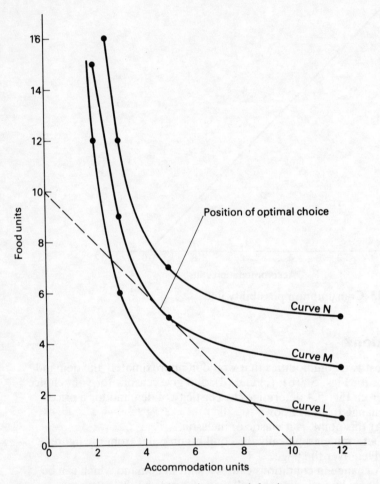

Fig. 5.14 Determination of maximum satisfaction

Demand		Supply	
Price (£)	Quantity/month	Price (£)	Quantity/month
7.00	50	1.00	100
4.75	100	1.75	200
2.75	200	3.50	350
1.25	450	5.00	450
1.00	600	6.00	500

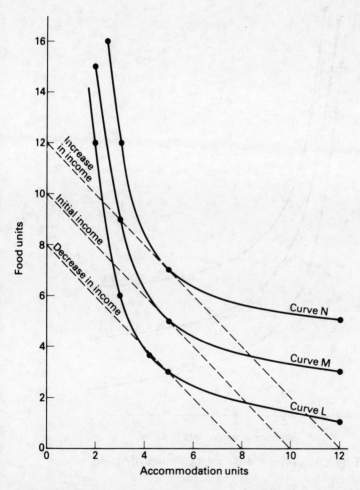

Fig. 5.15 Effect of change of income on an indifference curve series

86

Demand

Price (£)	Quantity/month
7.00	150
5.50	175
3.50	275
2.00	500
1.75	600

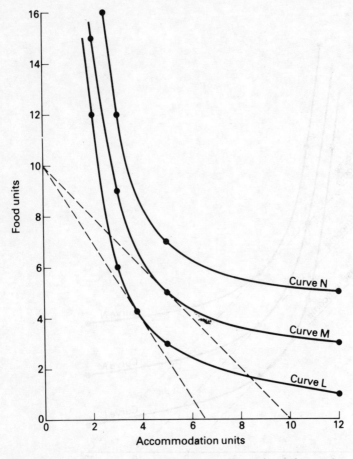

Fig. 5.16 Effect of a price change on the optimal demand

Chapter 6

The use of supply and demand in helping to formulate government policy

Supply and demand analysis is useful, not only to producers or other parties engaged in trading, but also to government. By the adoption of various policies, government can help to guide:
(a) Manufacturers in their choice of goods produced.
(b) Buyers in their choice of goods to consume.
(c) Importers and exporters in their choice of goods handled.
(d) Farmers and food producers in their choice of products grown.

Fiscal control is the tool used to try to achieve these various policies, and this comprises the selective use of taxes and subsidies, in order to achieve certain objectives. All democratically elected governments, irrespective of which party is in power, have certain general or normative objectives, which are considered necessary in the present day, for the good of the nation and its population. These objectives cover the following areas, and some will be discussed in more depth in later chapters.
(a) Improvement of living standards.
(b) High level of employment.
(c) Ensuring a good balance of payments.
(d) Curbing of inflationary tendencies.
(e) Equalisation of the distribution of wealth.

Supply and demand, and particularly elasticity analysis can be used in many ways, to help achieve the objectives above.

Consider the following examples.

The effects of taxation on commodities of different elasticities

Taxes on goods can be classified under two headings, *specific taxes*, which is where a fixed amount of tax is paid per unit, or *ad valorem* taxes, where a percentage of the price is added on as tax. A typical example of a *specific tax* is excise duty, which is payable on cigarettes, spirits and petrol. Value added tax on the other hand is a good example of *ad valorem* tax.

The effect of specific taxes

Consider the following statistics which are put into graphical form in Fig. 6.1.

Demand		Supply before tax		Supply after tax	
Price (£)	Quantity (1 000's/wks)	Price (£)	Quantity (1 000's/wks)	Price (£)	Quantity (1 000's/wks)
6.00	1	0.4	1	2.4	1
4.50	4	2.5	5	4.5	5
3.50	7	4.0	8	6.0	8
3.00	9	6.1	12	8.1	12
2.50	12				

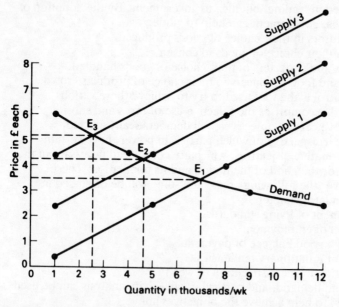

Fig. 6.1 Effect of a specific tax on an elastic demand

From the figures above it could be deduced that a specific tax of £2 per item has been imposed, but the effect of the tax is not immediately evident. Figure 6.1 however shows a very shallow demand curve, and if the elasticity is calculated between supply curves 1 and 2, that is from a price of £3.50 rising to £4.20, a figure of 1.60 is obtained, indicating an elastic demand around these prices.

The £2 tax on the selling price has in effect made fewer manufacturers able to supply goods at the existing price. Initially 7 000 could be supplied at £3.50, but after tax only 3 100 could have been supplied at £3.50. This meant that if 3 100 were supplied, due to the shortage of supplies, prices would have risen to £4.90. This in turn would have encouraged more manufacturers to produce which would cause prices to drop until a new equilibrium point E_2 was reached.

What is the effect as far as government revenue is concerned?

It would receive 4 700 units at £2, which equals £9 400/wk. If the government now anticipated adding a further £2 tax per unit, what would be its revenue then?

This would result in supply line 3, which would lead to E_3. The revenue would be 2 600 units at £4 each which equals £10 400/wk.

Although the government tax revenue has increased, the much higher burden of tax is being borne by only about half the number of consumers, had only £2 tax been imposed. Such a situation also poses other problems. If E_3 was the new equilibrium point, then only 2 600 units would be needed, instead of the original 7 000. This reduction can only normally come about by redundancies. Thus the action of adding £4 tax would go against one of the government's basic objectives, for it would reduce employment.

The difference between supply line 1 and 2 measured vertically is the £2 tax. The difference between E_1 and E_2 measured vertically is only £0.70. Although the government gets £2 tax per unit, only 0.70 comes from the consumer, the other £1.30 is added to the supplier's production costs. Producers then bear the burden of the majority of the tax. From the above it can be seen that there are several problems with imposing a specific tax on an elastic demand.

Consider now another set of statistics which again are reproduced in graphical form, this time as Fig. 6.2.

Demand		Supply before tax		Supply after tax	
Price (£)	Quantity (1 000's/wks)	Price (£)	quantity (1 000's/wks)	Price (£)	Quantity (1 000's/wks)
8.00	5	0.40	1	2.40	1
5.50	6	2.50	5	4.50	5
3.50	7	4.00	8	6.00	8
0.50	9	6.10	12	8.10	12

This product has the same supply lines as Fig. 6.1, it also has the same initial equilibrium of 7 000 units at £3.50. If the elasticity is worked out, however, between E_1 and E_2 it will be seen to be relatively inelastic.

What difference will this make to the arguments from the previous example?

From Fig. 6.2, it became evident that the imposition of the tax has resulted in only a slight reduction in demand, compared to Fig. 6.1, and much more of the £2 tax is now borne by the consumer, rather than the producer.

Government would raise revenue of 6 200 at £2 which equals £12 400, which is considerably more than that raised in Fig. 6.1.

If the tax was raised to £4 per unit, the revenue would be 5 500 at £4 which equals £22 000. This massive revenue would result in only a relatively small drop in the quantity demanded and supplied and so would not cause excessive redundancies.

Commodities with inelastic demands are much more likely to find themselves the targets of the Chancellor's budget policies than those with elastic demands, as the quantity demanded is less likely to change.

Table 6.1 Summary of specific tax

On elastic demand commodities: it causes a large contraction in demand.	On inelastic demand commodities: it causes small contraction in demand.
Most of the tax is borne by suppliers.	Most of the tax is borne by consumers.
Tax is borne by relatively few people.	Tax revenue comes from many consumers.
Relatively small potential tax revenue.	Relatively large potential tax revenue.

The effect of ad valorem *tax*

Figure 6.3 has the same demand line and initial supply line as Fig. 6.1. Instead of a specific tax of £2 however, the government has decided to operate a 50 per cent *ad valorem* tax. This results in supply line 2 of Fig. 6.3. This tax results in similar changes with respect to supply and demand to those of Fig. 6.1, there is however one major difference. With the specific tax, the same amount per unit was recovered as tax, irrespective of price. This resulted in the parallel supply lines of Fig. 6.1. With the *al valorem* tax, whatever the price was originally, it is

91

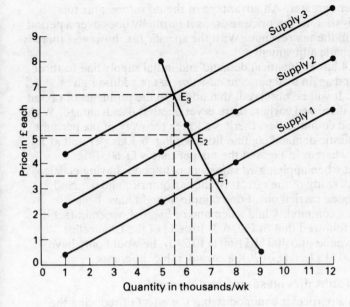

Fig. 6.2 Effect of a specific tax on an inelastic demand

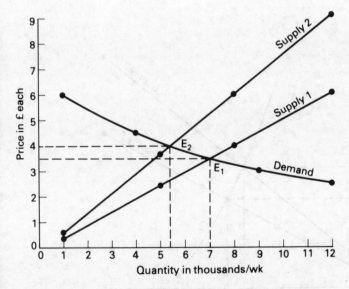

Fig. 6.3 Effect of *ad valorem* tax on an elastic demand

92

now 50 per cent greater. An advantage of the *ad valorem* tax for government is that, as the price rises, as it normally does over a period of time, so will the tax revenue. With the specific tax, however, there is no such automatic adjustment.

Figure 6.4 has an identical demand and initial supply line to those of Fig. 6.2, and again a 50 per cent *ad valorem* tax addition gives supply line 2. It will be observed, that added to the problems of tax on elastic goods discussed earlier, there is yet another disadvantage. With elastic demand commodities, there is a lower recovery of tax per unit, than with inelastic demand commodities. In Fig. 6.3 tax per unit at E_2 is only £1.30 whereas in Fig. 6.4 the tax per unit is £1.60. It is essential, that when applying *ad valorem* tax to goods having elastic demand, a full study of the effects of the tax on price and demand should have been carried out. For example it might have been assumed that a commodity had a demand of Fig. 6.4, when in fact it more closely followed that of Fig. 6.3. Instead of the Chancellor realising a revenue of 6 400 at £1.60 (£10 240), he would only have obtained 5 400 at £1.30 (£7 020), a considerable difference.

The effect of subsidies on supply and demand

A subsidy on a particular commodity has the effect of reducing the production costs. As stated previously this will result in a new supply line with a shift to the right.

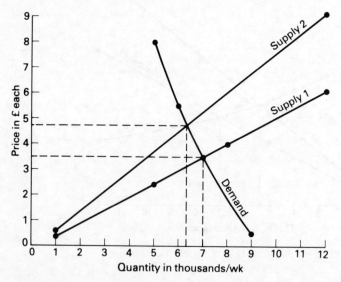

Fig. 6.4 Effect of *ad valorem* tax on an inelastic demand

Figures 6.5 to 6.8, show the results of a £2 subsidy per unit on various combinations of elastic and inelastic supplies and demands.

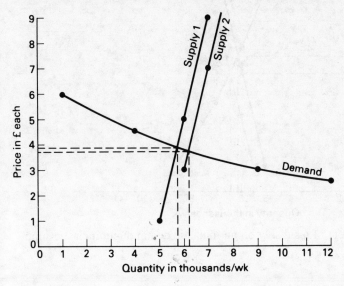

Fig. 6.5 Effect of a subsidy on an elastic demand, but with an inelastic supply

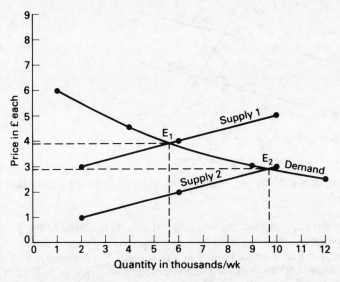

Fig. 6.6 Effect of a subsidy on an elastic demand and elastic supply

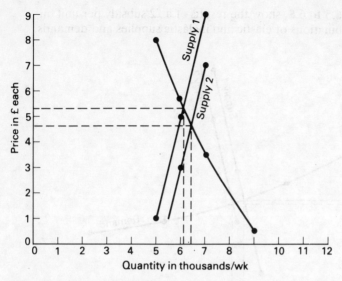

Fig. 6.7 Effect of a subsidy on an inelastic demand and inelastic supply

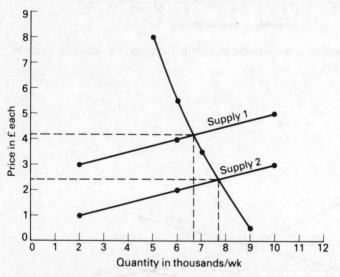

Fig. 6.8 Effect of a subsidy on an inelastic demand, but with an elastic supply

Figure 6.6 perhaps shows best the workings of a subsidy. Initially the equilibrium point is at E_1, but after being subsidised, the supply line drops £2 to supply line 2 which results in a new equilibrium point at E_2. It can be seen that the demand has increased from 5 600 to 9 700 per week and the total subsidy that the government will have to pay will be 9 700 × £2 (£19 400). The consumers however do not pay £2 less, they do in fact pay only £1 less, the other £1 then must be kept by the producers. From studying the four graphs Figures 6.5 to 6.8 the following conclusions can be drawn.

(a) Figure 6.6, that with elastic supply and demand, shows a fairly large drop in price, coupled with a large extension of demand. The more perfect the elasticity of supply and demand is, the greater is the extension in demand.

(b) Figure 6.8, that with elastic supply and inelastic demand, shows the greatest drop in price, coupled with a small extension of demand. To enable the full £2 subsidy to be passed on to the consumer, there would have to be perfectly inelastic demand and perfectly elastic supply.

Uses of subsidies and taxes

Both taxes and subsidies can be used to help achieve the normative objectives stated earlier.

Subsidies can help curb certain economic problems; to help alleviate unemployment, demand could be stimulated, and conditions as in Fig. 6.6 would be sought to carry out the exercise effectively. In the past, subsidies have been introduced on agricultural products, in order to make Britain self-sufficient in times of war. See Chapter 16 for further details on current subsidies.

If subsidies were being used to reduce the cost of necessities and aid the poor, then situations like those depicted in Fig. 6.8 would be chosen.

In both the above cases, it will be seen that subsidies are of little benefit when used on inelastic supply curves.

Taxes are used by government for two main reasons:

(a) To raise revenue.

(b) To cut back demand.

Taxation is discussed more fully in Chapter 16, but the revenue raised by government is needed to pay for social services, health, defence etc. From time to time it becomes necessary for the government to increase its taxes. Ideally the government would look for situations resembling Fig. 6.2, where the demand is relatively inelastic. The more inelastic the demand, the greater will be the revenue obtained.

The taxing of luxury items, tends to help redistribute wealth within the country. Rich people pay the tax, which means that the poorer sector of society needs to pay less tax. The problem here is that many luxury goods have very elastic demands, so that as more tax is imposed, demand rapidly falls.

Taxes may be imposed to cut back on demand for various reasons:

(a) To reduce home demand for a product, in the hope that the manufacturer will turn to exporting.

(b) To reduce consumption of socially undesirable goods, such as tobacco and alcoholic drinks. This group however tends to be very inelastic in demand, due to the habit forming nature of the goods.

(c) To cut back on imported goods to help the country's balance of payments.

Questions

1 From the following figures, construct the supply and demand curves and find:
(a) The total government revenue.   (b) That total revenue borne by the consumer.   (c) That total revenue borne by the supplier.

Demand		Supply	
Price(£)	Quantity (1 000's/wks)	Price	Quantity (1 000's/wks)
6	2	2	2
5	4	4	3
4	6	6	4

A specific tax of £2 per item is added to the price of the good.

2 Construct the supply and demand curves from the following figures, and compare the results with those of question 1.
Discuss the benefits or costs of the two situations with respect to:
(a) Society in general;   (b) Government;   (c) The suppliers.

Demand		Supply	
Price	Quantity (1 000's weeks)	Price	Quantity (1 000's weeks)
7.00	3.0	2.00	2.00
4.00	3.50	3.00	5.00
1.00	4.00	4.00	8.00

A specific tax of £2 per item is added to the price.

3 The government is trying to decide whether to subsidise the cost of all meat produced in the country. Discuss the possible outcome of such a policy with regard to: (a) Producers and consumers;
(b) Importers and exporters;   (c) The society in general;
(d) Government.

Chapter 7

The clients and the different sectors of the construction industry

The projects undertaken by the industry are very wide ranging, but can be classified by work type under two main headings:
(a) Building.
(b) Civil engineering.

The construction industry is perhaps one of the few industries that encompass such widely differing sizes of job, such as the replacing of a roof slate, to the building of a multi-storey office block or motorway. In size of firm, again there is a great variation between, at the one extreme, many sole traders who concentrate mainly on local maintenance work, to the other extreme of national organisations whose turnover is measured in millions of pounds.

There are many aspects of the industry that could be analysed and in this chapter, five will be looked at:
- The sectors of the industry as defined by type of work.
- The size of firm.
- The trade of firm.
- The clients of the industry.
- The gross domestic fixed capital formation.

The classification of sectors

The construction industry can, as has already been stated, be split into building and civil engineering. It is necessary, however to divide the industry down further in order to analyse more accurately current trends in construction activity.

One system of sector classification is that used by the Department of the Environment (DOE) in their quarterly publication *Housing and Construction Statistics*, which gives current output figures for the industry.

The headings are as follows:
1. New work
   (a) Public housing.
   (b) Private housing.
   (c) Other new work:
       (i) industrial.
       (ii) commercial.
   (d) Other new work – public.
2. Repair and maintenance
   (a) Housing.
   (b) Other work – public.
   (c) Other work – private.

The *public sector* can be defined as any public authority, such as local authorities, nationalised industries, new town corporations etc.

The *private sector* is any private owner, developer or private organisation.

Industrial work would encompass such projects as factories, warehouses, chemical treatment plants etc.

Commercial work includes work carried out on shops, offices, farm buildings, dance halls etc.

Table 7.1 shows the output of the various sectors over the last thirteen years, but with all work priced at 1980 prices. This allows comparison of the actual amount of work carried out.

If a particular year is analysed, say 1986 the various sectors can be compared by analysing their outputs.

Total construction output was approximately £22.6 billion, at 1980 prices (in this book 1 billion is taken as 10^9). Total new work was approximately £13.5 billion, with maintenance work at £9.1 billion.

Therefore new work represents $\frac{13.5}{22.6} \times 100 = 59.7$ per cent with maintenance representing 40.3 per cent.

These figures surprise many people, as it is generally not realised that over ⅓ of all money spent in the construction industry is on repairs.

The rest of the sectors can easily be calculated, and can best be shown on a pie chart as in Fig. 7.1.

From Fig. 7.1 it can be seen that the largest sector is Repairs to Housing, which includes both private and public dwellings. It should be remembered that DIY is not included in these figures. This section is followed by Other works public, which includes roads, schools hospitals etc.

The figures from Table 7.1 can be plotted on graphs (Figs. 7.2 to 7.4) which show up any trends in the sector outputs. It should be

Table 7.1 The value of output of the construction industry at 1980 prices £ million

Year	New housing		Other new work			All new work	Repair and maintenance			All repair and maintenance	All work
	Public	Private	Public	Private	Commercial		Housing	Other work Public	Other work Private		
1974	2 439	3 455	4 989	2 401	2 844	16 128	3 655	2 443	1 165	7 263	23 391
1975	2 689	3 114	4 672	2 383	2 581	15 439	3 205	2 402	1 008	6 615	22 054
1976	2 970	3 318	4 641	2 276	2 268	15 473	2 957	2 267	1 004	6 228	21 701
1977	2 702	3 142	4 425	2 268	2 268	15 175	3 073	2 276	1 093	6 442	21 617
1978	2 539	3 558	4 238	2 803	2 520	15 658	3 559	2 550	1 342	7 451	23 109
1979	2 108	3 283	3 905	3 004	2 390	14 689	4 320	2 718	1 532	8 570	23 260
1980	1 711	2 585	3 524	2 806	2 430	13 055	4 480	2 920	1 597	8 997	22 052
1981	1 124	2 351	3 343	2 339	2 601	11 758	4 075	2 681	1 434	8 189	19 947
1982	940	2 701	3 493	2 100	2 957	12 190	4 052	2 655	1 362	8 069	20 260
1983	1 001	3 238	3 556	1 879	3 014	12 688	4 326	2 711	1 377	8 413	21 101
1984	910	3 118	3 602	2 364	3 156	13 149	4 532	2 694	1 468	8 693	21 842
1985	751	2 968	3 396	2 702	3 365	13 182	4 688	2 595	1 607	8 889	22 072
1986	665	3 272	3 374	2 387	3 834	13 533	4 874	2 463	1 746	9 082	22 615

Source: Housing and construction statistics

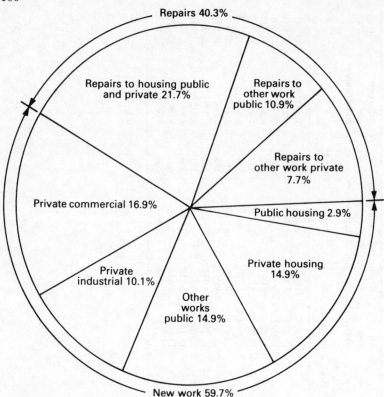

Fig. 7.1 Construction industry outputs by sector, as a percentage of total work done in 1986

remembered however that such graphs are only a representation of historical figures, and are open to many interpretations.

The sectors described above, are the ones most often used when the industry is discussed. There is nothing to stop further division by more detailed analysis of the type of work. Indeed this is done in some DOE statistics tables, so that more detailed examination of both government and private expenditure can be undertaken.

The size of the firms

As the role of the industry is being portrayed, it is important to set the scene, by ensuring that the student has the basic information about the many building firms regarding their size and function.

Consider the following figures in Table 7.2 which are taken from the housing and construction statistics.

(a) 94.5 per cent of construction firms employ less than 14 men. The number of firms employing over 13 men only constitutes 5.5 per cent of the total number of businesses.

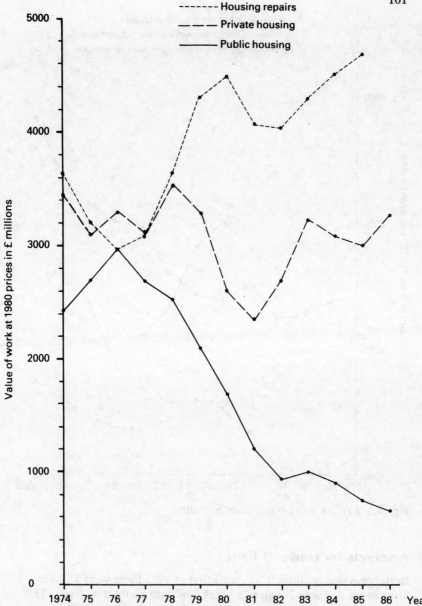

Fig. 7.2 New housing and housing repair sectors

(b) This 5.5 per cent of large businesses accounts for about 67 per cent of the industry's output, and about 61 per cent of the industry's workforce.

At this stage, the student may be asking himself, 'Why are there so many small firms, and why so few large firms?' These questions will hopefully be answered when marketing and types of business organisations are dealt with later in the book.

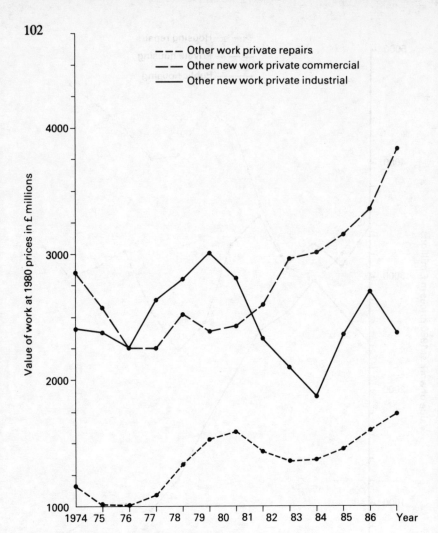

Fig. 7.3 Private work other than housing

Analysis by trade of firm

In the previous section, it was seen that in 1985 there were 167 825 firms in total. Table 7.3 gives a breakdown of this total by trade. This table at this stage may appear as a jumbled mass of figures, but hopefully the student will refer back to these, during the reading of the rest of the text, where appropriate. The figures in Table 7.3 tend to show fairly well, that the number of firms engaged in a particular trade is of course related to the demand for that type of work. Hence there will always be more general builders than floor and wall tilers, as people do not require the services of the latter very often.

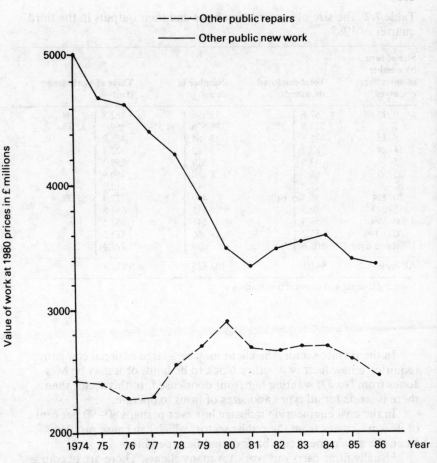

Fig. 7.4 Public work other than housing

Clients of the industry

Almost everyone in the country must at some time during his life be involved with the construction industry. It may be in the course of his work, or it may be in private life. The clients of the industry then are many and varied, and it again becomes necessary to categorise them. To a certain extent this has already been done in Table 7.1 where the two main client sectors are either public or private.

Much of the work for public bodies is subject to open or selective tendering, which tends to favour firms already specialising in the type of work under consideration. As much of this work is on a large scale, then the firms doing public work tend to be of medium or large size.

104

Table 7.2 The size of construction firms and their outputs in the third quarter of 1985

Size of firm by number of operatives employed	Total employed thousands		Number of firms		Value of work done (£m)	
0–1	67.8		72 896		382.8	
2–7	228.8	39%	78 576	94.5%	1 159.2	32.7%
8–13	71.8		7 164		405.2	
14–24	83.2		4 582		522.4	
25–34	43.6		1 519		269.3	
35–59	65.7		1 480		450.9	
60–79	29.9		441		212.2	
80–114	38.8	61%	409	5.5%	272.4	67.3%
115–299	89.3		512		654.8	
300–599	59.3		141		462.1	
600–1 199	55.2		66		413.5	
1 200 and over	108.6		39		779.4	
All firms	941.1		167 825		5 974.3	

Source: Housing and construction statistics

In the private sector, the client may be a large national company, requiring a new factory or office block to be built, or it may be Mrs Jones from No 37, wanting her front door eased. In this sector then, there is scope for all types and sizes of firms to operate.

In the civil engineering industry however perhaps 80–90 per cent of its work comes from the public sector, which can cause problems when the government cuts back on public expenditure.

Usually firms carry out work for many clients. There are of course exceptions to this, for instance: A civil engineering firm may specialise in carrying out roadworks for the Coal Board, or a small general builder may specialise in doing maintenance work at a large factory, where it was deemed uneconomical to have a direct maintenance labour force. The obvious problem of this dependence upon one client is summed up by the proverb, 'Never put all your eggs in one basket.'

The smaller building firms tend to carry out smaller works, and there are many reasons for this:

(a) Small firms have lower overhead costs, and so can do smaller jobs cheaper than the bigger firms, who have to carry higher overheads to cope with larger jobs.
(b) Small firms may lack the expertise or experience of carrying out the larger works.
(c) Lack of finance for carrying out larger works.

Table 7.3 Analysis of construction firms by trade in the third quarter 1985

Trade of firm	Number of firms		Work done	
	Total	%	£m	%
General builders	67 475	40.2	1 956.8	32.7
Building and civil engineers	3 623	2.1	954	16.0
Civil engineers	2 662	1.6	462	7.7
Plumbers	14 934	8.9	188.1	3.1
Carpenters and joiners	10 949	6.5	128.4	2.1
Painters	14 662	8.7	223.8	3.7
Roofers	5 818	3.5	194.4	3.2
Plasterers	4 019	2.4	64.7	1.1
Glaziers	4 387	2.6	121.4	2.0
Demolition contractors	559	0.3	22.9	0.4
Scaffolding specialists	996	5.7	90.1	1.5
Reinforced concrete specialists	515	0.3	35.3	0.6
Heating and ventilating engineers	8 461	5.0	391.1	6.5
Electrical contractors	15 449	9.2	492.1	8.2
Asphalt and tar sprayers	856	0.5	133.2	2.2
Plant hire specialists	3 664	2.2	149.4	2.5
Flooring contractors	1 400	0.8	45.8	0.8
Constructional engineers	1 560	0.9	88.0	1.5
Insulating specialists	1 308	0.8	66.0	1.1
Suspended ceiling specialists	842	0.5	25.3	0.4
Floor and wall tilers	1 167	0.7	23.5	0.4
Miscellaneous	2 549	1.5	118.4	2.0
All trades	167 825	100.0	5 974.3	100.0

Source: Housing and construction statistics

(d) Personal attention by a small builder is appreciated by clients.

To sum up, in general terms: Small firms carry out small general works for private individuals and also highly specialised work such as glazing or air conditioning, for large public or private clients. At the other extreme, large firms tend to carry out work for large public and private clients.

The size and distribution of firms will be discussed further in Chapter 9.

Gross domestic fixed capital formation

Capital goods are those tending to have a durable nature. The formation of domestic fixed capital (DFC) can be said to be the amount of new factories, roads, plant, equipment and housing produced within the country.

From Table 10.2 of the UK National Accounts 1986, the following figures of Table 7.4 were extracted.

It can be seen from Table 7.4 and from Fig. 7.5 which is derived from it, that the construction industry plays a significant part in the formation of DFC.

Table 7.4 Domestic fixed capital formation. £million at 1980 prices

	1975	1977	1979	1981	1983	1985
Private sector						
Dwellings	5 537	5 560	6 468	5 454	6 069	6 481
Other buildings	6 744	6 537	6 374	6 119	6 184	6 965
Total construction costs	12 281	12 097	12 842	11 537	12 253	13 446
Total capital formation costs	24 138	26 510	30 732	27 712	29 908	36 163
Total construction as % of total capital formation	51	46	42	42	41	37
Public sector						
Dwellings	3 554	3 382	2 893	1 720	2 342	1 994
Other buildings	7 414	6 556	6 038	5 284	6 314	6 512
Total construction costs	10 968	9 938	8 931	7 004	8 656	8 506
Total capital formation costs	17 184	14 840	13 222	10 104	11 782	10 147
Total construction as % of total capital formation	64	67	67	69	73	84
% overall both sectors	56	53	50	49	50	47

Source: National income and expenditure

Consider the year 1985

The public sector incorporating all industries accounted for £10 147 million, the construction industry having 84 per cent of this at £8 506 million.

The private sector had a total of £36 163 million of which the construction industry produced 37 per cent at £13 446 million.

Overall however the industry generally produces about 50 per cent of all gross domestic capital formation.

How important are these figures? It should be remembered that fixed capital formation represents an investment in the future of the economy of the country. This applies whether it is for the private sector in the form of houses or factories, or for the public sector in the form of new roads, town halls, schools etc.

Hopefully all these projects will lead to greater output or greater efficiency within this country, and ultimately to a higher standard of living.

Future trends in gross Domestic Fixed Capital formation

In the past, construction work for the government and other public bodies has contributed a higher percentage to the DFC than work for the private sector. Will this continue to be the case? Several factors have to be taken into account when considering this.

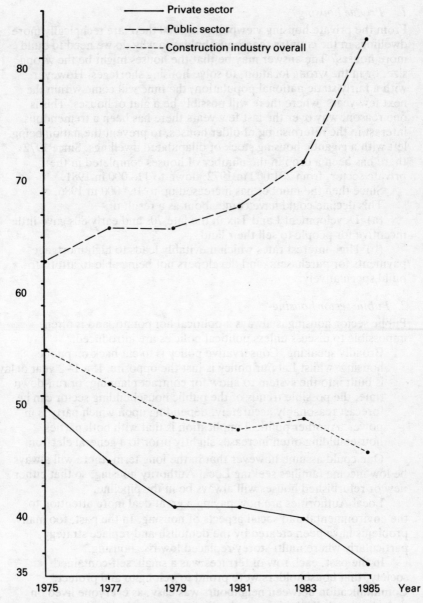

Fig. 7.5 Gross domestic capital formation. Construction industry sectors as a percentage of total fixed capital formation

1.   Private housing

From the private housing viewpoint, in 1980 there are technically more dwellings in the country than households, so why do we need to build more houses? The answer may be that the houses might be the wrong size, or in the wrong location, to solve housing shortages. However, with a fairly static national population, the time will come within the next few years, where there will possibly be a glut of houses. This is one reason, why over the last few years there has been a tremendous interest in the refurbishing of older houses, to prevent the nation being left with a gigantic housing stock of dilapidated dwellings. Since 1972 there has been a drop in the number of houses completed in the private sector, from 201 000 in 1972, down to 118 000 in 1981.

Since then the number has increased up to 164 000 in 1986.

This decline could have come about as a result of:−

(a) Development Land Tax in the late 70s and early 80s gave little incentive for people to sell their land.

(b) High interest rates which inevitably leads to high mortgage payments for purchasers, and developers not being able to afford to build speculatively.

2.   Public sector housing

Public sector housing is always a political hot potato, and is often impossible to discuss unless political policies are introduced.

Broadly speaking, Conservative policy is to cut back on public housing, whilst Labour policy is just the opposite. If a 1−2 year delay is built into the system to allow for contract planning, or run-down time, the possible trends of the public housebuilding sector can be forecast reasonably accurately, depending upon which party is in power. Another political implication is that with both parties, housebuilding often increases slightly prior to a general election.

One could assume however that in the long term, there will always be low income families seeking Local Authority housing, so that either new or refurbished houses will always be in the pipeline.

Local Authorities are now paying a great deal more attention to the environmental and social aspects of housing. In the past, too many problems have been created by the demolish-and-replace strategy, particularly where multi-storey replaced low rise housing.

In the past, each row of terraces was a small, self-contained society, that householders were proud to belong to and protect. Communication between neighbours was easy, as everyone lived on the same level. With high rise dwellings, communication is much more difficult, as one family lives on top of an other.

The modern approach to the problem is to try to preserve the local community environment, by moving people out of their houses, refurbishing, then moving the people back into their own houses. By doing this, communities remain intact and the local environment is not too disrupted.

3. Public sector other than housing

This sector has possibly the blackest future in the short term, with longer term prospects being uncertain. With the ever increasing price of oil, there seems little possibility of any new large motorway projects after the completion of those already in progress. Also many towns have by this stage constructed their inner and outer ring systems. The road building sector therefore looks to be set for a very hard time, especially as the majority of its work is controlled directly by government, which during times of depression tends to cut back on such public expenditure. Work in the service industries, i.e. gas, water, electricity and sewerage systems will in the future probably be concentrating less on new schemes, whilst employing more resources in the maintenance and replacement of outdated supply systems. Possibly around the turn of the century there will be much work created when it may be found necessary to revert back to town gas from natural gas.

When service industries have their capital budgets cut by central government, this often deals a blow to private housebuilders, and to industrialists. They may find that they have to pay more to get services laid on to premises under construction, and also pay higher charges for the energy used.

Projects such as reservoirs, oil depots, gas storage tanks etc. are becoming ever more difficult to plan for, due to environmentalist pressure groups opposing many such schemes.

4. The private industrial and commercial sector

A large proportion of the buildings used in industry and commerce were built prior to 1940. Although many of these buildings are still serviceable, it becomes more and more expensive to adapt them to changing technologies and systems required in modern industry. A great many factories still exist with insufficient headroom for modern machinery, and with workshops compartmentalised. Modern trends are towards higher ceilings which then enables the use of gantry cranes, conveyor tracks etc, with the whole area open plan, thus giving flexibility for future changes. Warehouses now use fork lift trucks, but many earlier buildings incorporating split levels and low headrooms cannot use these efficiently.

Position too, plays a large part in efficient distribution. In the past, rail and canal often dictated the town centre position of many factories and warehouses. Ideally, today these are best built on the fringes of towns, but close to a good road system.

Older properties are constantly being replaced, and this should lead to a fairly steady flow of work for many years to come in this sector.

There are however specific factors which affect this sector:

(a) A business investing in a new factory, must have reasonable faith in the sales of its products. This is most likely to happen in a boom period rather than a recession.

(b) The new factory must be financially viable. High interest rates often cause the shelving of many new industrial projects, as they would not be profitable after paying high interest charges.

(c) The accelerator principle. This is based upon the idea that a change in demand for durable capital goods leads to a greater change in activity in the industry supplying them.

For example. A large brick-making business uses 100 kilns. If each kiln has a life of five years, a constant investment programme of replacing 20 kilns every year will be necessary to maintain production (assuming a steady replacement situation is in operation).

Thus it will be seen that the construction industry has to maintain an output to this client of 20 kilns per year.

From Table 7.5 it can be seen that in years 1 and 2, there is a normal demand for bricks. However in year 3, an increase in brick demand causes a 20 per cent increase in the total demand for kilns. This gives a total of 40 new kilns to be built (20 replacements + 20 extra kilns), thus causing a 100 per cent increase in kiln building. In year 4, demand for kilns still rises, but the percentage change in demand for kilns drops to 4 per cent. This leads to a drop in kiln building of 37 per cent on the previous year. In year 5, fewer kilns are required which results in only ten kilns being built, a reduction of 60 per cent in kiln building. In year 6, 120 kilns are again needed, but because kiln building activity in the previous year was so low, this results in an increase of 150 per cent in kiln construction.

It can be seen, that the change in kiln construction is highly geared to the demand for kilns. A greater percentage increase in demand for kilns over the previous year leads to greater activity in kiln building. A smaller percentage increase, or a decrease from last year's demand for kilns, leads to a fall in kiln building activity.

Table 7.5 The accelerator principle applied to brick kilns with a 5 year replacement period.

Year	Demand for kilns		Construction of kilns			
	Total required	% change on previous year	Replacements	Extra required	Total	% change on previous year
1	100	0	20	—	20	0
2	100	0	20	—	20	0
3	120	+20	20	+20	40	+100
4	125	+4	20	+5	25	−37
5	115	−8	20	−10	10	−60
6	120	+4	20	+5	25	+150

If Table 7.6 is compared with Table 7.5, it becomes obvious that the greater life span of the capital goods concerned, the greater the fluctuation in the industries supplying them.

In year 3 for example, should the kilns last five years, kiln building would have increased 100 per cent. If the kilns lasted 20 years, kiln building would have increased 400 per cent.

Direct labour organisations

Many Local Authorities run non-profit-making departments, to carry out maintenance work on their dwellings. The direct labour organisations (DLOs) of some authorities tender alongside contractors for some new public works. Also, in some areas new Local Authority housing is constructed by DLOs. The following figures in Table 7.7 give an approximate guide to the value of work done by LA DLOs compared with the rest of the sector. It should be noted, that as the content of work varies under the different headings between DLOs and the industry in total, figures should not be strictly compared. They do however serve to give an idea of the amount of work carried out by DLOs. Direct labour, it should be remembered, is often used by private business for maintenance work in large factories and offices.

There is often much criticism of DLOs in that many do not work efficiently, and this results in the taxpayer and ratepayer ultimately paying more than if the work had been put out to tender.

The contracting industry dislikes LA DLOs as it is said that they take much work away from private businesses, which could in any case carry out the work quicker and more cheaply.

Before condemning DLOs the advantages and disadvantages should be considered.

Table 7.6. The accelerator principle applied to brick kilns with a 20 year replacement period.

Year	Demand for kilns		Construction of kilns			
	Total required	% change on previous year	Replace-ments	Extra required	Total	% change on previous year
1	100	0	5	0	5	0
2	100	0	5	0	5	0
3	120	+20	5	+20	25	+400
4	125	+4	5	+5	10	−60

Table 7.7 The value and proportion of work undertaken by L.A.D.L.O.s in 1985 at 1980 prices (£m)

	Public new work			Public repairs			Total
	Housing	Non-housing	All work	Housing	Non-housing	All work	All work
Undertaken by LADLOs	24	179	203	717	1 153	1 870	1 356
Total work done by construction industry	750	3 407	4 157	1 610*	2 597	4 207	8 367
% of total work load carried out by DLOs	3.2	5.2	4.9	44.5	44.4	44.4	16.2

*Estimated

Source: Housing and construction statistics.

Advantages of DLOs

(a) Direct labour should in theory be more economical, by at least the amount of the profit margin, as their prime aim is to provide a service, not to make a profit. Profit is therefore not included in their costings.
(b) With a workforce totally under one's control, greater flexibility is possible, plus faster reaction to emergency work.
(c) Operatives ultimately acquire an intimate knowledge of the buildings upon which they work.
(d) The management is more able to ensure that operatives carrying out the work have been properly trained up to a certain standard.
(e) There is no delay whilst contracts and/or specifications have to be produced to enable private contractors to tender.

Disadvantages of DLOs

(a) There is no profit motive, therefore in many organisations there is little incentive to maximise efficiency.
(b) There may be periods when there is little work for the operatives to do.
(c) It often works out dearer than if a private contractor was employed.
(d) A direct labour force requires the provision of back up facilities of stores, workshops, vehicles, plant etc. plus administrative staff.
    Generally DLOs are used for general non-specialised work, where a fairly even flow can be arranged, within a reasonably small geographical area.

Trade cycles

In all economies, there tend to exist trade cycles. In the past, many statistics have been studied, and figures produced, to try to validate the existence of a regular trade cycle, with a period of from 7 to 11 years.

It is important to realise at the outset, that there is no such thing as a regular trade cycle which will repeat itself with unfailing accuracy every few years. Nearly all fluctuations leading to the occurrence of trade cycles have been caused by numerous different external factors outside the control of industry generally.

Consider the following, which are some of the factors likely to lead to fluctuations.

Government action

This may affect the construction industry either directly or indirectly, as follows:

1. Directly
From Fig. 7.1, new public work accounted for 32 per cent of all new

work carried out by the industry in 1986. The government therefore has a large say in how much work the industry will be allocated, and it could reduce considerably the output of the industry if no new government or LA contracts were issued. This however is very unlikely to happen, as the government is frequently reminded by employers' associations of the problems caused by government stop–go policy.

The construction industry is therefore one of the first to suffer during times of recession. There are however problems for government with the operation of a stop – go policy. Governments are unlikely to stop work on projects already under construction, and as most public works tend to be large-scale, long-duration projects, little effect will be felt for possibly 12–18 months, until the contracts have been completed. A longer time lag may be experienced when the government wishes construction activity to increase. The design functions will become overloaded with work and thus the design and planning stages would not be able to cope. Added to this is the problem of planning permission delays and the actual tendering procedure. This could again lead to a 12–18 month period from the initial authority to proceed, to the placing of the contract. Here another point should be considered. The turnover of work is very slow during the early stages of a contract, and so a marked upturn in construction activity may not become apparent until 12 months after a job has started. This means two years after the government has taken off 'the brake'.

2. *Indirectly*

Government can affect private construction development indirectly by the application of fiscal and monetary policies. These are considered fully in Chapter 16 and 17, after the workings of such policies have been studied.

Reasons for government action: There are an infinite number of possible reasons for government implementing policies likely to affect the industry, but a few examples are:
(a) The country may be involved directly or indirectly in a war which would affect trade.
(b) Economic policies of other governments might affect the level of imports to, or exports from, this country.
(c) Energy factors, either the discovery of new reserves within the country, or the cutting off of supplies by other governments often results in changes of policies.
(d) Effects of inflation.

Demands on industries, leading to the application of the accelerator

It was seen earlier in the chapter, how a change in demand for bricks led to a greater change in demand for new kilns. If this is extended over many industries, whose boom periods coincided, it can be seen that the construction industry might be considerably overworked at these times. Conversely, a small change in demand downwards in the industries concerned would lead to a considerable recession in the construction industry.

Increasing propensity to save

During a recession, people tend to save money rather than spend it. This tends to exacerbate the trough of a depression, and so increases the period of the depression. See later chapters on Keynesian policies, and the multiplier.

Questions

1 Why, when old houses can be modernised or refurbished, do we tend to pull down and replace old factories and warehouses, rather than adapt them.
2 If the country ever reaches the situation where very few new houses are required, will the value of property still tend to increase annually, or will it tend to depreciate, as a new car does now.
3 In which country would you think the accelerator principle is most likely to operate, and why.
  (a) A country with a very stable economy, good standards of living, and a slowly increasing relatively high national income.
  (b) A country with a fairly volatile economy, fluctuating standards of living and widely varying national income.
4 From Table 7.3, building and civil engineering contractors comprise 2.1 per cent of the firms in the construction industry, and yet they carried out 16 per cent of the total value of work. Painters comprise 8.7 per cent of the firms in the industry and yet they carried out only 3.7 per cent of the total value of work.
  Discuss these statements.

Chapter 8

Employees' and employers' organisations and communication within the industry

No discussion of the construction industry would be complete without a brief consideration of the organisations representing both employees and employers.

In Chapter 4 was discussed the start of such organisations, with the advent of the craft gilds. Several major differences exist however, between the organisations of the Middle Ages, and those of today:

(a) In the craft gilds, both employees and employers belonged to the same organisation. Today, each party belongs to different organisations.

(b) Workers in the gilds were not generally trying to acquire better wages as many of today's unions do. They knew that with the system that operated at the time, they would eventually become masters, and they would then improve their standard of living. Later, however, the journeymen's associations closely resembled today's unions, in that they tried to obtain better wages and conditions for their members, from the employers.

(c) The earlier organisations tended to be formed on a local basis, whereas today all the large associations are national.

(d) A major activity of craft gilds was the checking of standards, and weights and measures. Although it is obviously in an employer's best interest to ensure that work is up to standard, regulations and inspections have largely been taken over by the various government bodies. Similarly, many of the social benefits, such as sick pay, schooling for children, widows' payments etc. which were introduced by the earlier organisations have now been taken over by the State.

Employees' organisations

Represented on the National Joint Council For The Building Industry (NJC) are four unions to which construction operatives belong.

The Union of Construction, Allied Trades and Technicians (UCATT): Trades belonging to this union are bricklayers, masons, slaters and tilers, joiners, painters and some labourers.

The Transport and General Workers' Union (TGWU): Plasterers, scaffolders, steel fixers, labourers, and Scottish slaters and tilers belong to this union.

General and Municipal Workers' Union (GMWU): Construction industry labourers generally belong to this union.

Furniture, Timber and Allied Trades Union (FTATU): In general, it is only wood machinists and a few carpenters who belong to this union.
    Another union not represented on the NJC, but to which construction operatives belong, is the Electrical, Electronic, Telecommunication and Plumbing Union (EETPU). The needs of electricians and plumbers are catered for by this union.
    Prior to 1972, there were thirteen unions represented on the NJC, but due to amalgamations, these were reduced to the four detailed above. Many people hope that further rationalisation and amalgamation may eventually lead to there being just one widely based union, representing the construction industry. This would inevitably lead to faster communication, and easier decision making during negotiation or dispute.
    The reorganisation resulted in a reduction of members on the council from 46 to 24, comprising 12 employers and 12 trade union members.
    The main aims of the construction unions, as with all unions is to promote social and economic advancement of the members, and the obtaining and maintaining of just wage rates, hours of work, and working conditions.

Employers' organisations

The employers are represented on the NJC by the National Federation of Building Trades Employers (NFBTE), and the National Federation of Roofing Contractors (NFRC), the former being much the larger organisation of the two, with a membership of about 11 000.
    A selection of other employers' associations which are not represented directly on the NJC are:
- *The National Association of Plumbing, Heating and Mechanical Services Contractors* (NAPH).

- *The Electrical Contractors' Association* (ECA).
- *The Federation of Master Builders* (FMB): The Federation looks after the needs of the builders and contractors.

The National Federation of Building Trade Employers

The NFBTE operates at local, regional and national level, and acts on behalf of building contractors as a whole, also carrying out negotiations with government bodies. It has direct links with affiliated organisations such as the Metal Window Federation, and the National Federation of Plastering Contractors etc. It also has good communications with many government departments through joint committees and working parties, such as its links with the DOE via the housing Working Party, and the Construction and Housing Research Advisory Council.

The many committees within the organisation of the NFBTE consider such aspects as: Training, safety, wages and conditions, management, finance, contracts, public relations, membership, taxation, insurance, Construction Industry Training Board (CITB), etc. The Federation is in constant touch with the Confederation of British Industry (CBI), which as the name suggests, represents British industry in general, when considering such problems as legislation, government policies and the economic situation of the country.

The many contacts that the Federation enjoys, thus makes it truly representative of the construction industry as a whole, from manufacturers of components through to government departments.

The Federation of Civil Engineering Contractors

This organisation holds a similar position in the civil engineering field to that of the NFBTE in the building industry. It was formed in 1919 and at present has a membership of approximately 550.

Its main function is to represent the employers in the civil engineering field, and to this end, employs various committees to look after: Training, wages, safety, health and welfare, research, conditions of contract, daywork schedules, future planning, and the effects of the Common Market.

The Federation has access to the National Joint Council for the Building Industry via the Building and Civil Engineering Joint Board.

The National Joint Council for the Building Industry (NJCBI or NJC)

In 1932, the NJC was formed jointly by the NFBTE, and the construction unions operating at that time. The main functions of the council are:
1. The administration of the National Joint Training Scheme for building operatives.
2. The determining of wages and working conditions of building trades operatives, through the National Working Rules.
3. The settlement of disputes, between employers and employees.

Other organisations within the construction industry

So far, a selection of employers' organisations has been briefly outlined, together with the major unions, and the NJC. Within the industry however, there are many other associations, which unfortunately are too numerous for them all to be mentioned here. The majority of these bodies can, however be put under one of three following headings:

Professional bodies

These have somewhat different aims to the associations so far discussed.

They maintain the professional standing of the various specialist functions, by:

1. Ensuring that codes of conduct are adhered to.
2. Keeping the profession informed of current and new practices.
3. Organising an examination and membership scheme to ensure that standards are upheld.
4. Maintaining links with industry, and the other professions.

Examples of such bodies are: The Chartered Institute of Building; The Royal Institute of British Architects; The Royal Institute of Chartered Surveyors; The Institute of Quantity Surveyors; The Institute of Civil Engineers.

Trade organisations

These bodies are formed generally for the promotion of certain products. They are responsible for communicating to the industry new developments in, and uses for, the product in question. The organisations are generally financed by the manufacturers whose products they promote. Some examples are: The Brick Development Association; The Cement and Concrete Association; The Copper Development Association; The Calcium Silicate Brick Association Ltd; Gypsum Products Development Association; Lead Development Association.

General organisations

These are bodies which cannot be classified under any of the previous headings.

The aims of these general organisations are varied, but can generally be said to look after, in general or specific terms, certain aspects of the industry. A selection of such bodies are given below:

1. National Building Agency

This body was formed by the government, for the purpose of improving techniques and productivity throughout the industry. It is financed by charging fees for its services and by a grant from government. The agency carries out its function by disseminating information to contractors, manufacturers and Local Authorities.

2. The Building Advisory Service

This body which was formed by the NFBTE, is split into four sections:
(a) Management training.
(b) Consultancy.
(c) Appointments to positions.
(d) Safety.

These four different sections look after their respective specialisms within the construction industry. The service is financed by fees and payments charged to the users, which are normally contractors or Local Authorities.

3. Agrément Board

The aim of this government-sponsored body is to test newly developed techniques and materials, for use in the industry. Manufacturers send their products to the Board, and are issued in due course with a certificate, providing that the test results are satisfactory. The obtaining of a certificate enables architects to specify new products with greater confidence than would have been possible by believing unsubstantiated manufacturers' claims.

4. Building Research Establishment (BRE)

This again is a government-sponsored body, that looks after three distinct areas of research.

The Building Research Station (BRS): This section tests, researches and publishes its results in the well known BRE digests, covering a wide range of topics on construction materials and methods. The station also advises on the preparation of British Standards, and the Building Regulations.

The Fire Research Station (FRS): This, as the name suggests, is a research organisation specialising in fire resistance. Its work comprises testing materials to destruction in fire.

The Princes Risborough Laboratories: Research is carried out at this establishment into many aspects of timber use, including seasoning, machining, forming of board products, preservation etc.

It must be obvious from the many organisations so far mentioned in this chapter, that much information has to be passed to the various parties within the industry. Here we have hit upon one of the first problems of communication within the construction industry, that is, knowing where to go for the information required. Unfortunately due to limitations of space, it is impossible to detail all organisations and information sources. The student should research further to get to know suitable sources for information relevant to his particular specialisms.

Communication within the industry

Good communications are one of the main prerequisites for the smooth and profitable running of any organisation. This is particularly so in the construction industry, as communications in this industry are often hampered for the following reasons:

(a) Lack of co-operation and early consultation between the various stages of construction, i.e: Clients' conception and brief stage; Design stage; Planning and other legislative approvals; Erection stage.
(b) The increasing proportion of subcontract labour over which the main contractor often has no direct control.
(c) The problem of the erection site being many miles from the specialist head office functions often leads to instructions being issued by phone, rather than more concise written instructions being given.

Concerning construction projects in Britain, it is often said that erection times are longer, and efficiency is lower than in other countries. Could poor communications within the design and build process be the cause of this low output from the industry? In the following pages, four particular areas of communication problems will be considered under the following headings:

(a) The design team and the planning/building control function.
(b) Communication between the design and erection functions.
(c) Communications within the contractors' organisations.
(d) Communication between the parties on site.

(a) The design team and the planning/building control function

The role of the construction industry in society, is to satisfy the wants of the consumers in terms of construction projects, whether they are houses, places of work, entertainment, or transportation routes.

This task is often frustrated by problems of planning or building regulation approval. Under the Town Planning Act of 1947 Local Planning Authorities are required to produce development plans. These can be considered at two levels.

1. Structure plans:
These look at the overall area in relation to its surroundings, and lay down policies within the areas of employment, transport, recreation, housing, industry, population and education etc. These plans are not detailed, but tend to be proposed statements of policy for the area with regard to the various considerations.

2. Local plans:
These are prepared to examine in detail the local area under

consideration. They usually take the form of a map, which indicates how the structure plan will be carried out in practice. It is these plans which will show the zoning areas of a particular locality.

It is essential that the designer of building projects keeps abreast of any changes in development plans, which might affect projects under consideration. It would be foolish, for example, to proceed with a planning application for a roadside extension to a client's factory, if there is a local plan proposing a road widening scheme in the future, which will affect the factory.

All development plans are available for inspection at Local Authority planning offices, and it is a great pity that more of the public do not take the opportunity of finding out how their future environment is being shaped.

When a design for a building is likely to come up against problems with certain clauses in the Building Regulations, it is essential that the designers confer with the building control departments to decide what is, or is not allowed, and whether a relaxation of specific clauses must be applied for. It is pointless putting in plans, in the hope that the Local Authority will 'stretch' a point. This inevitably ends in much wasted time for everyone.

Architects are specialists in designing buildings, builders are specialists in constructing them. What an ideal combination if only the two would join forces and work together right from the early stages of design. It is unfortunate that in the recent past the two functions have been usually totally divorced from one another. The main reason for this is the continuing use of the competitive tender.

(b) Communication between the design and erection functions

On nearly every job certain difficulties arise, usually practical difficulties in constructing to certain detailed drawings. These problems in many cases could have been overcome, had there been consultation between architect and builder at an earlier stage. Builders are seldom aware of many such problems until the job has progressed considerably, because of the usual procedure of issuing detailed drawings long after the project has started. This point alone raises communication problems, in that the builder may have to order purpose made components, and the contract could be delayed during their manufacture.

On the other hand many builders bring a lot of delays upon themselves. There are many situations where it is obvious to the site agent that he is going to have to seek the architect's advice, or ask for details about certain points, but it is not mentioned until such a late stage that delays occur.

It is strongly recommended that a communication system is built up between the architect and builders, or via their representatives, to ensure a smooth running contract.

Many methods of communication are used within the industry,

ranging from plans, details and specifications, to simple site diaries and memoranda between departments. The building industry, unlike many others, is dogged with the problem of dealing with many variations claims, which often form a substantial proportion of the contract sum. For this reason all communications likely to be important in this context must be written, preferably with a copy kept at another location, to safeguard against destruction by fire.

(c) Communications within the contractors' organisations

Within a building company, the type of communication system, and the speed with which it works, are to a large extent a function of the size of the organisation. The smaller the company, the faster will information be disseminated. With large companies, a communication network has to be developed, that ensures that the information necessary for decision making gets to where it may be wanted. This can sometimes lead to overloaded 'in' trays, with the majority of the information being irrelevant to the particular department. It is therefore important to design the flow of information, so that where possible only the required information goes to each department.

(d) Communication between the parties on site

On site, communications can be greatly improved with the aid of weekly site meetings, which could be attended by all relevant parties, viz. architect, contracts manager, general foreman, clerk of works, main subcontractors etc. At such meetings, information and problems can be discussed, which helps to bring other people's problems into perspective. Such meetings will lead to a faster flow of information which in turn leads to a more harmonious working environment, and often to an early completion of contract.

Questions

1 Why is it necessary to have employers' organisations.
2 Discuss reasons why it is unlikely that employers' and employees' organisations will ever amalgamate.
3 From your own experience, discuss the existing communication system operating in your own firm, or on site, and state how you think it could be improved.

Chapter 9

Marketing

What is marketing, indeed, what is meant by a market?

A market is said to exist, where buyers and sellers are brought together, so that goods can be exchanged for money. In the construction industry, the market has to be defined with care. One may talk of the market for the services of the construction industry, in which case the products dealt with would be all those produced by the different sectors of the industry. This would include, housing – both private and public – schools, hospitals, industrial work, roads, etc.

Alternatively, one may talk of the markets for purpose made joinery, or housing, or for road building.

Besides defining the market by product, it can also be classified by the type of client. This in its broadest sense could mean the different sectors as discussed in Chapter 7.

Yet another method of defining market is by location. For instance, a market could be:

(a) Local.
(b) Regional.
(c) National.
(d) Overseas.

It can be seen then that there are three ways of defining market.

(a) By product.
(b) By client.
(c) By location.

On studying the construction industry in depth, it is found that certain products tend to be purchased by certain clients, and that

certain products fit into specific location definitions, as far as a single
company is concerned.

From Fig. 9.1, it can be seen, that builders specialising in
maintenance work will generally deal with individual householders,
and because profit margins are fairly tight, and competition fierce, it
would not be worth their while venturing far afield for work. Their
market as far as location is concerned, would be local.

At the other extreme, large civil engineering contractors who are
looking for projects valued in £ millions are prepared to work
anywhere in the country, or even abroad, provided it is profitable.
These companies will be dealing with clients at the other end of the
scale, i.e. domestic and overseas governments. Their location market
would be national or international.

In between the extremes of the two examples given there exist
many medium-sized operations, but generally they all fit within the
broad band as shown in Fig. 9.1.

Why should the pattern of Fig. 9.1. exist? The question of
company size and location will be dealt with more fully in Chapters 12
and 13, but a brief discussion on the company's relationship with the
market would help at this stage. Consider the two examples given
earlier.

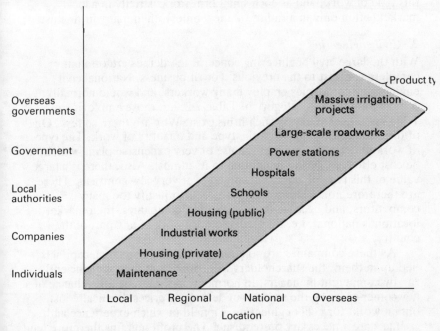

Fig. 9.1 Diagram indicating the inter-relationship between the product
market, the client market and the market as defined by location

1. Maintenance work

It has often been said that a man can go into a local ironmongers, buy a few tools and set up in business as a builder doing maintenance work. Without doubt, this still happens today, and such people often have little or no knowledge of the pricing of work, and often put in low prices in order just to obtain work. There are always such people in the small works area of building. Another group of people operating are moonlighters, who carry out work often without the taxman knowing, and so are able to charge less. In every locality there are many such people keeping down prices, and for this reason it would not be worth a bone fide builder travelling any great distance to obtain work. For his costs would be higher than those in the locality in which the potential work exists. With small jobs, a builder does not have expensive plant to keep working, indeed it is usual to hire much of the expensive equipment needed. He therefore has no worries about keeping plant working in order to get the maximum value from his investment.

From Chapter 7, it was seen that 95 per cent of the number of building firms in the country employ less than 14 operatives. The reason why there are so many small firms is linked to the type and amount of work undertaken by these firms. The smaller firms concentrate mainly on small works. As there is a large total value of this type of work, and as each small firm works strictly in a local market (often only in a radius of a few miles), then many firms exist.

2. Civil engineering

With the large civil engineering concern, the details are often in complete contrast to the previous type of business. National civil engineering companies employ many workers, and would normally come within the last category of Table 7.2, i.e. those employing over 1 200 operatives. Only 39 such firms exist. Why are there so few? One of the main reasons again, is the type and quantity of work. The type of work undertaken involves the use of very expensive plant, which, to be cost effective, has to be utilised to its utmost. Also, there is a large value of this type of work, but spread over very few contracts. There are therefore not the number of contracts to justify too many competitors, and because there are so few companies, their market location is national, i.e. they will consider work in any part of the country.

As these companies are so large, and because so much capital is tied up in them, the shareholders will ensure that they are efficiently run by competent managers. In normal times, there is little chance of a newcomer entering the market, undercutting prices drastically just to obtain work, for civil engineering is a field in which experience and contacts are a necessary prerequisite. The profit margins therefore tend to be fairly good. By the very nature of the work, there would be little difference in the costs of carrying out a contract in say South Wales, or in Edinburgh, as these sites often have all the specialist functions on site. Distance from head office tends to be immaterial.

Many national companies do however have regional depots, which may split up the country into four or five regions, but basically they are still national companies.

To define a company's market, it is necessary to bear in mind the following:

(a) The competition expected.
(b) The degree of capital tied up in plant etc.
(c) The management of the company, including expertise in particular fields.
(d) The type of work.
(e) The economic climate.

Marketing

Marketing can be considered as the management function responsible for the determining, promoting and satisfying of the client's needs whilst following the criteria laid down by the company's policies.

Every business irrespective of size has a marketing policy. This may range from an unwritten set of ideas in the mind of the owner of a small business, to a formally presented document, so essential for the larger company.

Why is a marketing policy necessary, and what should be included in it?

Many people consider marketing as a practice carried out with the sole intention of benefiting only the company itself. This is not so, for marketing can be said to benefit society in many ways, as follows:

(a) By providing products or services at the most economical prices, by the optimum allocation of the company's production factors.
(b) Greater company efficiency leads to greater profits, which flow back into society.
(c) Reducing business risk, thereby helping to ensure continuing employment.

It will be argued by most people, that the most important aim of any business organisation is to make a profit on its trading operations. To this end, a marketing policy which is formulated after a properly conducted investigation should help to guide the company into the most profitable markets.

Before a marketing policy is formulated, four areas, as indicated on Fig. 9.2 (p. 132), should be thoroughly investigated, and the results analysed ideally by several people, to allow for possible different interpretations of the results.

The company itself

An in-depth analysis of the company itself is necessary, to show whether or not it is capable of entering certain fields, or whether others need to be expanded, or contracted.

The following areas should be considered.

1. Organisation

- What is the existing structure of the company?
- How are the different fields managed, i.e. is the work split into building, and civil engineering; or is it split by value, such as projects up to £200 000 and those over this figure?
- What is the communications network within the company? Both the formal and informal pathways should be investigated.
- What are the areas of operations, and the levels of resources in terms of skilled operatives, plant, supervisory personnel, stores facilities and specialist functions?

The results of this analysis should show whether the company can deal adequately with any new work, or whether major reorganising is necessary before new fields are entered, or workloads within existing fields are altered.

2. Management

- What is the experience and ability of the management?
- What is the outlook of management, is it very staid, or is it dynamic and enthusiastic?
- Will change be readily accepted or not? Too staid a management can lead to stagnation, whereas too enthusiastic a management could lead to overtrading in terms of finance and organisation, with bankruptcy as the outcome.

3. Trading records

These should be split up into the different fields of operation, and checked back over the previous years to determine the trends in the company's performance, with regard to overall profitability, capital employed, source of capital, profit as a percentage of capital employed, growth in turnover.

It is advantageous to compare the record of one's own company, with those of similar companies engaged in similar work.

The results of these enquiries will show which are the most profitable areas of operations, and which require the most capital etc.

This section of the investigation is one of the most important, but is often the one that is carried out the most badly.

Materials sources

Types of materials can be classified as follows:

(a) Those that are generally problem free, with regard to quality, shortage in supply, or excessive price increases.
(b) Those prone to shortages in peak periods, such as bricks, cement, plaster and associated products. These are generally relatively low cost items compared to their bulk, where the manufacturers find it difficult to stockpile in times of industrial recession. This results in shortages, when the level of industrial activity is high.

(c) Those always having long delivery periods. This refers to such items as purpose made components, steelwork etc. Many companies set up their own manufacturing units to produce joinery and concrete products, as these are then within the direct control of the parent company.

(d) Those prone to excessive price increases. Often these are due to actions beyond the control of industry or government, particularly where goods or raw materials are imported, such as copper from Zambia. These price increases may result from price increases at source, or from shortages.

The methods of acquisition of materials should be investigated, which will be from one of three types of source.

(a) Materials purchased from merchants. This is usually restricted to small items from manufacturers whose sales policy it is to operate through wholesalers only.

(b) Those materials purchased directly from the manufacturer. This often involves ordering in large quantities which may result in stockpiling being necessary.

(c) Materials purchased from within the company itself, e.g. aggregates from pits owned by the company, timber and joinery, precast concrete, bricks and blocks etc.

By analysing materials, degrees of risk and economies relating to materials can be investigated.

Analysis of the market

1. By client

Lists of details of the main clients within the different fields should be drawn up, including such details as:

- Size of client's organisation.
- Value of potential contracts.
- Does the company deal with all clients in the market?
- Has the company stopped dealing with particular clients, and if so, why?
- Are the clients creditworthy?
- Does each client generally deal only with one contractor for all its work, or many?
- How is the work placed; by package deal, or open tender etc?

2. By type of work

The potential work that is available in the different fields within an area should be investigated for as far into the future as possible. It would be pointless investing in specialist capital equipment that would not be fully utilised.

3. By competition

As much information as possible should be accumulated concerning the level of operations of competitors in each field, together with, if possible, details of their trading figures and organisation structure.

What is the company's share in each field of the market? Do the trends show an increasing or decreasing market share over the last few years.

4. Changes in consumer demand

Although this should have shown up in the market analysis, the volume of certain types of construction work are often difficult to foresee, due to the type of work being in or out of favour with the consumers. High-rise development is a case in point. In the 1950s, tower blocks provided an answer to the problem of providing dwellings quickly, whilst at the same time taking up very little land. By the 1960s, it had become apparent that these were not the ideal choice of dwelling. Social problems developed, especially vandalism, and stability and maintenance problems were rife.

Today, very few companies would class high-rise housing as a possible growth market in the near future.

Analysis of relevant external influences

Many of the following examples cannot be foreseen with any degree of accuracy, but it must never be forgotten, that these occurrences do happen, and as such, contingency plans should always be built into any marketing strategy.

1. Government action

Due consideration must be given to the existing and future policies of government. For example:

- Economic recession;
- High interest rates;
- Lack of import controls;
- Low public expenditure;
  Leads to a low level of construction work.
- Grants;
- Special development programmes such as airports, motorways etc;
- Export drives;
- High public expenditure;
  Could lead to a higher level of construction work.

2. Technology

Technological advances in construction methods and materials are constantly creating potential new markets for the building industry. For example, in the early 1960s, few people had heard about cavity wall insulation. In the 1980s, there are now many businesses specialising solely in this work. Double glazing is yet another similar example of a booming industry, thanks to the soaring energy prices, which started in the early 1970s.

Plastics have revolutionised the industry, saving much labour on many sites. Manufacturers obviously saw great potential for the industry with such products as rainwater and drainage goods, septic tanks, window frames etc.

Companies must keep abreast of developments that may ultimately lead to increased demand from consumers.

3. Overseas governments

Political instability in the world can lead to fluctuations in the value of the pound. This may affect certain exporting companies, as a strong pound means that people abroad have to pay more for the goods that they are buying from this country. A drop in export sales could result in a cutting back in expansion programmes for exporting industries which leads to less work for the construction industry.

Construction companies that are proposing to enter the overseas market must bear in mind the types of government that they will be dealing with. An appraisal of the country's past performance often helps to determine whether it is worth trying to carry out work there. For example the following points should be considered.

Is the country politically stable, or is it volatile, with frequent military takeovers?

Does the country in question enjoy good relations with Britain and the rest of the world?

Although this practice is tending to die out, in some countries in the past, bribery was often the only way of securing work; this still persists to a small extent in some countries. In Britain bribery is illegal, in some overseas countries it is tolerated. Should a company pay bribes to obtain work in such countries? If your answer is no, then the company will not obtain work there, for companies from other countries will certainly go along with the old saying 'When in Rome do as the Romans do.' This book does not want to make moral judgements, but merely points out that when a company starts dealing outside the range of its normal activities, many different types of problems may occur.

- What level of inflation is there likely to be in the country, and what types of contract do they work to.
- Is the country wealthy, in its own right, or are contracts likely to be funded by western governments or world banking organisations.
- The attitude of local labour to construction work is important, are the workers lethargic, or energetic in their approach to work.
- Are there likely to be any problems from labour unions.

Following the analysis of the four areas under investigation, the marketing policy can be drawn up. This will include recommendations regarding the existing company, the materials sources and the markets.

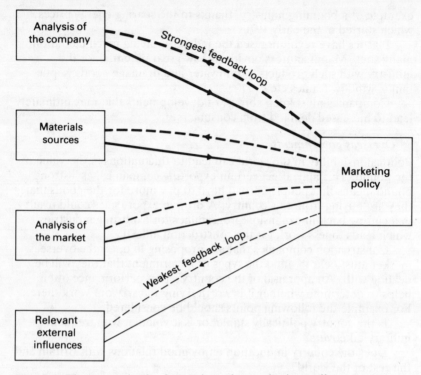

Fig. 9.2 The stages in the formation of a marketing policy

The marketing policy should be regularly reviewed, in all four areas, and any changes made.

Figure 9.2 shows the feedback loops which indicate that change may be necessary to the policy in one of the four areas. The first area, that of the company structure and organisation, is the one most easily changed, as the company has direct control over it. The next group in which changes are most easily made is that of materials sources. Markets can be altered but often only slowly. The external influences generally cannot be affected at all by a single company. It is most important to remember that a marketing policy should be dynamic, and that it is not a once and for all operation.

Sales promotion

The construction industry does not use many of the expensive advertising techniques used by other industries. Few construction companies advertise on TV for example. Unless the company is predominantly concerned with speculative development, there will not actually be a product to promote.

Some businesses promote services in which they specialise, e.g. glazing, thermal insulation, wall tiling, design and build for industry, etc. Most construction companies try to promote their good name, by keeping the company name or symbol in the public's eye. This can be done in many ways:

(a) Ensuring that there are clean site boundaries and entrances, with well positioned signboards, and by inconveniencing the public as little as possible.

(b) Many companies adopt a symbol which is usually displayed alongside their name.

(c) The adoption of a company colour, with standard lettering or symbols on plant, lorries etc.

(d) Prestige buildings often have many large company nameboards, not only at the site entrance, but on tower cranes, scaffolding etc.

(e) Prestige buildings often have foundation or topping out ceremonies, which are made much of in the local press.

(f) Good quality literature and stationary for the company can be well worth while, as this is often the first approach by the company, to a client.

(g) Where a company has a particularly interesting contract, a film unit may be commissioned to produce a film which can be shown later to prospective clients.

Again it is important to have a formal sales policy, with budgets for particular promotions. The return derived from money spent on advertising or other promotions is very difficult to assess, for a prospective client seeing a company advertisement today, might not require their services for several years.

Questions

1 Discuss the difficulties of marketing within the construction industry.
2 Within the construction industry, discuss the advantages of marketing, to the various parties concerned.
3 The construction industry spends relatively little on sales promotions, compared to some consumer good industries. Discuss reasons for this.

Chapter 10

Housing

Building societies

By 1775 much of the common land in Britain had been enclosed and the agricultural revolution was just about to be replaced by the Industrial Revolution.

This change created a landless rural population of men and women who moved to towns looking for work. This led to two distinct classes, the working class, and the middle class which earned its income from trade and commerce.

No welfare state existed at this time, and this led to mutual self-help in the working classes. Two examples are sick and burial clubs, and friendly societies. It was at this time that building societies began, indeed they are still administered today by the Chief Registrar of Friendly Societies. Men clubbed together and pooled their money in order to own their own houses. The earliest society was founded in 1775 in Birmingham, and within the next 50 years, at least 250 building societies were formed.

The usual plan was to use the accumulated savings to buy a plot of land and build houses on it. Each member would agree to pay the society a certain amount of money each month, until all the members were housed. The problem with this system was that it took many years to house all its members, and also that it was difficult to decide who should have the next completed house. The latter problem was often settled by pulling names out of a hat or by auction. When everyone was housed, the society was disbanded. About 1840 the long-time periods that operated were reduced by the societies borrowing from the wealthy middle classes, and giving interest on it. This necessitated charging interest on the money borrowed by the members. It was now realised that societies no longer needed to be terminated, but could be permanent, a name which still persists in the titles of many societies.

Various Acts were passed in 1874 and 1894 to help prevent frauds. By 1919 the assets of the societies were about £77 million, by 1939 this had increased 10 fold to £773 million. After the Second World War, there was a housing shortage, and mortgages had to be rationed. By 1945 the assets totalled £825 million but by 1950 this had grown to over £1 200 million and in 1964 it was £4 400 million.

From the beginning of this century, the number of societies has fallen, often due to amalgamations, from 2 250 in 1900 to 900 in 1945 to 650 in 1964. Many of the earlier societies were terminating, so were due to close in any case.

The scene today is dominated by the large national building societies, but many smaller provincial ones still exist. At the end of 1984, 190 societies had assets of about £102 689 million, the amount lent in 1984 was £23 771 million.

Today, societies borrow money from investors and offer interest, tax paid, to the investor. The interest offered will depend upon the length of time the money will be invested for, and whether regular monthly deposits are going to be made. The invested money is then lent out to people wishing to buy a new house or extend an existing one. The interest paid is variable depending upon market forces, but is tax deductable up to a certain limit.

Housing associations

These are non-profit-making organisations which have to conform to the relevant statutes in order to become eligible for subsidies or loans from public funds. Housing associations should not be confused with building societies, as building societies are concerned solely with providing loans, whereas housing associations are concerned with providing accommodation.

Housing associations started about 1830, with 'The Labourers Friend Society'. It began its housing work in 1844 and survived until the 1960s when it was taken over by another trust. The main aim of this society was to provide housing for lower paid workers at low rents. In the early years, the societies borrowed capital from people, often at 2–4 per cent and also sought gifts and endowments. In 1919 local authorities were empowered to assist in the promotion of housing associations, as a means of accelerating the formation of a greater stock of dwellings.

These days, housing associations are formed as charitable trusts, or
as limited companies, and at the present time they own about 300 000
dwellings, which offers an alternative to the accommodation provided
by the local authorities or private landlords.

The National Federation of Housing Associations (NFHA) is the
parent body to which 2 200 member associations are affiliated. There is
also a Scottish Federation of Housing Associations which has 124
members.

Housing associations can be divided into several different
headings, as set out below, which generally denotes their area of
activity. It should be noted however that there is considerable overlap
between the various types.

General family associations

This is the largest group of housing associations, and they provide
accommodation for families mainly, but also for the elderly and
disabled. Both new buildings, and renovation and convertion work are
carried out by this group.

Old people's housing associations

This is the second largest group, with many of the associations being
charitable trusts. They are concerned mainly with the provision of
warden supervised bungalows, or specially converted houses for the
elderly.

Self-build associations

These are formed by people who are willing to co-operate in the actual
physical construction of their own houses. Generally when the houses
are completed they are sold to the members, but in some instances the
ownership remains with the association and they are let to members.
Loans can be arranged from the housing corporation, or from local
authorities to enable land and materials to be purchased. If properties
are sold to members, an allowance is made for the time that the person
has devoted to the project, and the buyer then arranges a normal
mortgage. The association can then pay off its loans, and be wound up.

Industrial housing associations

In certain industries, the employers or sometimes the employees have
at times formed housing associations. In general they were formed to
offer accommodation along with a job, or to use better housing as an
incentive to persuade people to move to a new area and job. The Coal
Board housing association is just such an example.

Co-ownership housing associations

With this form of organisation, houses or flats are provided for the
occupation of their members, who collectively own all the dwellings
they individually occupy.

All the members are responsible for the total estate, and a management committee must be elected. The members initially have to pay a small deposit and subsequently rent, which pays off the mortgage on the total estate, plus payments for building maintenance and ground maintenance.

If a person leaves, then he or she will receive back the loan possibly together with a further payment, based upon the increase in value during the tenancy. The new member will become a member of the association, and so it will continue as before.

Co-operative housing associations

These are similar to the co-ownership associations, except that the members do not have an interest in any particular dwelling.

Special purpose housing associations

These are associations generally registered as a charity, that help provide accommodation for particular sectors of society, e.g. students, the disabled, immigrants, battered wives etc.

In many cases these associations work closely with local authorities to repair and let on short term many dwellings that are awaiting redevelopment.

The housing corporation is required under the 1974 Housing Act, to keep a register of all housing associations, which at present total about 2 600. Only those registered are eligible for government grants and certain tax privileges, and local authority loans.

Housing associations finance the building of properties generally by loans from local authorities or from the housing corporation at rates approaching those of building societies over a period of usually 60 years for new work, and 30 years for improvement work.

The terms of payment for accommodation vary with the different types of association, but generally the occupier pays a rent, fixed by the rent officer, to the association. This rent will cover the costs of loan repayments, and management and maintenance costs.

Types of housing

Housing accommodation is provided by three main sources.

(a) Local authorities or new town corporations rented properties. There are about 6.5 million properties in this group, which comprises 32 per cent of Britain's housing stock.

(b) Owner occupied properties. There are about 11 million, or 54 per cent of the housing stock in this sector.

(c) Private owner rentals, or rentals from housing associations accounts for 3 million properties, or 14 per cent of the housing stock.

The total stock of dwellings in Britain is currently about 20.5 million.

The sale of local authority housing stock

The 1980 Housing Act gave a statutory right to nearly all council house tenants to buy their dwellings at a considerable discount. Certain properties were exempt, and the act has been updated. Here briefly are the main points of the scheme as it operates under the 1985 Housing Act.

(a) A tenant who has been in occupation for at least 2 years can obtain an initial discount of 32 per cent on a house with an additional 1 per cent for every extra year of occupation, up to a maximum of 60 per cent. With a flat, the initial discount is 44 per cent with an additional 2 per cent for every extra year of occupation up to a maximum of 70 per cent.

(b) Where the purchaser is unable to obtain a mortgage from normal sources, then the local authority has to provide a 100 per cent mortgage subject to status.

(c) Where the tenant desires to purchase the property, but has insufficient income to make the repayments, he can have the valuation price frozen for three years, on payment of a small refundable deposit. Hopefully within the three years his income will have risen sufficiently to enable a loan to be obtained.

(d) After purchase the tenant must remain the owner for at least three years otherwise a portion of the discount must be repaid.

The implications of this Act have been debated by many economists already, and will be for many years. It is possible, that in time the Act will have far reaching effects, or will it? Consider the outcome from the following viewpoints: Local authorities; Tenants; Housebuilders; Society in general.

Local authorities

Financially it seems that in the short term, the overall sales of property will be to the local authorities' advantage. It is felt however that there are likely to be greater sales in the better types of estates, possibly also in newer houses. At present, the tenants of the better housing stock are subsidising to an extent the older properties, and if the better properties are sold off, this inevitably leaves the council with a relatively higher maintenance bill.

Against this argument it is said that properties in the less desirable areas would receive a low valuation anyway, this hopefully leading to more bargain sales. Is this not a golden opportunity for local authorities to rid themselves of many of these older properties, and save themselves a large annual maintenance bill? At the present time in many areas the rent income nowhere near covers the maintenance costs, plus repayment of interest and capital on the construction or rehabilitation loan. If local authority maintenance could be reduced, this would lead to a reduction in local authority staff which might tend to make local authority rented accommodation more cost viable.

The government has stated that much of the monies received from the sale of properties will be ploughed back into local authority building programmes. Again this seems to benefit the local authority, by replacing old with new. The problem is, what is going to be the cost of the new properties? Land is getting more and more expensive, and so is the cost of borrowing money. It could be that few new properties will be built by local authorities, as economic rents could not be asked. One then starts to ask, 'Would we not have been better off keeping the old properties?'

Socially, there will always be people who need help with accommodation, and it is important that the local authority maintains a certain level of housing stock, for the lower paid, disabled, elderly, or agricultural workers in rural areas.

The tenant

Financially, the basic question to be asked is how does the cost of buying compare with the cost of renting. There is no easy answer to this, but the following points should be included:

(a) What age is the tenant, and what length of mortgage can be obtained?
(b) The rises in rent over the next 15–25 years is highly unpredictable, but to a large extent will follow inflation.
(c) The mortgage interest rate is likely to fluctuate, but which way, up or down? The rate does not tend to increase in line with inflation, which means that if a mortgage is taken out now, at some time in the future the mortgage repayments will become cheaper than the rent.
(d) How long is the tenant likely to remain in the property?
(e) How long has the tenant been in the property? This will affect the discount obtainable.
(f) Will the property be easy to resell? (Generally houses on local authority estates are valued 10–20 per cent below similar houses on private estates.)
(g) Will the tenant sell the property as soon as possible, with quite a capital gain, and move into a new house?
(h) Is the tenant in a position to have the valuation frozen for three years? Obviously if property prices rise 10–20 per cent annually, then it is in the tenant's interest financially to try for this.
(i) Will the tenant be so financially 'stretched' by the mortgage repayments, that he could not afford to adequately maintain the property?
(j) The tenant must ask himself, 'Do I want to live in this area for the next X number of years?' The question is very pertinent in the case of the less desirable areas which are possibly more prone to vandal attack.

It can be seen that it is no simple decision for the tenant when all the above factors have to be carefully weighed, and the unknown estimated.

Housebuilders

There has been great concern from the housebuilding sector that potential customers will now buy their own council houses, rather than new privately constructed dwellings. Is there really great need for concern? It is said that about 60 000–70 000 local authority tenants move into owner occupied houses annually. Although only a small proportion of these move into new houses, some of the people who have moved out of the older houses would also have bought new properties as the buying chain takes effect. This means that somewhere along the line, a good proportion of the 60 000–70 000 houses will not now be required from housebuilders, until the bulge of council house buying has passed and sales level off.

From the mid-1980s, when the original statutory five years' retaining period has been passed for the first batch of buyers, many tenants who have bought their council houses will sell, to gain the capital advantage, and move over to new houses. If this comes about, this could mean a picking up of new private sales from this date. This is however somewhat optimistic, as people likely to gain the greatest advantage, i.e. those in the largest discount group, are probably at an age where they are unlikely to want to move.

Society in general

What is the object of this mainly Conservative policy of selling off council houses?

There are many areas, where the local authority cannot set a rent sufficiently high enough to cover the cost of maintenance, and the repayment of interest and original loan. Consequently a heavy burden for local authority housing falls on the ratepayer.

In 1978/79 out of a total income of £662 million for the local authority housing revenue account for the London boroughs £122 million was contributed from the general rate fund. This represents a subsidy of 18 per cent.

By encouraging more people to opt for owner occupation, in theory this should cut down the burden on the ratepayer and on the taxpayer via the rate support grant. In practice the local authority will still have to maintain a certain housing stock, and so as houses are sold more will need to be built. If the balance does swing significantly towards greater owner occupation, then properties should be better cared for and hopefully vandalism will also be reduced.

It is possible that there will be no great rush initially to take advantage of the Act. Many people will try to go for the three year freeze on valuation, whilst those who can afford the mortgage repayments may wait in the hope that interest rates will drop.

Factors affecting the erection and sale of housing

Demand for housing

The price of housing relative to incomes will undoubtedly affect what type of housing is sold or let. There is always a great demand for local authority rented accommodation, because compared to other forms it is generally cheaper, this often only being accomplished at the expense of the ratepayer.

Where rented accommodation is not available, or is in very short supply, then people have to think about becoming owner occupiers. Whether or not they buy houses will often be determined by the cost and conditions of taking out a mortgage. Many large developers now operate their own mortgage schemes thereby ensuring that buyers of their houses will not have great problems in acquiring a mortgage.

Certain jobs carry significant benefits when it comes to house purchase. Traditionally, employees of building societies and banks have been able to take out loans at much lower rates of interest than normal.

The demand for housing in a particular area will be affected by the level of employment and the security of employment in that area. The south-east of England for example has house prices between 50–100 per cent higher than the rest of the country, for similar properties. This being a reflection of the need for accommodation in a relatively prosperous area, coupled with the problem of land shortage. Properties in South Wales however, particularly in areas hit by heavy redundancies in, for instance, the steel industry, will now be selling for prices lower than if there was greater employment. This reflects the lack of demand, due either to people moving out of the area, or there being a lower average income in the area.

Supply of housing

When the construction industry is working at peak capacity, the rate of completion of dwellings can be held up by non-availability of land, labour or materials. Land on which to build is becoming harder to find, and it is not unknown for large companies to employ land negotiators, whose job it is to seek out suitable parcels of land, often by air reconnaissance.

Labour and material shortages often occur, and are easily exacerbated by the government's stop – go policy. (see Ch. 19).

The process of developing housing sites needs the availability of large amounts of money, which will not turn over quickly if houses stand unsold. Housing development is very sensitive to the level of interest rates. High rates can turn a potentially profitable site into a definite loss maker. One of the main determinants of housing availability is government policy. In the 1970s there were many suggestions and policy statements in government publications concerning housing policy.

It was suggested that there should be a fairly detailed though flexible national housing policy. This would be supplemented by local authorities preparing comprehensive Local Housing Strategies (LHS), which take into account the housing needs in a particular area. Coupled with these LHSs local authorities have to produce Housing Investment Programmes (HIP) covering their capital expenditure over a set period, normally four years. These HIPs are revised each year and central government will make capital spending allocations to each authority on the basis of these plans. It is hoped that by allowing local authorities to individually produce these plans, they will better cater for the particular housing needs within an area and will help make the local authorities more autonomous.

In the past, the criticism of unfairness has been levelled at government housing policy as local authority housing has been heavily subsidised by the central government and by local ratepayers. Owner occupiers have enjoyed very little in the way of subsidies. Current policy is tending to clear up this anomaly and to give people a fairer choice on their mode of occupation.

In order to encourage the growth of owner occupation, the government has introduced a scheme whereby a first time buyer can obtain a loan of £600 interest free for the first five years. The government policy to allow tax relief on mortgages up to a certain figure has also encouraged the growth of owner occupation.

The government has tried to control the use of land in various ways, two such examples are:–

(a) Development Land Tax, (operating from 1976 until 1985), discouraged the sale of land for development, as a significant proportion of the increase in value was paid in tax. People often held on to the land in the hope of government eventually abolishing the tax, as has happened.

(b) The supply of suitable land is fixed to a certain extent by the various development plans of the local authority.

The effect of government policy is discussed in more detail in Chapter 19.

Land values and use

The value of land can be looked at from various viewpoints. Up until the start of the twentieth century, the value of land was discussed mainly in *economic* terms, i.e. using the land to its greatest financial advantage.

Throughout history, and even today, land in many instances holds a significant *political* value. It may be that it is a strategic position for the military overseeing of a strip of nearby land or water. A particular piece of land may contain valuable mineral deposits, essential to the economy of a certain country.

In the last few decades, there has been an ever increasing awareness of the *social* value of land. Playing fields and parks for instance hold a social value for the local community.

The *ecological* value of land is a subject which only in the last couple of decades has started to receive the attention required.

Economic value

The economic value of land is set by the demand for a particular plot, and this in turn is set by its location, climate, and environment, which gives rise to competition between the possible users. On purely economic grounds, the use that land is put to is based on deciding which alternative gives the greatest financial return within the timespan considered. Land on the edge of a green belt for instance will tend to be used for development rather than farming, providing, of course, planning permission is granted. For land gives a much lower return as farmland than it does as development land.

Development tends to have an irreversible mushrooming effect. For example, the decision to allow the building of a factory, often leads to other factories, then houses, schools etc.

Town and Country Planning Acts however now ensure that land development is not the 'free for all' it was in the nineteenth century. Without town planning, the use of land would be unlimited, disorganised and very uneconomic.

The actual valuing of a plot of land is often fairly easy. One simply compares it with similar pieces recently valued or sold to arrive at a figure. If the land is to be sold, and an interest is shown by several people, it is often auctioned. There are sometimes situations when only one client is interested in purchasing; it is then necessary to try to determine the client's demand for the land. This may happen in the following situations, where it is often very difficult to arrive at a figure, as the value to this particular client may be many times the normal market value for the land.

(a) Part of a garden is sold to enable an access to be formed for an existing factory.
(b) Gardens of several houses are sold to a developer to form a viable building plot.
(c) One or two houses are sold and demolished, to allow access to land at the rear which can now be developed.

Social value

This could be defined as the value to the community, of a piece of land, in terms of health, well being, safety and general environment. Economic values as stated earlier are often fairly easy to fix quantitatively, whilst social values can only be discussed in qualitative terms, as described in Chapter 3.

Consider the following examples.

Example 1: A plot of land may be used for a library, a sports ground, or as a site for houses. As a library, it is a place for gaining enjoyment from literature; it aids society as a whole via education, possibly it even aids society economically. A sports ground provides a place for enjoyment, it also aids health which again could be said to aid society as a whole economically. Houses aid the community by providing accommodation.

Example 2: A plot of land is vacant in a town centre, what should it be used for?

Economically land is normally used for the purpose for which it is most suited, as the prospective users can each determine what utility it would hold for them. The client to whom it would give the greatest utility would normally pay the highest price, all things being equal.

A town centre position would economically dictate a use as shops, or offices, not houses or farmland. Social pressures may, however require the provision of a library or police station.

A problem that often occurs, is that what might at first seem a social benefit, often ends up a social problem. For example, the repositioning of a heavy engineering factory to provide jobs, may result in pollution in the form of smoke, dust, noise, traffic etc.

Government tries to set certain social values with the aid of legislation, such as the Town and Country Planning Acts, and various environmental health Acts. Encouragement is also given to the preservation of trees, historic buildings and monuments, and national parks.

Political value

The political value of land can be viewed from two standpoints:
(a) Where it is politically advantageous to own or control a piece of land, for military reasons.
(b) In certain circumstances, government tries to encourage owners of land to use it in a particular way. This is done, in order to benefit the country as a whole. For example:
  (i) During the Second World War, the 'dig for victory' campaign encouraged people towards self-sufficiency.
  (ii) In the 1930s, food subsidies were given to farmers to encourage them to grow sugar beet and wheat for self-sufficiency.
  (iii) In development areas, the government tries to help the setting up of new industries by offering grants. This is often to try to relieve an unemployment problem.
  (iv) In the national interest, government may sanction the working of open cast coal mines in a farming area. Here conflict arises between the social value of beautiful countryside, and the economic value to the country of coal reserves.

Ecological value

This is really concerned with factors which affect the continuation of various forms of life. A few examples might be:

(a) Pollution of rivers by industrial effluent is likely to kill off fish stocks.

(b) Urbanisation in general leads to the destruction of many natural habitats of fauna and flora.

(c) The destruction of hedgerows by farmers to produce larger more easily worked fields again destroys natural areas so often used for nesting.

(d) The increase of agricultural output by the use of pesticides has led to the decline of many bird populations.

In nearly all the above situations, a conflict arises between the ecological and the economic value of land.

Who benefits from the use of land

When considering land value, it is very seldom one person who derives the benefit from a particular use. Consider the following:

Many people derive a benefit from a high street shop in a town centre.

- The owner obtains an income.
- The employees obtain an income.
- The customers obtain satisfaction for their needs.
- Suppliers of goods and services to the shop are kept in employment.

In general town centres are used for the benefit of society, whereas suburbs and farmland tend to give greater benefit to the individual.

Questions

1 Why is there still a need for housing associations in modern society?
2 Should local authorities be forced to sell their dwelling units to tenants?
3 In the past there has been talk by certain governments of nationalising land. If such a measure ever did come into effect, what would be the advantages and disadvantages?
4 In your opinion, should there be more local authority housing, or more private housing, and why?

Chapter 11

Production equilibrium of the firm

When studying the action of any production unit, it is necessary to take into account the type of competition likely to be met in the market in question. In the eyes of the economist, competition can exist anywhere between two extremes. These extremes are known as perfect competition and perfect monopoly. Like the concept of planned and free economies discussed earlier, they are unreal situations which are only assumed, to try to simplify interactions into simple processes that economists can use to interpret the actions of real situations. See Fig. 11.1.

Perfect competition

Perfect competition is a concept much used by economists, to study the

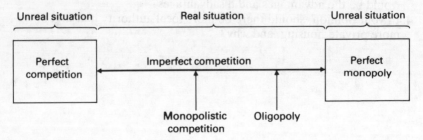

Fig. 11.1 Types of competition

effect on production and consumption of the action of supply and demand. The conditions necessary for perfect competition were detailed in Chapter 5 but to reiterate, they were:

(a) All products are homogeneous.
(b) A large number of buyers and sellers.
(c) There is perfect market knowledge.
(d) All factors of production are perfectly mobile.
(e) All commodities produced are perfectly mobile.
(f) All firms are free to enter or leave the industry.

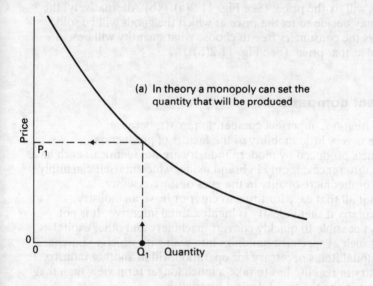

(a) In theory a monopoly can set the quantity that will be produced

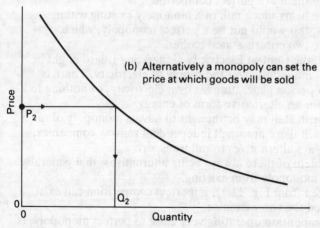

(b) Alternatively a monopoly can set the price at which goods will be sold

Fig. 11.2

Perfect monopoly

For perfect monopoly to exist, there are two conditions to be met.
(a) There must be no substitute for the particular commodity. This is usually the more difficult of the two conditions to comply with, as nearly all commodities have alternatives.
(b) There is only one producer.

Under perfect monopoly, the supplier has complete control over the supply of goods, and may choose to do one of two things: (a) He may fix the quantity of goods that will be produced. In this case the customers will fix the price. (See Fig. 11.2(a).) (b) Alternatively, the supplier may decide to fix the price at which the goods will be sold. This leaves the consumers free to choose what quantity will be demanded at that price. (See Fig. 11.2(b).)

Imperfect competition

In a real situation, imperfect competition exists, because:
(a) There is very little mobility of the factors of production.
(b) Products produced by modern industry are not identical, each have small differences, if only in brand name, which in itself can imply good or mediocre quality in the eyes of the consumer.
(c) It is not all that easy for firms to enter or leave an industry, particularly if that industry is highly capital intensive. It is not always possible to quickly convert machinery and other capital items such as specialist buildings into cash with which to purchase the capital items necessary for operation within another industry. Industry in real life has to take a much longer term view than that implicit in the theory of perfect competition.

Although one hears much talk of a monopoly existing within certain industries, this would not be a perfect monopoly, which complied with the two criteria stated earlier.

For example, the Central Electricity Generating Board might be thought to hold a monopoly over the supply of electricity. There is nothing to stop a person generating his own electricity, or nothing to stop him opting for an alternative form of energy.

Similarly British Rail may be thought to have a monopoly of rail transport, but again there are small independent railway companies, and there are always alternatives to rail transport.

It is this problem of there always being alternatives, that generally prevents perfect monopoly from existing.

As can be seen from Fig. 11.1., imperfect competition can exist anywhere between the two extremes.

A type of competition operating very close to perfect monopoly, is oligopoly. Here, there are only very few suppliers, and each commands a significant market share. As there are so few suppliers, if one reduces prices, then the others have to follow in order not to lose sales. It is because of this potential price war situation, that price fixing, or the forming of cartels is often attempted. In these circumstances, competition for sales is concentrated not on price, but on such things as advertising, the benefits of after sales service, or even free gifts.

Another type of imperfect competition is monopolistic competition. This occurs very often in modern trading, and is where there are large numbers of manufacturers, whose products are close, but not perfect substitutes.

For example, many manufacturers produce cars, but there is only one Rolls Royce. Other cars could be classed as an alternative means of transport, but if a person specifically wanted a Rolls Royce, then there is no substitute.

Similarly, a coffee processing firm may sell its coffee under the name of 'Brown bean'. As this would be a registered trademark, this company would have the monopoly of selling Brown bean coffee. Again there is no substitute for the real Brown bean, but there are many substitutes within the market for coffee.

Monopolistic competition is close to perfect competition, except that the products are not homogeneous, but individual.

In the UK there is much legislation concerning monopolies and restrictive practices. The Monopolies and Restrictive Practices Act 1948 caused the formation of the Monopolies and Mergers Commission. Under the present law, a supplier is defined as being in a position of monopoly if he holds 25 per cent or more of the market. This legal definition of monopoly must not be confused with the economic definition.

Since 1948, many Acts have been passed to try to encourage freer competition and better service in the public interest. Some of the relevant Acts are listed below:

The Restrictive Trade Practices Act 1956.
The Fair Trading Act 1973.
The Restrictive Trade Practices Act 1976.
The Resale Prices Act 1964 and 1976.

Returns to scale

In this chapter are discussed the various criteria which affect the attaining of the optimum production enterprise. The external influence of competition has been investigated, the internal problems of the scale of operations will now be considered.

In Chapter 1, the law of diminishing returns was demonstrated. Broadly speaking, this was defined as the effect of adjusting a variable factor, or factors, in combination with one or more fixed factors. The returns to scale refers to the outcome of varying all the factors of production, to cater for increased production requirements.

If for instance all the factors were increased by 50 per cent but the output only increased by 40 per cent, then this would be an example of decreasing returns to scale. If on the other hand the output had increased by 50 per cent then this would represent constant returns to scale. If, however a 50 per cent increase in all factors resulted in a 60 per cent increase in output, then this would show increasing returns to scale. This last example is the most common of the three, and is related to the advantages of economies of scale discussed in Chapter 12.

At this point, this effect of varying the factors will be analysed more fully. The object of trying to determine the optimum criteria is, so that within any particular time period, the maximum returns can be obtained for the minimum cost, which is another way of saying that the profit is maximised.

The costs borne by a producer can be divided into two types:

Fixed costs: These are those that do not vary in the short term. In a typical manufacturing business these would be represented by the buildings, large machinery, the management itself, etc., in other words the items that could not be changed quickly. Over a wide range of output, it can be seen that the fixed costs can remain constant.

Variable costs: These are those that vary with the amount of output. In a typical producing business, this would be represented by raw materials, labour costs, energy costs in using the machines etc.

From a study of the nature of a firm's costs, the short term or short period can be defined as the period of time in which a firm's fixed costs remain constant.

Similarly the long term, or long run, or long period, can be defined as any length of time greater than that in which it takes to change fixed costs.

The definition of short and long period is therefore likely to be different for various industries, as their costs are built up differently.

The following can be deduced:

Total costs = Fixed costs + Variable costs

Production equilibrium

This takes into account the fixed and variable costs, and can best be seen using an example as follows.

A small joinery manufacturer, specialising in the production of timber staircases, has the following cost figures, as in Table 11.1. These figures can be interpreted into graph form, as on Figs. 11.3, 11.4 and 11.5.

On Fig. 11.3, it can be seen that the fixed costs remain constant

Table 11.1 Output costs of staircase manufacture

Output/day (staircases)	Fixed cost (£)	Average fixed cost per unit (£)	Variable cost (£)	Average variable cost per unit (£)	Total output cost (£)	Marginal cost (£)		Average total cost per unit (£)
0	100	—	0	—	100			—
1	100	100	80	80	180	} 80	75	180
2	100	50	150	75	250	} 70	67.5	125
3	100	33.3	215	71.7	315	} 65	65	105
4	100	25	280	70	380	} 65	72.5	95
5	100	20	360	72	460	} 80	95	92
6	100	16.7	470	78.3	570	} 110	137.5	95
7	100	14.3	635	90.7	735	} 165	195	105
8	100	12.5	860	107.5	960	} 225	262.5	120
9	100	11.1	1 160	128.9	1 260	} 300		140

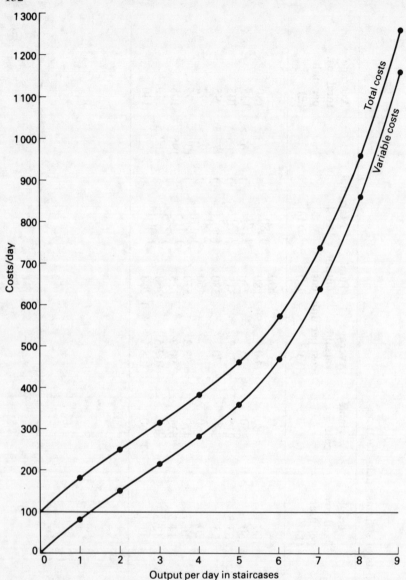

Fig. 11.3 Fixed and variable costs

over the whole range of outputs considered here. If it was decided to expand output to say 20 or 30 units per day, it would probably be necessary to increase the fixed costs involved. If this was not done, then the law of diminishing marginal returns would set in.

Figure 11.4 shows the relationship between the average variable cost and average total cost. Looking at the average fixed costs line, it

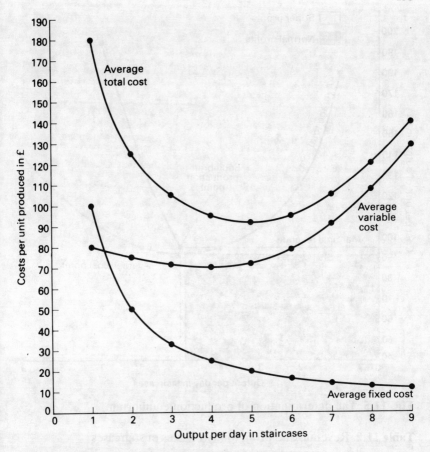

Fig. 11.4 Average production costs per unit

can be seen that the more goods that are produced from an enterprise with a certain mix of fixed costs, the lower will be the fixed cost commitment per unit.

Variable costs on the other hand can be seen to drop, up to a certain level of output, then rise steeply again, this demonstrating yet again the law of diminishing returns.

The average total cost is the addition of the two lower lines, and this too follows in general the pattern of decreasing to a certain level of output, then increasing again.

Figure 11.5 compares the average total cost with the marginal cost. Marginal cost is defined as the incremental cost involved in producing one more unit of output in a given period. Conversely, a marginal return or marginal revenue is the incremental return obtained from the sale of one more unit of output in a given period.

To be able to determine the production equilibrium point, which is

154

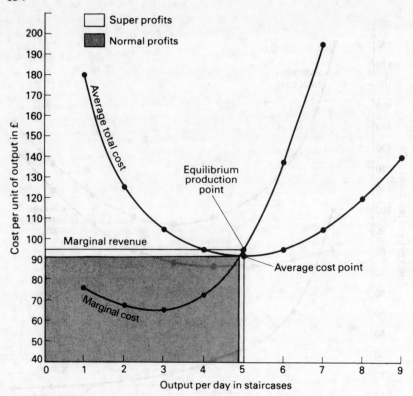

Fig. 11.5 The determination of production equilibrium

Table 11.2 Revenue and profitability of sales of staircases

Output/day (staircase)	Total Revenue (£)	Marginal revenue* (£)	Total costs (£)	Marginal cost (£)	Profit (£)
0	—	—	100		-100
1	95	95	180	75	- 85
2	190	95	250	67.5	- 60
3	285	95	315	65	- 30
4	380	95	380	72.5	0
5	475	95	460	95	15
6	570	95	570	137.5	0
7	665	95	735	195	- 70
8	760	95	960	262.5	-200
9	855	95	1 260	405	-405

* Marginal revenue is constant.

the optimum level for production, it is necessary to investigate the returns from sales. Consider Table 11.2, and Fig. 11.5.

As can be seen in Fig. 11.5, after a certain point the marginal costs of production increase. It is, however, most profitable for the business, if production is increased as long as the marginal cost of producing the last unit of output is less than the marginal return.

The maximum profit equilibrium point is attained where marginal cost equals marginal revenue.

If a business is operating below this output, then it will be more profitable to increase output. If the marginal cost is higher than the marginal revenue, then obviously it will be more profitable to reduce output. This can be seen from Table 11.2; the greatest profit is made where the marginal cost equals the marginal revenue with an output of five units per day. In this particular case, if the output is varied up or down by one unit, then there is zero profit.

Over the long term, the marginal return must at least equal the average total cost. If this were not the case, then the enterprise would have to go out of business. If many firms were in this state, because of a recession, then below normal profits would be made which would

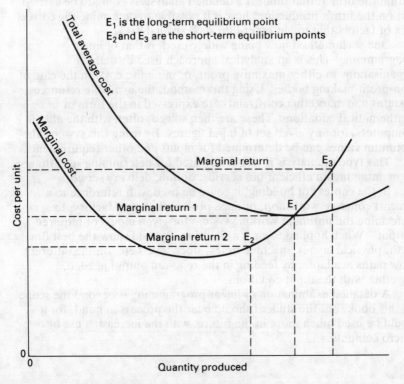

E_1 is the long-term equilibrium point
E_2 and E_3 are the short-term equilibrium points

Fig. 11.6 Short-and long-term equilibrium positions

induce firms to leave the industry. This is shown on Fig. 11.6 at position E_2. If on the other hand large super profits were being made as at position E_3 of Fig. 11.6, then many firms might enter the industry. When only normal profit is made then firms neither join nor leave the industry, and the industry is said to be in a state of equilibrium.

If a firm was operating at a point where only normal profits were made, then the firm is said to be operating at a long-term equilibrium point. See Fig. 11.6 point E_1. If it was operating so that either below or above average profits were made, then assuming the theory of perfect competition, changes would occur. The firm in these circumstances would be operating at a short-term equilibrium point.

Linear programming

After following through the previous example, based on fixed and variable costs, and the revenue obtained, it is possible to determine the equilibrium production point for the particular circumstances existing within the firm at that time. If a detailed analysis is going to be carried out on the firm's production, how is it possible to determine the correct mix of factors that might enter into such an analysis?

One such method now being widely used, is that of linear programming. This is an analytical approach used by many organisations to either maximise profit, or minimise costs in the case of non-profit-making bodies. Using this method, the available resources, systems and marketing constraints are expressed in the form of mathematical equations. These are then solved, often with the aid of computers, for any given set of input figures. By using this system, the optimum values can be determined for inputs and other requirements.

This type of analysis is frequently used for determining such things as maintaining an efficient bus service, or milk delivery service.

In the context of building, it could be used with reference to a precast concrete workshop, or mass produced joinery factory, to determine the optimum working system for given inputs or required outputs. When applied to such a situation, it could show the best flow path, physical layout, machine times, stock levels etc. on the different flow paths available, by feeding in the required output needed, together with the input equations.

A detailed examination of linear programming is beyond the scope of this book, but the student should bear the process in mind, for it could be used much more in the future, with the increasing use of micro computers.

Questions

1 Discuss the difference between perfect competition and perfect monopoly.

2 (a) Determine the production equilibrium point for the staircase manufacturer discussed earlier, given the following information.

Selling price £145.

Fixed costs £90 per day.

Variable costs/day	110	210	300	400	530	680	860
Output/day	1	2	3	4	5	6	7

(b) What profit is made at this point.

3 Discuss why a firm can not exist at a short-term equilibrium point for a long period, assuming perfect competition is in operation.

Chapter 12

The scale of production

If the type of business enterprises existing today is compared with those of 50–100 years ago, it will be seen that there are many more larger businesses today, than in years gone by. One important reason for the growth of larger companies is the advances made in communications at all levels over the last few decades. In particular, with reference to telecommunications, postal services, transport, and data distribution systems in general. These have enabled faster distribution of goods and information, from a few large national production units, rather than from many smaller locally based industries. This has led to firms operating not only on a national level, but often multi-nationally.

Why, one may ask, do firms grow to such large sizes, for there must be reasons other than communications?

The main reason for the existence of a business is to make a profit, and very often, the larger the firm, the greater the profit, due to economies of scale.

Economies of scale

These may be classified either as internal or external economies of scale.

Internal economies of scale

These are economies that arise from within the firm itself. They can be described as follows.

Bulk purchase of raw materials

The larger the production operation, the more raw material will be required. This generally enables the firm to obtain bulk supplies at a reduced cost. By moving from purchasing on a small scale to purchasing on a large scale, very often the middleman or wholesaler can be bypassed. This is particularly so in the construction industry, where for example a small company might buy cement or bricks in small lots from a builders' merchants, whereas a large company would have large direct loads which are despatched straight from the factory, at a much lower cost per unit.

Bulk sales

By increasing the production of the firm, more goods will need to be sold. Again, favourable rates can often be obtained for selling large lots rather than small. A typical example is where an estate agent might normally require 2 per cent commission on the sale of a few houses erected by a developer. With a site of 100 houses, however, the same agent might agree to sell the houses for 1 per cent commission.

Division of labour

The larger the firm, the greater the opportunity to carry out division of labour, with all its associated advantages, as discussed in Chapter 4.

Borrowing money

It is often said that large firms have a better facility for the borrowing of money, as the larger the firm, the more stable and secure it seems in the eyes of an investor. The actual cost of borrowing large amounts of money is, however often higher than that of borrowing smaller amounts.

Research and development

A large company can afford to employ specialists, and carry out detailed research, that would not be financially possible for a smaller firm. This often results in large firms remaining market leaders, as they maintain a flow of technological developments which enables them to stay ahead of their competitors.

Administrative economies

Large-scale production often leads to economies in administration. For instance, if a manufacturing firm doubled its turnover, it is unlikely that the numbers of managers and clerks employed would be doubled.

Improved benefits

Large firms often provide much better social facilities and fringe benefits than could be offered by smaller companies. This has the benefit of improving working conditions and reducing the turnover of staff.

External economies of scale

A firm may gain benefit by virtue of the industrial environment within a location, rather than from any internal changes in the firm. Such points to consider might be:

1. Existing service industries

Where there is a large multi-industry population within an area, then many service industries will already exist to service a wide range of industries. For example, transport facilities, banking and insurance facilities, suppliers and wholesalers of all materials, electric motor rewinders etc.

2. Specialist industries

Where a similar industry exists on a large scale within a region, then the operation of division of labour will often have created specialist firms, that can carry out certain types of work cheaper than a large multipurpose firm.

A good example is a typical industrial area in the Midlands. Here engineering work of all types is carried out, and has led to many specialist firms, e.g: pattern makers; toolmakers; chromium platers; galvanisers; specialist waste disposal firms.

3. Local labour and training

If a firm is thinking of entering an area in which the industry already exists, then there is likely to be an existing supply of labour trained in the particular skills required. Should labour have to be trained, however, then there often exists good training facilities locally for the skills required.

The optimum size of firms

Firms engaged in different types of industries, will be most efficient at different sizes of production unit. Consider the following:
(a) A blacksmith will operate best when he is self-employed with possibly a couple of staff to assist. In other words a very small-scale operation.
(b) The manufacture of motor cars needs a production unit on a vast scale, if it is to achieve the economies of scale necessary to make a profit.

Although earlier it was stated that firms grow in order to make greater profits, some firms are more profitable on a small scale by virtue of the type of work they do. Some reasons why certain businesses stay fairly small follow.

1. Specialists providing personal attention

Work requiring the personal attention of a specialist. Architects for example are nearly always to be found in fairly small practices, as their personal attention is required by the client.

Once a private architect's practice grows to a certain size, it is difficult to maintain the personal contact, and much more time would be spent by the senior partners in supervising and correcting the mistakes or inadequacies of the other employees. This example demonstrates a fairly low threshold for the setting in of diseconomies of scale.

2. Small specialist businesses

Within a particular geographical region, there is sometimes only enough work for one or two small business units of a particular type, e.g. tree surgeons. As there is normally so little demand for a tree surgeon within any particular area, if he tried to expand the firm, a great deal more travelling would have to be done in order to obtain work. This would increase costs, and so again diseconomies of scale begin.

3. Specialist craft businesses

Where particular craft skills are required, for example in the production of hand-made goods, whether they are jewellery, pottery, sculpture or exclusive women's fashions. With craft skills, it is very difficult to employ labour and therefore expand, as there are so few people with the exceptional skills that would be required.

As was seen in Chapter 7, there are a great many small firms within the construction industry, who cater mainly for the repair and maintenance and specialist subcontract market.

When there are no constraints keeping the optimum size small, then firms may grow in different ways.

Expansion of the existing operation

This is the most common form of growth, and it is quite simply where a firm will increase its turnover by carrying out more of the same sort of work that has been handled in the past. For instance, a contracting firm may decide to carry out more or larger contracts than in the past. Hopefully this will lead to greater profits.

Combination

Here a firm will either take over, or amalgamate with another or others, to form a single more efficient unit. Combination can take place in two forms:

1. Horizontal combination

This is where a firm will join with another firm, where both are carrying out similar business. For example a building firm may decide to take over another building firm in the same area for various reasons. It may be that the two firms are in fierce competition with one another, and so by getting rid of this competition, profit margins could increase. Another reason for this merger is where the firm being taken over might hold considerable land banks, that would be useful to a building development company.

2. Vertical combination

This is where firms combine, so that the different levels of the production and possibly distribution of a product are brought under common ownership.

For example a building company might take over a builders' merchants, so that in times of materials shortages, the building company will have security of supply. This would be a backwards combination, as the building company would be combining down the production chain.

Alternatively, a speculative development company may take over an estate agents, in order to hold power in the selling of their properties, and to enjoy the benefits of associated building society backing, which is often allied to estate agents' work. This particular type of merger is known as a forward combination, as the builder is combining up the production chain.

In order for company A to take over company B, it is necessary for company A to obtain 51 per cent of the voting shares (a majority holding) of company B. Company A, is then known as a holding company with full control over company B. By this method of takeover, very large groups or combines of businesses are possible.

The growth of multinational companies

In the last 20 years, there has been considerable growth in the size of many companies, to the extent that their area of operations now covers several countries. There are several possible reasons that might persuade a company to expand in this manner.

(a) Many businesses try to combine vertically to take under their control raw material supplies that have to be imported. A good example of this is where tea and rubber firms operating in Britain own extensive plantations abroad. By doing this, they can ensure that the raw materials are not sold to competitors.

(b) In order to improve sales and widen the market for its goods, a company may set up an operation in another country, to sell goods. This can take many different forms. For instance, American oil companies set up subsidiary companies in Britain, in order to sell their petrol to British motorists.

In some instances, to overcome restrictions on the importing of finished products, it is necessary to build an assembly plant in the country in question in order to be able to bring the goods in, in

163

Table 12.1 An example of a simple input output table

Figures are in £100 000	Manufacturer A	Manufacturer B	Manufacturer C	Manufacturer D	Manufacturer E	Inter-mediate output	Home market	Export market	Final output	Total output
Manufacturer A	—	5	1	0	2	8	2	2	4	12
Manufacturer B	1	—	0	3	1	5	4	2	6	11
Manufacturer C	4	1	—	0	0	5	1	0	1	6
Manufacturer D	1	0	3	—	5	9	0	12	12	21
Manufacturer E	2	2	0	0	—	4	10	0	10	14
Inputs other than goods and services	3	3	2	12	4	24				24
Imports	1	0	0	6	2	9	10		10	19
Total inputs	12	11	6	21	14	64	27	16	43	107

component form, assemble into finished form and sell them.

(c) In the past, many companies have developed manufacturing and assembly plants in countries where either labour costs were low, or where there was little disruption to production caused by strikes etc. This helps to ensure that costs are kept low, and that production targets will be met.

(d) Very often, where there is high unemployment in a particular region of a country, the government will offer financial assistance, in the form of grants, to encourage foreign firms to set up businesses there.

(e) Where a company has many production units in many countries, this is frequently done in order to offset the problem of recession that might occur in any one particular country. This spreads the risks of the total enterprise over as wide a base as possible.

(f) In some countries, there is a very low rate of 'corporation' tax. This encourages companies to carry out business in these countries, for this could lead either to higher direct profit margins, or to lower productive costs which in turn should lead to higher demand and eventually to more profits.

Input output analysis

In the study of the economy of the firms of a particular country, it is necessary to try to collate the information concerning the various inputs and outputs of the different industries, to see how all industries relate to one another. The study of such interactions can be carried out with the aid of an input output table.

An input output table is a matrix, where the various producers and consumers are each allocated a row, and a column within the table. The inputs and outputs of these producers and consumers, can then be analysed.

Consider Table 12.1. The total output from manufacturer A is £1 200 000 worth of goods, of which £800 000 worth goes to other manufacturers, £200 000 worth to the home consumers, and £200 000 worth is exported. The value of inputs into manufacturer A balances the output, with £800 000 coming from other manufacturers, £300 000 being the value of labour, profits and taxes, and £100 000 worth of goods coming in directly as imports. By studying the table, it can be seen to what extent each industry is dependent upon another.

Likely repercussions of possible actions can easily be seen. For example:

(a) If the government decided to restrict the sale of exports to 50 per cent of the existing (not a very likely action in practice), then manufacturer D would lose £600 000 of sales immediately, and would have to try and sell more in the home market.

(b) If government policy was to restrict imports, then again manufacturer D may be hard hit, as this firm uses a large proportion of imported inputs.

(c) From the table, it can be seen that manufacturer A supplies £500 000 of goods to manufacturer B. If A went out of business, then B might be in serious difficulties, as $\frac{5}{8}$ of its inputs come from A.

From Table 12.1 which, it must be stressed, is a very simple example, the ratio of imports to exports can also be deduced.

Very complex tables can be drawn up, to show the inter-relationship of all industries, services, consumer sectors etc. within a country. By doing this, it is much easier to study situations than by wading through masses of figures in statistical lists.

Questions

1 The optimum size for a building firm is large. Discuss this statement.
2 What could be shown by considering input output analysis applied to the construction industry, its suppliers and customers.

Chapter 13

The location of industry

In the past there were many factors influencing the location of industry. Today, in developed societies, some of these factors are now less important, thanks to the developments in education, transport, communications and power supplies, as will be seen.

A firm needs to operate at its most efficient level, if it does not, its competitors will be able to undercut its prices and eventually the firm will go out of business. By carefully locating the place of business, certain costs can be minimised. The following five factors may need to be considered.

Nearness of power supply

In the Industrial Revolution, with the beginning and growth of industry, it was essential to have a nearby source of power. This was one of the main reasons for the development of the woollen industry in Yorkshire. Here were ample streams which would provide power for the looms and other machinery, with the aid of waterwheels. Later on, with the advent of steam power, it became important for industries to be centred on or near coal producing areas. Hence the reason for the positioning of many power requiring industries in the Midlands, South Wales and around Manchester.

With the coming of the twentieth century, other forms of power were being developed, so that with the completion of supply networks for electricity and gas, and with oil being fairly easy to transport, the location for reasons of power supply is no longer so critical in many cases.

Coal, when required in large amounts is still a very important factor, for due to its bulk, it is very expensive to transport. It is for this reason, that electricity power stations designed for burning coal are still constructed close to coal mines, to cut down transport costs.

Nearness of raw materials

The transporting of any raw material involves costs which vary with the distance, unless there is a set price delivered anywhere in the country, or within certain regions. The price of cement for instance would be the same in many areas, for the price is fixed nationally, to a certain extent. It is obvious that transport distances should be cut wherever possible in order to cut costs. This is especially important with low cost, high bulk materials. These are said to only have a high value close to their place of origin, and so are termed high place value materials. Examples of these would be sand and gravel used for roadworks and concrete, and clay for brickmaking. A businessman wishing to set up a production plant for precast concrete, or brick manufacture, would be extremely foolish if the site chosen was not close to good raw material sources.

As the cost of oil rises, so do transport costs. In the future, when transport costs could form a much larger proportion of the selling price of an article, the nearness to raw materials could be even more important than it is today.

Nearness to a market

Certain types of goods have to be near to potential markets, again these are goods which are heavy to transport. Again as in the last section, precast concrete products and bricks fall into this category. It can be seen already that when locating an enterprise there is often a compromise between nearness to raw materials, and nearness to markets. A factory that had to transport its products over long distances would be at a price disadvantage, compared to a competitor who only transported a short distance. Where breakable goods are being transported, long hauls can often be very expensive if many breakages occur.

Other goods, which tend to be fairly scarce, and where transport costs only form a small percentage of total cost, for example motor cars or televisions, do not need to be too close to markets. Indeed, at the present time, Japan is selling both these commodities to Britain.

Pilfering is a major problem that must be borne in mind, when transporting high cost, scarce goods, over long distances.

High future transport costs could again make the nearness to markets another more important factor in the future.

The external economies of scale

These were discussed in the last chapter, and they all help to form a decision as to the ideal location for an industry. One point is particularly important, however, and that is the closeness of a suitable source of labour, and specialist suppliers. If skilled and trained labour already exist in an area then much time and money could be saved, through not having to train operatives.

As was mentioned in Chapter 2, labour tends to be very immobile and so it is difficult to attract trained labour to an area. This is yet another reason for establishing an enterprise in an area where a pool of labour exists.

The intervention of government

(See also social problems and attitudes in Chapter 4.) Over the last few decades, there has been a decline in certain industries, particularly those associated with the North of England, such as shipbuilding and the textile industries. The new technology industries, however, have tended to concentrate in the Midlands and the South East. This has led to an imbalance of industrial activity within the different regions of the country.

The various governments since the 1930s have tried to overcome this problem, by the granting of certain types of aid to those areas needing assistance. There are at present three types of assisted area:
(a) Special Development Areas, where the needs are most urgent.
(b) Development Areas, where the needs are less severe.
(c) Intermediate areas, where some help is needed, but not urgently.

Regional development grants, for machinery and buildings in specified manufacturing industries are made under the 1972 Industry Act, whilst other grants are available, providing they aid employment in an assisted area.

Government also helps these areas in two other ways:
(a) Firms in assisted areas get preferential treatment when tendering for government contracts.
(b) Government is keen to give fast approval to Industrial Development Certificates (IDC) in assisted areas. Approval for an IDC in a non-assisted area generally takes a little longer.

Since joining the EEC, areas of Britain suffering industrial change or severe unemployment are eligible for grants from the European Regional Development Fund.

The development of rural industries and small firms is carried out through the Council for Small Industries in Rural Areas (CoSIRA). Technical and managerial advice is given, and loans and credit facilities are arranged. This has helped develop many small businesses in areas where there was previously little chance of increasing employment.

The previous five factors are those particularly relevant to many industries in Britain today. In Britain in the past, and indeed in other, less developed countries today, there are different factors which often have to be taken into account

The stability of the political situation

Businessmen, wishing to develop a production unit in countries abroad, will look very seriously at this problem. Where the political climate is volatile, with much unrest, production from industries within this type of environment can be seriously disrupted, as can transport facilities. There are also many situations, where governments have compulsorily nationalised foreign investments, sometimes without compensation.

Climate

This was very important for certain industries in the past. A good example of this is the production of woollen cloth in Lancashire and Yorkshire, where the correct degree of humidity existed for the processing of the fibres.

Today, climatic problems are only really considered a problem in the food and other organic industries, such as the growing of cotton or rubber trees etc. Manufacturing is not now so worried by extremes or wrong types of climate, for thanks to technology, almost any type of climate can be created artificially using air conditioning techniques.

Close to main centres of commerce etc.

It is often a great advantage to have a business operation close to centres of commerce, finance and government. Close links can be formed with other types of commerce, and large contracts can often be won, purely because of public relations exercises, or by personal contact which is possible when many industries are grouped together.

Many large industries operate a branch office, if not the head office, from London, purely because it is the centre of commerce and government, and because much trade is negotiated there.

The speed and efficiency of modern modes of passenger transport, however means that two business meetings, which took place at opposite ends of the country, could be managed in the same day.

Transport and communication

Closeness to transport has in the past been very important. In Britain, many industrial centres developed around the networks of canals and railways, in the eighteenth and nineteenth centuries. With the advent of a good road system, all markets now become easily attainable.

When transport is a major factor however, especially when hauling heavy materials, then a considerable financial advantage can be gained over competitors by siting the production plant close to a motorway junction, or in certain circumstances a separate rail link may be run to the factory.

At present, thanks to relatively cheap transport, many industries can afford to have one, or only a few, production centres, and can transport the goods all over the country. As transport gets relatively more expensive, will the economic market area for industries become smaller? This may lead to regional markets where national now exist, or local markets, where regional now exist.

How the location factors affect different industries

In Table 13.1, the letters A,B,C, have been used to try to give some indication of the importance of a particular location factor to each industry considered. A, being the most important, C, the least.

Some of the table is left blank, and as an exercise, after reading this section, the student should fill in the spaces, and discuss his choice of weightings.

As power is so well distributed in this country, the positioning of an industry close to power is no longer so critical here. The table, however tries to give some idea of the importance power has to the industry, as this would still often be considered in overseas locations.

Car industry

Here much power is used in total, from the pressings and castings of the manufacture of components, to the assembling and finishing processes.

The car industry can be defined at different levels of operation.

It is possible to talk of the car industry as virtually an assembly and finishing process, or one could include all the preliminary basic manufacture of components. The latter example is the one favoured here, and, as so much steel is used in the production of cars, it is fairly important to have good local sources of supply in sheet and other form.

A close market is not nowadays all that important, for cars are shipped between many countries of the world, and as the cost of transporting cars within a country bears an insignificant part of the total cost (about 1–2 per cent of the selling price), other factors are more important.

The closeness of specialised suppliers to the car industry is very important. Within the industry, components for just one type of car are often manufactured by hundreds of different suppliers. An ideal situation then would be to position a car assembly plant within close

Table 13.1 The importance of different location factors in various industries

Location factor Industry	Near power	Near raw materials	Near market	External economics	Government intervention	Political situation	Climate	Near to commercial centres	Transport
Car industry	A	B	B/C	A	A/B	A	C	B	B
Brick manufacture	A	A	A	B	B	B	C	B	A
Construction	C	B	A/C	B	B/C	A	B	B	B
Shipbuilding	B	B	C	A	A	B	C	B	A
Electronics									
Jewellery									
Craft industries									

A = Very important; B = Fairly important; C = Not very important.

proximity to these suppliers. Specialist service industries, such as machinery manufacturers, should also be close at hand.

A car assembly plant complete with machinery, costs many millions of pounds, therefore any help with loans or grants, as in development areas, might help sway a decision on the location of a plant.

As so much money is at stake in capital investment, it is unlikely that car production plants would be set up in politically volatile countries.

Climate, as in most factory based industries, is of secondary importance, although in other countries extremes of heat and cold can cause the expending of much energy on air conditioning or heating.

Brick manufacture

The firing of bricks uses a great deal of energy, whatever form of fuel is used. Traditionally it was coal, and very often coal was mined on the same site as the clay. Modern methods, however, use oil fired kilns, and so nearness to energy sources is not today, so important in Britain.

Bricks have a low cost/weight ratio. As the total cost is still relatively low, then much money cannot be spent on the transport of heavy raw materials, or finished goods. Traditionally bricks were manufactured on the site of the clay workings, and this still goes on a great deal today. The transport of finished bricks is almost invariably by lorry, and many brickworks have an economic distribution area of only a few tens of kilometres, before their delivery costs become higher than those of a nearer competitor.

The government can chiefly affect the brick industry, by whether or not it allows the extraction of clay in a certain area. It could be argued, that extraction of clay would expand employment, but mar the countryside. (An ideal situation for the use of cost benefit analysis (CBA))

Brick manufacture in less developed countries is a fairly stable industry necessary to the local environment. It is unlikely to be affected greatly by politically volatile situations, much less so, than say a car assembly plant, where components may be imported, and finished cars exported.

Construction

The location of the construction industry needs to be viewed in a different light to other industries, as the industry will always be found where work is needed to be done. The reason for this is, of course that the products of the construction industry are not mobile. Therefore given any flourishing sector of business, the construction industry will be there, building factories, houses or service buildings.

Although there are many power tools used on construction sites, any site, if necessary, could become self-contained from the power point of view.

The construction industry could in some respects be looked upon as a service industry, as it provides the service of constructing buildings or other structures where the client wants them. The choice of position is the client's, and is often made with a view to long-term operation of the building:

(a) If a factory, it may be near markets or raw materials.
(b) If an office block, it may be within a commercial centre, close to passenger transport facilities.
(c) If a private house, the position and views over the countryside may be of prime importance.

The actual cost of the construction is often of secondary importance to these examples of other factors, and as any building material can be transported anywhere, the closeness to raw materials is not critical.

The closeness to market becomes more important, the smaller the construction business. As discussed in Chapter 9, a maintenance builder has to operate within a fairly small geographical market, whereas a constructor of motorways operates nationally.

The political situation in countries abroad, where firms foreign to that country have secured contracts is most important. Many companies have carried out such contracts, only to discover that final payments are held up indefinitely, or that actual war or government intervention, has caused the closure of the site.

Climate can affect construction sites, but, if a building is required in a climatically bad area, then this is just reflected in the price.

Shipbuilding

The most fundamental factor in the siting of this industry is that it should be on the coast, and adjacent to water deep enough to allow the transporting of the finished vessels.

The need for power is fairly important, particularly in the initial stages of cutting and shaping of steel etc.

The nearness to markets is not all that critical, as orders in Britain are obtained from many foreign countries.

External economies are especially important, particularly with regard to having a trained labour force nearby.

As a large proportion of shipbuilding is carried out by the nationalised industry, British Shipbuilders, many government contracts come automatically to this company. As shipbuilding is nearly always centred in development areas in this country, the government is under considerable pressure to maintain employment in this area.

In the past in this country, and today in certain countries abroad, pressure could be exerted by the government to establish shipbuilding facilities, either to produce warships for defence, or cargo ships, that would cut out the need to buy from abroad.

The above descriptions of the four industries have been fairly brief, as it was intended to give only the major factors concerned with industrial location.

The relative importance of the various factors in the particular

174

industries will not remain static, as commerce, politics, social effects, communications and transport are changing constantly. What today may be a major factor, tomorrow may be insignificant.

Question

1 Complete Table 13.1, and discuss reasons for your weightings.

Chapter 14

Types of business enterprises and their financing

Business enterprises can exist in one of several forms: **Sole traders;**
Partnerships; Companies; Nationalised industries; all of which are
described below.

The choice of business enterprise will depend upon two basic
factors, to which are related many others.

(a) The size of the business operation is an important factor, for this
will determine the amount of capital required, the need for
experienced specialists in the various functions of the enterprise,
and the number of managers, and possibly owners of the business.

(b) The type of product being produced is the other major factor. This
is partly linked with (a) above, in that the type of product often
dictates the scale of operations possible in a particular field.
Woodcarving, for instance, would not take the form of a
large-scale operation, whereas standard joinery manufacture
would. The production of certain products is inherently more risky
than others, fashion clothes for instance may not sell, so that large
losses are likely.

Sole traders

This is the simplest form of organisation, and it exists where there is
one owner of a business.

It may take the form of a one man business, where no other people
are employed, or the owner may employ several people to work for

him. This form of business is very common in small building firms, as it
is an ideal type of unit for carrying out small works.

Little capital is required and this is usually provided by the owner,
or through limited borrowing from banks.

Small businesses of this type are very flexible, in that the owner
can quickly make decisions, and as the organisational structure is
small, communications travel quickly between the associated parties.

One major problem with this form of organisation is the fact that
there is unlimited personal liability for any debts incurred.

Advantages of sole traders

(a) Easy to start this form of business.
(b) Little capital is required.
(c) The owner can work as hard as he wants to, for the rewards are all
his.
(d) Good communications, and personal contact with staff and
customers.
(e) Flexible, due to small organisation and fast decision-making.

Disadvantages of sole traders

(a) Scope of activities often limited to the experience of the owner.
(b) Problems of administration, when the owner is ill, or on holiday.
(c) Expansion is limited, as further capital is often difficult to obtain.
(d) Unlimited liability for debts incurred.

Partnerships

A partnership may be formed by two or more people, generally up to a
maximum of 20. Partnerships are often formed by sole traders taking
on a partner to form a partnership, between the original sole trader
and the newcomer. The new partner would be chosen for his ability to
provide additional skills or money. A partnership can be formed with
just a verbal agreement, but it is advisable to have drawn up a proper
partnership agreement, to include such items as:
(a) The duration of the partnership.
(b) The amount of capital each partner will contribute.
(c) The allocation of profits and losses.
(d) Amounts of salaries of each partner.
(e) How any dispute between the partners will be settled.

Ordinary partnerships help to spread the load of responsibility, but
because all partners are responsible for the actions of an individual
partner, it is essential to ensure that they are trustworthy, and act in a
reasonable manner. With partnerships, there is still unlimited liability.
so that if one particular partner incurs debts, on the partnership's
behalf, then the personal possessions of all the other partners could be
claimed in payment.

It is possible to form a limited partnership. In this case, at least one partner must still be accountable for the partnership debts, whilst the other limited partners enjoy limited liability. This means that they will not be asked to pay more money than they have agreed to invest, should debts be incurred.

A business run as a partnership lacks permanence, for if one partner dies, the whole partnership has to be dissolved, and recreated in a different form.

Many professional firms, such as architects, quantity surveyors etc. are run as partnerships.

Advantages of partnerships
(a) Fairly easy to form.
(b) Allows for the combination of the different skills of the partners.
(c) It provides a method of obtaining a financial backer.
(d) Eases the administrative load, compared with that of a sole trader.

Disadvantages of partnerships
(a) Unlimited liability.
(b) Great degree of personal harmony required between the partners.

Companies

A company can exist as one of three types, and in either a public or private form.

Private companies have between two and 50 shareholders. They do not have to publish a balance sheet, although they do have to send in copies of accounts to The Registrar of Companies, Companies House, Crown Way, Cardiff, and for a nominal sum these can be inspected by the public. Shares of private companies cannot be acquired by the general public, and any transfer of shares must be in accordance with procedure laid down in the articles. This normally involves offering shares to existing shareholders first.

Public companies have at least two shareholders, with no maximum number being stipulated. Balance sheets are published in the press, and there is no restriction on the sale or transfer of shares. The company name must end in PLC (public limited company).

Companies can be formed as:

1. Unlimited companies
For these the liability of the members is unlimited. These are very uncommon.

2. Companies limited by guarantee
Here the members guarantee to provide a certain amount of money, should the company go into liquidation.

3. Companies limited by shares

Here the shareholders liability is limited to the total price he has agreed to pay for the shares. This category of company is by far the most important in business today.

The operation of these limited companies can be very simply described as follows.

People purchase shares in the company, and should the company make a profit, the directors decide what proportion of the profit will be allocated to the shareholders as dividend. The dividend is expressed as a percentage of the fully paid up face value of the share. Whilst the shareholders are the owners of the company, the actual policies of the company are laid down by the board of directors, which is selected by the shareholders. Should the directors fail to declare a dividend one year, although a profit was made, then possibly the directors' jobs will be in jeopardy.

The normal day-to-day running of the company is controlled by the managing director who will be a member of the board. Under him would be the normal business organisational structure, which will vary according to the size of the enterprise.

A limited company is seen in law as a separate legal entity, and is able to 'sign' contracts and be sued in its own right. A company also enjoys permanence, for a company is not affected by the death of a shareholder, as the shares simply pass to the heir. The company itself stays in business until it is liquidated, either compulsorily, or voluntarily. A company can plan ahead for longer periods in the knowledge that its existence is not dependent upon the skills of one, or a few people.

The formation of a company offers the ability to acquire much more capital than a partnership or sole trader, and public companies can obtain much more than private companies, as they are open to wider subscription. Investors will be willing to invest, knowing that their risk is limited to the amount they agree to pay. It provides a means whereby a large amount of capital can be accumulated, for large capital intensive projects, from many relatively small investors.

Advantages of limited companies

(a) Limited liability means that the personal possessions of the owners are not at risk.
(b) It provides a means whereby people can invest small or large amounts, without the worry of being involved in the running of the business.
(c) It enables businesses to grow quickly. In the past, businesses often grew as a result of the ploughing back of profits. Today with greater competition resulting in lower profits, it is often essential to start off at a large scale of operation. This needs much capital.
(d) A limited company has perpetual life.
(e) People often have more faith when dealing with a limited company.

(f) Mergers and takeovers are relatively easy with limited companies.

(g) The company is not dependent upon the knowledge or skill of any individual. Any specialist can in theory be hired by the company, in any capacity.

(h) The shares of public companies are dealt with on the stock exchange. This means that the shares in such companies can be easily converted into cash, although the value of the shares on the day of sale has to be accepted.

(i) In public companies, there are often facilities for investment, with varying degrees of risk and profit potential (see the section on types of shares).

Disadvantages of limited companies

(a) It involves following a strict procedure for formation and operation, as laid down in the 1948, 1972 and 1976 Companies Acts.

(b) Some degree of privacy is lost, as any member of the public can obtain financial details from The Registrar of Companies.

(c) There is often disagreement between the shareholders and the directors, on matters of policy. Thus the divorce of control from ownership is not always a good thing. The directors have to look after the interests of the company. The shareholders primarily look after the interests of their investment, and are often more concerned about their dividends rather than future expansion of the company.

Formation of a limited company

The Companies Acts require that those wishing to form a limited company should supply the following documents to the Registrar of Companies together with the necessary registration fee and the stamp duty payable on the nominal capital.

1. The Memorandum of Association

This contains information defining the company's relation with the factors outside the business.

The following points should be included:

The company name: The Registrar may refuse to register any undesirable name, or one which is misleading.

The address of the registered office: All legal and statutory information will then be sent to that office. The European Communities Act 1972 now requires that the registered office address is shown on all business letters and order forms.

The objects clause: This sets out the type of activities of the company. It is necessary to include everything that the company might wish to become involved with in the future, as well as the present, for a company cannot legally operate outside its range of operations as defined in the objects.

The limited liability clause: This will state whether the company is limited by shares or guarantee. If by shares, then there will be a statement to the effect that the total liability is limited to the fully paid up value of the shares. If by guarantee, then the terms of the guarantee will be laid down.

The capital clause: This sets out the nominal or authorised share capital of the company, and its division into the different types of shares. As stamp duty is payable generally at the rate of 1 per cent of nominal capital, then there is some incentive to keep the nominal capital to a realistic figure.

Signature: The Memorandum must be signed by at least two people for a private company, or seven people if for a public company.

2. The Articles of Association

These relate to the internal workings of the company's activities. The rights and duties of members (shareholders) are set out, concerning the sale and transfer of shares. The procedure for voting, and the holding of the various meetings is laid down, as is the method of appointment and removal of directors, and the determination of their salaries.

Information relating to dividends and reserves should also be included.

3. A statement of names and particulars

The names and full particulars of the first directors and first secretary together with their signatures stating that they are willing to act in the capacity indicated.

4. A Statutory Declaration

This is a declaration usually signed by the solicitor forming the company, stating that the various Companies Acts have been complied with.

5. A statement of capital

This merely states the value of authorised or nominal capital of the company.

Providing all the documents are in order, then the Registrar will issue a certificate of incorporation, after which the company must acquire the capital with which to start trading. A private company will generally have subscribers already waiting, often the directors, and the money will be available almost immediately.

Public companies have to follow a different path however. A prospectus is issued by advertising in the national press, requesting the public to subscribe. Included in the prospectus will be the names of the company directors and the number, value and nature of the shares. The minimum subscription must also be stated in the case of the first share issue of a company. This is the minimum amount of money that the company can operate with initially. If this minimum subscription is not obtained by a certain date, then all monies received for shares have to be returned, and the particular share issue is void.

Public companies might not require all their nominal capital at once, in which case only part of it will be obtained initially, and a second and possibly a third issue of shares will be made at a later date. With these later share issues, the prospectuses must include:
(a) A report of the profits and losses over the preceding five years, and the assets and liabilities at the last balancing date.
(b) The dividends declared over the last five years.
(c) If another business is to be purchased with the proceeds of the share issue, then the information about that particular business as in (a) and (b) above is required.

Company capital

As was explained at the beginning of the book, there are different definitions of capital. In this section capital will be taken to mean the financial resources of the company. Even with this definition however, there may still be some confusion, for the capital of a company could refer to either the working capital, or various types of capital related to the share structure of the company, as follows.

Nominal, authorised or registered capital: This is the full amount of capital which the company has power to issue shares for, as in the Memorandum.

Issued or subscribed capital: The total value of the shares allotted, whether actually paid up or not. It is not necessary to issue shares for the total of the nominal capital, so the issued capital is that part of the nominal capital for which shares have been issued.

Called up capital: The amount of the issued capital which the directors have asked to be paid at this time. When shares are bought, the full price is not always asked for immediately. This often makes it easier to sell the shares. The called up capital is this amount that should have been paid.

Uncalled capital: That part of the issued capital that does not have to be paid at this time.

Paid up capital: The amount of called up capital that has actually been paid. The difference between called up capital and paid up capital is known as calls in arrears.

Unissued capital: That part of nominal capital not yet issued.

Reserve capital: Capital set aside out of uncalled capital, that will only be called in for use, if the company is wound up.

The above definitions can be better explained by the following example.

Example: A newly-formed company has a nominal capital of £100 000, and decides to issue 60 000 £1 shares, of which 75p per share is payable immediately, and 10p per share is set aside as a reserve. At the present time, only £37 000 of the £45 000 called up, has actually been paid.

Nominal capital	100 000
Issued capital	60 000
Unissued capital is therefore	40 000
Issued capital	60 000
Called up capital	45 000
Uncalled capital is therefore	15 000

Of this £15 000, £6 000 is reserve capital, which leaves £9 000 to be called in at some future date.

Called up capital	45 000
Paid up capital	37 000
Calls in arrears is therefore	8 000

Shares

A company may have issued only one type of share, or several different types. All shares however fall into two main types.

Ordinary shares: These are the most common type of share issued. They are the risk type shares, for dividends may be high or low or at certain times, non-existent. It is the holders of such shares, that are the financial risk takers of industry today.

Ordinary shares do not qualify for a fixed percentage dividend, for the return per share may fluctuate wildly between good and bad years. The dividend on ordinary shares is payable after that for any preference shares.

Ordinary shares are sometimes subdivided into deferred ordinary, and preferred ordinary. Preferred ordinary being paid their dividend before the deferred ordinary.

Preference shares: These have preference over ordinary shares, with regard to dividends. Preference shares are designated by a fixed rate of dividend payable, which has to be paid in full before ordinary shares are allocated a dividend. In the absence of any provision to the contrary in the articles, all preference shares are cumulative. This means that if there is insufficient money to pay the guaranteed dividend on the preference shares in a particular year, then next year the shareholders will receive any back dividend due, plus the current dividend.

Under normal circumstances, if a company made good profits one year, the preference shareholders would get their expected dividend, with probably a high dividend for any ordinary shareholders.

Participating preference shares again receive their guaranteed dividend, but once the ordinary shareholders have received a certain amount, the rest of the allocated profits are distributed between the participating preference shareholders and the ordinary shareholders in a predetermined manner.

The payment to the shareholder, for the risk of investing his money, is the dividend he receives. This is expressed as a percentage of the fully paid up face value of the share. The total amount of profits allocated to dividends is decided by the board of directors. It is important to note, that dividends must come out of profits.

To try to determine the profitability of a company by looking at its share capital structure, or the dividend paid, is not really possible. The nominal or issued capital gives little indication of the size of the company's operations, for it may be financing itself from past profits, or from other sources of borrowed capital. A statement of the percentage dividend offered has to be investigated carefully. A 20 per cent dividend might sound very good, but this may have been for a share whose face value was £1, but if the company has been doing well and showed good dividends in the past, the shareholder may have had to pay £2 for this share on the stock market. The actual dividend is 20 per cent of £1 or 20p. This represents a return on the shareholders investment of only 10 per cent.

Conversely, if the shareholder only paid 50p for the share, his actual return would be 40 per cent.

The Stock Exchange

The Stock Exchange is a market for second hand shares. Fully listed companies are now graded as either Alpha stocks – those most actively traded, Beta, or Gamma – those infrequently traded.

If a member of the public wished to buy shares in say ICI then he/she could approach a broker, which might be a firm of stockbrokers or a high street bank. The broker then consults his SEAQ (Stock Exchange automated quotations system) monitor which will indicate which market makers (the firms that actually make a market in the shares) operate in these stocks. In some instances the broker and the market maker will be different divisions of the same firm; however, 'in house' transactions are strictly controlled to avoid buying or selling which would be disadvantageous to the client. The broker will then make a deal with the market maker and the transaction is recorded.

The broker obtains his income from the commission on sales whilst the market maker obtains a profit from the difference between his selling price and buying price.

184

The prices of shares fluctuate, depending upon the supply and demand of individual shares. If a company is making good profits, or indeed if there is only a rumour of good profits, then people will want to buy shares in that company. People already owning the shares however will not want to sell, hence the market price for the shares will be high. If a company does not seem to be producing good dividends, then the share values will be low. The prices of the shares are listed daily in the national newspapers, but the most detailed information is to be found in the *Financial Times*.

The importance of the stock market to industry is that it ensures that investors will be willing to invest money in company shares, with the knowledge that their investment can be easily converted back into cash if they so wish. Besides shares, the stock exchange deals in stocks, which are another form of investment, but which are normally offered in this form initially by government, nationalised industries, local authorities etc. to finance capital projects.

Working capital

This is capital needed to finance the day-to-day running of the company, to buy materials and pay salaries and wages, until customers pay their debts.

The majority of the share capital of a company is used to purchase the long-term assets of the company, such as the premises and plant. There will occasionally be times when, due to recession, or after an expansion programme that has been financed from past profits, the company will be short of funds, and will need to seek sources of finance.

Sources of finance

When considering finance for a business the type of finance required will be categorised as:

(a) Short term. That required for up to 3 years.
(b) Medium term. That required for up to 3–10 years.
(c) Long term. That required for over 10 years.

It should be noted that the following sections are aimed fairly specifically at the construction industry, and many points may not be applicable to other industries.

When a company decides that it is short of funds, the managers' first thought is often to go out and seek a loan of some kind. There are however certain checks, that should be made on company finances before this step is taken. A few examples follows.

Example (a): Many small to medium construction companies own their own plant. This results in the tying up of large sums of money in capital items for which work may not always be available. There will also be money invested in the maintaining of a plant yard, together with service and stores facilities. Many such companies, after detailed analysis, have found it more economical to cut down on the amount of plant they own, which leads to considerable savings. The action of selling off plant, and possibly the yard, can also give a useful boost to working capital, and forestall the need for further finance.

Example (b): All builders maintain a yard or stores compound, either at head office or on site. If the level of stocks rises too high for the particular work being undertaken, then they should be reduced. Perhaps high stock levels are due to an over-enthusiastic ordering surveyor, who has tried to obtain very low prices, but has resulted in overbuying. Whatever the reason, if stocks can be reduced, then working capital will no longer be tied up.

Example (c): Medium to large companies often run specialist sections which might include such areas of activities as site investigation, plumbing, electrical work etc. A constant check should be kept on the profitability of the individual specialist areas, for it is sometimes so, that several profitable areas are having to carry one or two sections that constantly make losses. If this is the case, then after due consideration the unprofitable sections should be disbanded. This may seem an obvious action, but it is surprising how often companies allow this situation to develop and continue.

Example (d): An analysis of cash flow within the company might reveal that those clients owing money to the company are taking longer to pay their bills than is reasonable.

This problem might be solved by becoming firmer with the bad payers, or even operating on pro forma invoices. By this method the client pays before the work is carried out. Another method gaining popularity is that of factoring the company's invoices. Here the factoring company buys all the company's invoices at a discount, and takes over the responsibility of administering invoices and statements etc. and collects the money from the clients. The advantage of this is that the company gets its money very quickly, and it can also often cut down on the administrative staff.

The period of credit given by the company's suppliers is also of the utmost importance. The majority of goods supplied are on monthly account, which means that to qualify for discount, usually 2½ per cent, the goods have to be paid for by the end of the month following delivery. By ensuring that goods are ordered in the first week of the next month, rather than the last week of the present month, and also by ensuring no goods are purchased for cash, economies can be made.

Example (e): The hiring, rather than the owning of plant, has already been mentioned. In many companies the philosophy of contract hire has been extended to include office equipment, cars, offices, even staff; this inevitably leads to less capital being tied up.

Short-term finance

When sources of internal economics and financial resources have been fully investigated, only then should external sources be sought.

Short-term finance may be needed to cover periods when a contractor wants to take on or set up another contract. It can also cover short-term cash flow problems, where a client's payment is overdue. This form of finance can also be used to purchase land for development, or plant for a particular job.

Traditionally, the bank overdraft has been the most popular form of short-term finance. With this method, the bank manager gives agreement to a maximum overdraft figure for the company's account. Very often some form of security is needed for this facility. With an overdraft, the company only pays interest on the actual amount of the overdraft used, not the total overdraft figure granted. For example, if a company had an overdraft facility for £100 000, but at a particular time its overdraft was only £40 000, then at that time, interest would only be payable on the £40 000. The interest payable is generally about 2 per cent above bank base rates (BR), and overdraft facilities are generally reviewed annually.

Bank loans are another source of finance often used. Here the bank credits the account of the company with the amount in question, and the company has to begin repaying the loan with interest on the total figure borrowed, straight away, whether or not the money is being used by the company.

Overdraft interest fluctuates, following the movements of the BR, whilst interest payable on a loan is usually fixed for the period of the loan. Hence it is often better to take out a loan when BR is low, but likely to rise, whilst it is better to take out an overdraft when BR is high, and likely to drop.

Hire purchase is a form of short-term finance often used to buy capital items such as plant etc. With this method, the machine can be purchased, and set to work to start earning profit for the company, before it is finally paid for. By careful planning, this often works out very well.

Deferred creditors are those with long periods between payments. A typical example is the Inland Revenue. Here payment of VAT and PAYE etc. is only made every few months. The money set aside for these payments can be used to finance short-term ventures, providing the money will be available when required.

Medium-term finance

This is said to be one of the most difficult forms of finance to obtain. High street banks are reluctant to invest money for periods of up to eight to ten years, and very often if the money is needed for only three to eight years it is not really worth offering a new share issue to the public.

Finance can often be arranged from commercial banks, or finance houses, but at a fairly high rate of interest, and often they insist on a seat on the board of directors, just to ensure that the company will be managed properly.

Funds over the medium to long term can be provided by various finance corporations. Investors in Industry (known as the 3i) invests in a wide range of industries and during the year to March 1986 invested £320 million. Investors in Industry is owned by the clearing banks and the Bank of England. There are other finance corporations such as the Agricultural Mortgage Corporation, Equity Capital for Industry and the Commonwealth Development Corporation.

The National Enterprise Board, which used to assist industry with funds, was amalgamated with the National Research Development Group in 1981 to form the British Technology Group (BTG). The main function of the Group is to promote the development of technology arising from such public sector sources as universities, polytechnics, research councils and various government establishments. BTG follows an invention right through from development and funding to industrial production.

Long-term finance

There are three main sources of long-term finance.

Increasing the issued capital of the company: This involves the floating of a new share issue on the market. In order for this venture to be a success, the company must have a good past record of dividends in order to tempt investors to buy shares. With a public company, a prospectus will be placed in national newspapers. With private companies, further shares can only be issued in accordance with the Articles, which normally insists on the full agreement of the existing shareholders.

It must be remembered that the nominal capital, as stated in the Memorandum, is the maximum that can be issued. If more than this is required, then the nominal capital figure will have to be changed by a special meeting of shareholders.

If there is any uncalled capital outstanding on existing share issues, then it may be possible to call this in.

Debentures: The traditional form of long-term finance is the debenture. A debenture is a loan, generally a secured loan, and must not be confused with shares, which are concerned with the ownership of the company. Most shares carry voting rights, but debentures do not. A debenture is a fixed interest security, and in modern industry, they are generally repayable before a certain date, or very occasionally they may be irredeemable during the existence of the company.

A debenture loan may be raised by an issue open to public subscription, or a debenture may be granted by a bank, insurance or pension fund, or finance house. The debenture holder does not share in the risks of the company, for the interest must be paid, whether a profit is made or not. As the risk is less than that of owning shares, the return is generally less.

In order that a company may secure a debenture loan it must, over the long period, expect to make at least enough profit to pay off the interest. Also the company should possess assets which are unlikely to depreciate greatly.

The most usual form of debenture found in business today is the mortgage debenture. Under this form, the debenture is secured by the mortgage of a specific asset (usually land, premises, or sometimes large plant).

Floating debentures are also occasionally used. With this type of loan, it is secured by a charge on all, or certain sections of the company's assets.

In theory, unsecured debentures can exist, and these are known as simple or naked debentures, and are mere promises to pay, with no security given. In practise, as one would imagine, they are not seen very often.

Companies may make one debenture issue, or many. In the latter case, they are often designated A, B, or C debentures to indicate their order of priority. Generally the lower the priority the greater the rate of interest, to compensate for the lower degree of security.

The retention of past profits: Instead of distributing past profits in the form of dividends etc. they may be retained in order to build up a capital reserve within the company.

Finance for building projects

Many of the previous forms of finance discussed above, can be used to finance property development. The type of finance will obviously depend upon whether the building will be sold immediately it is finished, in which case the loan will be repaid quickly. Alternatively, the building may be owned by the developing company, and rented or leased to an occupier. With this latter situation longer-term finance would be required than with the former.

With housing development, at certain times, building societies will help finance the cost of erection of the dwellings, by giving stage payments to the builder as the work progresses. When the property is sold, the builder pays off the loan to the building society, and the buyer's building society takes over paying the stage payments, if the house is still not completed.

Where a company decides to move into larger office or factory accommodation, finance can sometimes be arranged with pension or insurance funds. With this method, the pension fund will pay for the construction by monthly payments, or at negotiated stages. On the completion of the structure, a lease will be signed with the occupying company. The pension fund remains the owner of a valuable appreciating asset, whilst the occupiers have effectively leased a new building tailor-made to suit their requirements.

Nationalised industries

These are organisations created by bringing certain operations under State control, e.g. coal mining, electricity, iron and steel production, shipbuilding etc.

At the head of each nationalised industry, there is a minister of the crown, who is responsible to Parliament. It is Parliament that lays down the general policy to be followed. The day-to-day management is in the hands of a committee, the chairman and members of which are appointed by the minister.

These organisations come into being, when the government of the day believes it is in the country's best interests to bring a specific industry under State control.

A major requirement of these enterprises is that the income should at least balance expenditure, and in many cases there will be guidelines laid down concerning the expected return on capital employed. There is also a requirement that consumers must be safeguarded, for in several instances the nationalised industry operates almost as a monopoly, for example in the supplying of gas, electricity and coal. This safeguarding is accomplished by the setting up of consumer councils which consider complaints and suggestions.

Capital can be raised by the nationalised industries by borrowing money from banks, or issuing stock; both forms of borrowing are backed by government guarantee. In 1968, the National Loan Fund was set up, to act as a central funding agency for nationalised industries and local authorities. Today, this is the major source of finance for nationalised bodies.

Some of the main nationalised industries are: National Coal Board: British National Oil Corporation; Electricity Council; British Steel Corporation; British Shipbuilding; British Rail; National Bus Company; Post Office.

From these it can be seen that two of the main types of industries that have been nationalised are energy industries, and transport industries. By putting these under government control it should be possible to produce viable national development plans for each industry, and thus ensure that the massive capital investment necessary is obtained.

Advantages of nationalised industries
(a) They enable government to control their activities more easily.
(b) Large sums of money can be invested to modernise plant, and to enable old inefficient systems to be replaced.

(c) It enables economies of scale to operate, e.g. one national rail network, rather than several smaller regional ones.
(d) Control where safety hazards exist, that might be dangerous in private hands, e.g. the work of the Atomic Energy Authority.

Disadvantages of nationalised industries

(a) Policy decisions may be influenced by politicians untrained in the realms of the type of business under discussion.
(b) They often result in almost monopolistic situations.
(c) As nationalised industries are not so profit motivated as private industry, waste and inefficiency can become rife.

Questions

1 What type of business enterprise is best for the construction industry?
2 Suggest what problems might be encountered, if it was proposed that the construction industry should be nationalised.
3 Discuss the main differences between bank loans, ordinary shares, and debentures.
4 Suggest why it would be inadvisable to use a new share issue for a short-term loan.

Chapter 15

Government objectives and their attainment

A government is generally chosen because its policies represent those required by the majority of the voting population of the country. It is not surprising therefore to find that the main objectives of government are those, concerned with improving the general conditions for the population.

This chapter will discuss the various objectives, and show their inter-relationships with one another. Chapters 16, 17 and 18 will show in detail the methods used to try to achieve these ends, and Chapter 19 will discuss in particular how application of these methods affects the construction industry.

In this chapter five government objectives will be considered: **Improvement of living standards; High level of employment; Redistribution of wealth; Curbing of inflation; Good balance of payments**.

Improvement of living standards

This is a very vague title, and can mean many things. There are however two factors that will be considered.

Improvement in the real earnings of society

By real earnings is meant whether a salary will buy more goods this year than last. An actual comparison of salary or wage figures over a succession of years will show very little, until the level of inflation (the rise in the price of goods), has been taken into account.

An improvement in real earnings can only come about by economic growth. This should ultimately result in greater productivity, and more efficient working practices.

Social welfare and the environment

If increased real earnings can improve the material surroundings of one's home, it can have little direct effect on social costs and benefits of society generally.

Pollution is one such problem that affects people's lives. It should be remembered that pollution is not just oily beaches but it could also include:

- Noisy environment.
- Dusty or smoky atmosphere.
- Dirty streets.
- Polluted waterways.

Even the encroachment of the urban sprawl on natural areas is a form of pollution.

Although pollution is often caused by individuals, only government can pass legislation to curtail it. It is ironic that economic growth often results in greater pollution, and because the prevention of industrial pollution can be expensive, it is often not put into practice until government demands it.

There are many social benefits which could be included in the improving of living standards. These might include:

- The peace of mind given, by knowing there is a good police force or army in existence.
- The operation of an efficient health service.
- State benefit and pension schemes.
- Libraries and education services.

Government has direct control over these areas, by passing the relevant legislation, or by increasing budgets for these schemes. Government, however has little direct control over the improvement of earnings, only the more efficient operation of industry and commerce can help here.

High level of employment

This is related to the real earning capacity of society. If unemployment drops, then society as a whole earns more money with which to purchase goods. In turn, the purchase of goods can lead to higher output from industry, which leads to more jobs.

High unemployment can lead to certain problems.

(a) As less people are employed, the government loses income in the form of income tax, that can not now be collected from those out of work. At the same time, unemployment benefits are paid out to these people, which throws a much greater burden on the smaller working force. It can be seen that should unemployment become too large, then the whole system of taxation and benefits and services will break down. The problem is similar to that of an ageing population. In such a situation, as the age structure of the population gets older, there are less workers to support the growing number of elderly.

(b) There is a sense of personal loss of dignity when one is unemployed.

(c) There can be undesirable side effects, such as an increase in vandalism and petty crimes. This in itself leads to more money being spent on preventing and remedying these actions.

Redistribution of wealth

In any society, there will be certain sectors whose relative earnings lag behind those of others. This is particularly relevant to people who do not or cannot take industrial action to force high wage settlements.

At the same time, there are certain other sectors of society who receive particularly high salaries. Government tries to even out the inequalities to a certain extent by taxing the higher paid, whilst the lower paid pay less tax and possibly even receive government benefits, to boost incomes.

Many people are of the belief that heavily taxing the higher paid takes away the incentive to work, as a greater percentage of the income is taken away as tax. Another criticism often voiced is that paying benefits to the lower paid and unemployed encourages people yet again to work less, if at all.

The controlling of inflation

Over a period of time, the cost of goods or services rises in terms of money. This increase is known as inflation, and is usually quoted over a twelve month period. Everyone is aware of the effects of inflation; it increases all materials costs, from bricks and cement, to the cost of land. Inevitably it leads to high wage demands in order to keep pace. What causes these increases in costs?

Economists talk of two situations leading to inflationary tendencies:

Demand inflation

This is where too much money is chasing too few goods, and by the action of supply and demand, the price of the relatively scarce goods will rise. This can most easily be seen to take place to a limited extent,

when there is a high demand for certain commodities, e.g.:
(a) Candles in a power cut.
(b) Sugar when there is a sugar shortage.
(c) Collectors' items in general.

   Across the whole spectrum of consumers' wants, however, it is unlikely that there is a considerable shortage of goods, so it is doubtful whether this is the main cause for inflation today.

Cost inflation

This is brought about by a rise in the price of goods leading to a demand for higher wages to compensate for this increased cost of goods. The increased wages then lead to further increases in commodity prices. This continues as an ever increasing spiral (Fig. 15.1). One problem with this theory is, that inflation tends to go up at a faster rate than it should, by just taking wages into account. It must be remembered that part of the cost of a commodity is made up of the raw material input. Another factor is the seemingly ever increasing cost of interest rates, or dividends needed to be paid to finance industry.

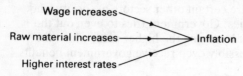

Fig. 15.1

   Ironically government often helps to fuel inflation, rather than cure it by imposing high interest rates, and especially by imposing high taxes particularly on fuels. An increase in the tax on petrol or diesel fuel immediately increases the cost of all goods which have to be transported; this increase is inevitably passed on to the consumer eventually.

Maintaining a good balance of payments

The balance of payments, is a measure of the ability of Britain's exports to balance its imports. A surplus balance of payments means that Britain has exported more than it has imported.

   If on the other hand Britain's imports exceeded the exports, then if this continued for a long period, economic decline would probably occur.

   The balance of payments is discussed more thoroughly in Chapter 18.

Methods of attaining government objectives

It is difficult to see how improvement could be made to social benefits. At present, with many it is necessary only to maintain the *status quo*. Admittedly it might be possible to improve the health service, or the education facilities, but it is doubtful whether an increase in the number of libraries for instance, could really be justified. An increase in certain areas might even have a detrimental effect. If, for instance, the police or army were greatly increased, an extreme condition might arise, as has occurred in certain countries, in that a police state emerges, with the loss of individual freedom.

The whole sphere of social benefits is under the direct control of government, via legislation and budgets. The types of benefits provided will however only be a reflection of those required by the population, for government, after all, is guided by the majority in a democracy.

Growth in real income can only come about by economic growth, and this is usually only possible during a period of low, rather than high inflation. There are various degrees and mixes of policies, adopted by governments, in trying to control inflation, whilst at the same time, trying to stimulate growth. They can, however be simplified into three basic policies, which are adopted in varying degrees of intensity.

Keynesian policy

In the 1930s, Lord Keynes developed and published his famous general theory. This used the idea of stimulating an economy in which there was high unemployment, back into a growth situation. His idea was that central government could stimulate the economy in two ways:

(a) By placing more government contracts, and generally expanding the amount of work executed in the public sector. This would lead directly to more workers being required to carry out the jobs, and so more money would be earned, which in turn meant more goods would be bought, and so the growth would continue.

(b) The alternative would be to lower taxation rates, thus effectively putting more money into the pockets of the consumers. They would spend the increase in money, causing a general increase in consumer demand which results in the need to produce more. In this way, more jobs would be created, which again would lead to continuing growth.

Both of the above policies would result in the government operating a budget deficit. This means that the government's income was less than its expenditure. Chapter 16 discusses this further.

The injection of investment into an economy will lead to the multiplier effect. For example: An injection of money as supplied by the Keynesian policy would lead to more employment and higher earnings. If these increased earnings were spent quickly, then more goods would have to be produced more quickly. If the money continues to be spent and not saved, then it can be seen that the circular flow of money has caused the initial investment to 'multiply' several times. This ability to spend quickly rather than save, is known as the marginal propensity to consume (MPC).

If, for instance, a person spent $\frac{3}{4}$ of a wage increase then the MPC would be $\frac{3}{4}$. Alternatively it could be said that the marginal propensity to save (MPS) was $1 - \frac{3}{4} = \frac{1}{4}$.

The multiplier in this example is:

$$\frac{1}{\text{marginal propensity to save}} = \frac{1}{\frac{1}{4}} = 4.$$

An increase of £1 million into the economy would eventually lead to an extra £4 million in consumption.

The lower the MPS, the greater the multiplier effect. If the MPS was 0.01, then the multiplier would be

$$\frac{1}{0.01} = 100$$

so that £1 million investment will lead to £100 million of consumption.

Monetarist policy

Monetarist policy is concerned with the regulation, either directly, or indirectly, of the availability of money.

In times of high inflation, if it is more difficult for people to borrow money, or more expensive to obtain loans or credit, then they will consume less. This is achieved in various ways, but the most popular is by the Bank of England increasing the Lending Rate. This has the effect that banks follow the lead, and alter their base rates. As soon as this happens, building societies and other financial institutions do likewise. Besides making the borrowing of money more expensive, high interest rates make it more desirable to leave money in deposit accounts, as more interest accrues. During periods of high interest rates, in the process of trying to reduce inflation, employment nearly always suffers. For as people spend less, so less has to be produced, and so some jobs are lost.

When the government wants to stimulate growth and employment, once inflation has been brought under control, then interest rates are lowered to encourage people to consume rather than save. Once again this leads to an increased consumer demand and eventually to lower unemployment.

If it is known that demand inflation exists, by cutting back the money supply, there will be less demand, so that in theory the price of goods may drop.

Price and wage restraint policies

These forms of policy have been adopted several times, for relatively short periods, by government in the recent past. In order to bring inflation under control, restraints are brought to bear, both on manufacturers, in the amount of the price increases they can impose, and on the allowable increase of wages and salaries. The problem with this policy is that it seems to operate fairly well in the short term of say two to three years, after which time it fails, often by massive union revolt, only to see wages rising again at a rapid rate.

Whilst wage restraint is in operation, it can cause considerable hardship to the lower income groups, paticularly where the allowable increases are well below the rate of inflation. A decrease in living standards can come about in such periods.

Restraint on manufacturers' price increases can seriously affect profitability, which can lead to a decrease in investment and so to slower industrial growth than would otherwise have been possible. Industry would be less inclined to invest, for two reasons:

(a) Due to low profitability, it may have to endure losses for a short period, which uses up capital that would have been used for expansion.
(b) More importantly, businessmen will see little incentive to invest, when there will be little or no return for their investment.

In these three methods of guiding the economy, there is considerable conflict between the various government objectives. It is very difficult to devise a policy which encourages an increased standard of living, with high employment and low inflation. There is no simple answer to achieving these objectives, and so the best solution is to try and maintain a reasonable balance of policies, not too extreme in their effects.

A common problem with all government policies is that a period of several months, even years in some cases has to elapse before the outcome of a particular action can be verified. It is essential, therefore, that a government should not jump from one policy to another, before the full effect of the first has had time to operate.

Questions

1 (a) Explain with the aid of calculations how there could be a multiplier effect of 1 000.
(b) If this figure were possible, what might be the effects, following an investment by central government?
2 Find out what the main objectives of the two principal political parties are in Britain; how do they relate to those discussed in this chapter.

3 Over the last few months, what policies has the government been following; do these relate to those discussed above, and in your opinion, are they working.

4 Distinguish between demand and cost inflation.

Chapter 16

Fiscal control in Britain

In Britain, and indeed in all countries, government needs to acquire funds, in order to pay for a wide variety of services and projects which are supplied from central government funds.

In 1985 the total income and expenditure of the government's current account was as shown in Table 16.1.

It should be noted, that the nation's financial year, that is when the country's accounts are balanced, runs from 1 April to 31 March the following year. The tax or fiscal year in Britain, however, runs from 6 April to 5 April the following year.

The majority of funds to meet government expenditure come from taxation, otherwise known as fiscal measures. The levels and types of

Table 16.1 *Source:* National income (1986)

Income		Expenditure	
Income taxes	51 959	Defence	17 946
Taxes on expenditure	43 232	Education	925
Soc. security conts.	24 068	Health service	16 710
Others	11 718	Other services	10 394
		Other payments	88 415
		Total expenditure	134 390
		Less deficit	3 413
	130 977		130 977

taxation are usually fixed annually on budget day, which is generally in early April, by the Chancellor of the Exchequer. It is the Chancellor's task, advised by many experts in the Treasury, to try to decide what levels of expenditure will exist in the various sectors of government spending over the next year. Once an estimated expenditure has been determined, then it has to be decided how the money will be raised. When deciding levels of expenditure, it is of course necessary to continue carrying out the policies of the current government, and much consultation goes on between the various departments to ensure a balanced expenditure programme. Such policies that may particularly affect decisions are: The increase of old age pensions will directly affect expenditure. A pledged reduction of income tax, on the other hand, will affect the means of gaining revenue.

It must be decided whether the budget will balance, or whether there will be a budget deficit. A balance indicates that income will equal the outgoings, whilst a budget deficit is where the outgoings exceed the income. The balance of the money necessary known as the public sector borrowing requirement (PSBR), may come from loans from abroad, or more usually by the issue of government stock, which is offered to the public, at a guaranteed rate of interest for fixed periods. This is in effect a loan to government by the public. It is also possible to have a budget surplus, where income exceeds expenditure.

The types of taxation can be classified under two headings, direct and indirect.

Direct taxation

This can be defined as taxes which are paid to government, when income or wealth is received. Examples of direct taxation are given below.

Income tax

The method of taxing income in Britain is known as a progressive income tax, which means that the more a person earns, the greater will be the proportion of it that will be paid as tax. Each year, a person in employment is required to fill in a tax assessment form. From the details filled in by the person a certain allowance will be given for such things as, wife, dependants, mortgages etc. This means that a certain amount of the income will not be taxable. In order that the employer knows how much tax to deduct from the employee, the tax office allocates a tax code to the employee, based on the value of non-taxable allowances. The higher the code number, the less tax is paid.

When a person runs a business, and is not likely to know his income until the end of the year, then tax is required to be paid retrospectively for that year, directly to the Inland Revenue. With the Pay As You Earn (PAYE) system, the tax is deducted from an employee's wages or salary by the employer, who then passes the money collected onto the Inland Revenue.

Income tax operating in the 1987/88 fiscal year, on 'taxable' income as follows ('taxable' is that remaining, after allowances have been deducted).

The first 17 900 is taxed at 27%
17 901–20 400 is taxed at 40%
20 401–25 400 is taxed at 45%
25 401–33 300 is taxed at 50%
33 301–41 200 is taxed at 55%
The remainder is taxed at 60%

Corporation tax

This is the tax paid by companies, on their profits, whether distributed as dividends or not. Corporation tax is fixed in the budget for the preceding year, and for the 87/88 year it was 35 per cent, with a reduced rate of 27 per cent for small companies. A small company being defined as that not exceeding a certain value of profit in a particular year.

Inheritance tax

This tax applies to property passing on death, plus the cumulative value of gifts made by the deceased in the previous seven years. Gifts made within seven years of death are subject to a tapering of the tax liability on earlier amounts.

This tax applies to:–
(a) Gifts between individuals within seven years of death.
(b) The transfer of property on a person's death.
(c) Gifts to certain trusts.

Again as with income tax inheritance tax is progressive. For 1987/88 the rates are as shown in Fig. 16.2.

Certain transfers of wealth are exempt from inheritance tax:–
(a) Transfers between husband and wife.
(b) Gifts to charities.
(c) Gifts to political parties and certain national bodies.
(d) Lifetime gifts up to a certain figure.

Table 16.2 Inheritance Tax 1987/88

Slice of cumulative chargeable transfer	Tax payable (%)
The first £90 000	Nil
90 000–140 000	30
140 000–220 000	40
220 000–330 000	50
Above 330 000	60

Capital gains tax

This is a tax, levied on a person or a company, in respect of any asset disposed of within the fiscal year, upon which chargeable gains accrue. For instance, if a person bought an area of land, as an investment, and later sold it at a profit, then tax is calculated on the profit or gain which is made. The basic rate, in the year commencing 6 April 1987 was 30 per cent, and is liable on the following assets:

(a) Investments such as antiques, jewellery, buildings, land etc.
(b) Any property produced by the person disposing of it, for example works of art.
(c) Any currency other than sterling.
The following assets are exempted however:
(a) A person's main place of residence.
(b) National savings certificates and 'Save as you earn' (SAYE) etc.
(c) Wins from betting, including football pools, and premium bonds.
(d) Compensation paid to a person for any wrong or injury incurred.
(e) Life assurance policies and annuities.
(f) Donations to charities.
(g) Tangible movable property with a life less than 50 years.
(h) The first £6 600 of your net gains.
(i) Private motor cars.
(j) Chattels sold for less than £3 000.
The chargeable gain is computed by totalling all the gains for the year, and deducting all the losses.

Advantages of direct taxation

There are three main advantages:

(a) It is a relatively cheap tax to collect, which results in a fairly small proportion of the income derived being used up in the collection costs.
(b) As it is administered in the United Kingdom at present, it is a progressive tax, so that the lower income groups pay little or no tax, whereas the higher income groups pay progressively more. This helps to fairly redistribute income.
(c) Government can determine, with a fair degree of accuracy, what level of tax income is needed, and adjust income tax rates accordingly.

Disadvantages of direct taxation

The major disadvantage is that all forms of direct taxation can be said to act as a disincentive to those being taxed. In the case of the individual, he may be reluctant to work overtime, because much of the extra he earns will be deducted in tax. It is possible that a worker's basic wage places him in the lowest or standard tax rate, by working extra hours however, the additional income may put him into the next highest tax range, so giving an even greater disincentive.

Relatively high corporation tax results in many companies finding ways of avoiding the showing of large profits. They may therefore reinvest in new plant and machinery, firm's cars, or other commodities that will reduce the tax bill.

Indirect taxation

This tax applies, when goods or services are paid for. It operates generally by an amount being added onto the selling price, this addition then going to government in the form of tax.

Value added tax

This is a tax charged on businesses, on most goods supplied by them. In 1987 the rate of tax was 15 per cent. In a particular VAT accounting period, usually three months, the businessman determines the output tax, i.e. the tax on the produce sold, and deducts from this the input tax which is the tax the business has paid on goods it has bought in. By computing in this manner, it is truly a tax on the added value of the goods.

For example, a businessman might have the following figures:

Total outputs	200 000	
VAT at 15%		30 000
Total inputs	100 000	
VAT at 15%		15 000
VAT payable		15 000

A particular commodity may go through many stages of production and several stages of selling, each involving a different business at each stage. Tax at the current rate will be added to the gain in value of the article at each of these stages.

Certain goods are zero rated, this means that no tax is charged on these particular goods when supplied, but any input tax paid on goods or services necessary for their manufacture can be deducted. A typical example is the construction of a new building. This is zero rated, so that the purchaser of the building pays no VAT, but the builder can claim back all input tax that he has paid out on the materials.

Other examples of zero rated goods are: food, books, fuel and power, transport, large caravans and houseboats, drugs and medicines, exports, children's clothing and footware. In the construction industry the various outputs are a little complicated regarding VAT, for whilst all new work, alterations or demolition is zero rated, repair and maintenance work is taxed at the normal rate.

Some goods and services are exempt from VAT, this means that like zero rated goods, no tax is chargeable on their sale. But unlike zero rated goods, input taxes paid out on purchases for their operation cannot be reclaimed. As these input taxes cannot be reclaimed, the costs are ultimately passed on to the consumer. The following are examples of exempt goods: land generally, insurance, education, banking, betting charges, postal services, charges for private health treatment, trade union and professional bodies membership charges.

Businesses with a turnover of less than £21 300 are not legally required to register for VAT purposes. This means however that they still pay VAT where applicable on their purchases, but this cannot be reclaimed if they are not registered.

Car tax

All new cars and motor caravans are charged car tax at 10 per cent of the wholesale price. This applies whether the vehicles are home produced, or imported. On this total figure VAT is chargeable.

Vehicle excise duty

This is a tax, payable for all motorised vehicles used on the roads. If any vehicle is used, or even kept on the public highway, then a current tax disc should be displayed. Some examples of 1987 rates are:

Motor cycles less than 150 cc	£10 p.a.
Private vehicles	£100 p.a.
Goods vehicles up to 16 cwt unladen weight	£100 p.a.
Goods vehicles can cost up to	£3 100 p.a.

Customs and excise duties

On many goods, a duty or tax is payable before VAT is chargeable. This applies to such items as tobacco, wines, spirits and perfume. Certain imported goods are subject to customs tariffs, which can be imposed to make imported goods more expensive to purchase than home produced goods. Some examples of duties charged during 1986 are:

Cigars	£47.05 per kg.
Hand rolling tobacco	£49.64 per kg.
Other smoking tobacco	£24.95 per kg.
Beer	from £25.80 per 36 galls.
Wine approximately	£95–£200 per hectolitre.

Advantages of indirect taxation

(a) It does not act as a disincentive to work, as many taxes, particularly excise duties and VAT are often paid without people realising it, for the tax is just included in the final retail price of the good.

(b) It has been said that government can regulate the consumption of certain goods, by the level of taxes imposed; this applies particularly to alcoholic drinks and tobacco. Whether or not the imposition of a high tax on these goods does have a beneficial effect on society in general is a matter of opinion, for it would be very difficult to prove such a statement. It should not be forgotten that these commodities are relatively inelastic in demand, therefore it is doubtful whether demand will fall greatly as tax is raised.

(c) Import tariffs can help protect home industries against fierce, often subsidised competition from abroad (see Ch. 17).

Disadvantages of indirect taxation

The major problem with indirect taxation is that it tends to be regressive. For instance, if a wealthy person and a poor person both buy the same type of refrigerator, the tax in the form of VAT might be £15. As the £15 would have greater utility to the poor man than the rich man, it would seem that this system of taxing is unfair, as the poor man is paying a larger proportion of his wealth in tax, than the rich man is paying.

Subsidies and grants paid by government

In order to further the government's aim of redistribution of wealth, subsidies can be given on certain goods. This means that instead of an item costing its true market price of say £1, by government giving a subsidy of 30p per unit, the consumer will now only pay 70p.

Besides direct subsidies on goods, government pays certain subsidies to industry in some circumstances, in order to further particular government objectives, as described below.

To directly encourage employment

1. Job release schemes

These are designed to encourage older workers to opt for early 'retirement' which creates vacancies for younger unemployed workers.

In 1980 people eligible for the scheme, namely disabled men of 60 to 64, fit men of 64 and fit women of 59, were offered an allowance in return for giving up employment. They undertook not to accept social security benefits, allowances or pensions, but could receive supplementary benefits.

2. Enterprise allowance scheme

This scheme is designed to provide financial help during the first 12 months that a person is working for himself. It is intended to help unemployed people who have a business venture in mind, but who may not have the financial backing to carry themselves over the initial period. People 18–65 are eligible, but must have some money of their own to invest.

3. Employment in development areas

Employment prospects in development areas can be enhanced by the
granting of Regional Development Grants, as mentioned previously.

These grants are given for new buildings or machinery used in
connection with industry. The grant given by government is of the
order of 15 to 20 per cent, subject to certain minimum costs and
eligibilities.

The encouragement of food production

Government has for many years subsidised certain forms of
agriculture, and there are several reasons for this.

(a) Farmers are subject to the vagaries of the weather; varying yields
of harvests and hence income, can play havoc with a farmer's
investment programme. By operating a minimum price, or
intervention system, they are assured of a certain income which
will hopefully encourage investment in particular fields.

(b) In the past, the idea of self-sufficiency was encouraged,
particularly in times of war. By giving good subsidies on foods that
the government wanted produced, farmers would be encouraged
to change over to production of these commodities.

(c) In order to cut down on imports, and so aid the balance of
payments, the growth of certain commodities is encouraged. An
example of this is sugar beet production.

Types of government aid to farmers

1. The farm capital grant scheme

This allows for grants to be paid to farmers, on capital expenditure
over a wide range of projects, including: land drainage, permanent
plant and equipment, water supply, roads, farm buildings etc. The
general rate of grant was approximately 15 per cent (in 1987), but for
farmers in less favoured areas, a higher rate is payable.

2. The hill livestock compensatory allowance

Under this scheme, the government gives a compensatory allowance to
the farmer for the breeding and rearing of sheep and cattle, in less
favoured areas.

3. By operating price guarantees in respect of the EEC Common Agricultural Policy

The intervention board, which is responsible for implementing these
policies, operates various schemes of direct subsidy, and support
buying.

Direct subsidy is paid to producers in respect of such commodities
as milk and hops.

Support buying or intervention buying, is a system operated
usually through marketing boards, whereby, when the normal market

price of a commodity falls below the intervention price, the government will buy the surplus at a guaranteed price, and put it into storage. This has two advantages, it provides the farmer with a guaranteed price, but it also has the effect of removing the surplus goods from the market thus ensuring that the higher market prices return all the quicker. When the market price becomes high enough, the produce is taken out of storage and sold. This operates particularly with regard to cereals, sheep and cattle. Instead of the government buying goods, aid is in some cases given to pay for the private storage of beef, butter, pigmeat etc.

The operation of the three forms of farming aid, all fall within the directives of the EEC Common Agricultural Policy (CAP). This tends to be a very controversial political issue, for three-quarters of the EEC budget goes on operating the CAP which has in the past led to the accumulation of massive surpluses of produce. The main criticism is that the intervention prices is too high, consequently this encourages inefficient farming methods and because the price mechanism is not free to operate, more and more farmers produce the goods that are already in surplus purely because they know the produce will be bought by government.

Questions

1 Find out the current levels of direct and indirect taxation at present operating in Britain.
2 What are the main fiscal policies that you would say government were following at present. Why are they operating these particular policies, and are they working.
3 Discuss the implications of changing Britain's tax system over to a wholly indirect system.

Chapter 17

Monetary control in Britain

Origins and functions of money

When the various civilisations began to develop, trading between nations became somewhat of a problem. From the earliest times, trading had existed, but was based on a system of bartering, whereby goods were directly exchanged with other goods. At times this form of exchange was very impractical, particularly when one tried to swop a large item, for a selection of smaller ones.

It then became necessary to have an intermediate medium of exchange. It was also necessary to have this money, as this is what it was, in a durable form, so that it could be stored to enable large items to be saved for. By valuing goods in terms of the particular money concerned, it was possible to compare values of goods. It was also necessary that contracts could be entered into, with the knowledge that when payment was made in the future, the money payment would be of a known value.

The four functions of money are therefore:
(a) A medium of exchange.
(b) A store of value, or wealth.
(c) A measure of value.
(d) A standard of deferred payment.

In order that money should fulfil these functions, it should possess the following properties:
(a) Its main quality should be acceptability. All people likely to come into contact with the money, should accept it at its understood value.

(b) The money should be portable. It would be ridiculous having bricks as a form of money, for they would make large holes in one's pockets.

(c) Durability is another important quality, perishable foods for instance would be useless as money as they would not last long. Paper money used today is not very durable, and because of this, it constantly has to be replaced, which is an expensive operation. It was for this reason that the £1 coin was introduced into the coinage system.

(d) Money should be capable of being divided into the smallest divisions likely to be required. Television sets could not be used as money, for they could not be divided into useable smaller segments.

(e) Money should be scarce enough to give it the required value. In Britain, fircones could not be used as money, for anyone could go out in the autumn, and collect lorry loads free.

(f) It should be difficult to imitate or forge. If forgery was easy, this would lead to large-scale criminal activities which could upset the whole monetary system.

(g) All items that are used as money must be homogeneous, that is they must be of the same material, and of the same size, so that each can be seen to have the same value.

In the past, many commodities have been used as mediums of exchange, but generally they failed to possess one or more of the above properties, and so eventually they went out of fashion. They have now been replaced with coinage systems. Some examples of old mediums of exchange are: Cowrie shells; cigarettes and nylon stockings during the last war; even cattle have been used at certain times.

Modern 'real' money generally consists in cash form of metal coins, or paper notes. Original coins were minted out of gold, and the printing of paper money was only allowed, when the value of the notes was backed by an equivalent value of gold bullion. The banknote issue since 1939 has not been backed by gold and is now known as a fiduciary issue. Today, as silver and gold have become scarcer, and also because these metals are not too durable, they are no longer used in coins in current circulation.

Prior to 1920 'silver' coins consisted of 0.925 fine silver. In 1920 however this was reduced to 0.500 fine silver, and in 1947 coins were minted of a copper nickel alloy which contained no silver at all.

Cash in the form of notes and coin is essential for small personal transactions, but to carry around large sums would be inconvenient, and would encourage crime. Various means of paying money from one person to another have evolved to overcome this problem.

A bank cheque

This is an instruction, signed and dated, given by person A to person B, instructing A's bank to pay from A's account, to B or B's account, a certain amount of money. Cheques are only valid if presented within six months of the signing date. In theory, cheques can be written on anything, but in practice, to facilitate mechanical checking they are standardised, with the bank's branch sorting code and customer's code imprinted on them. It must be remembered, that a cheque itself is not money, for it is not legal tender, although it can be passed on to a third person, if properly countersigned. It is only an instruction to transfer a deposit which must already exist, from one account to another.

Direct debit

This is a process whereby a creditor can make a direct claim on a customer's bank account. Approval is given for this by the customer signing an appropriate form. By using this system, single or multiple transfers (standing orders), for example mortgage repayments, can be facilitated. The whole system of direct debiting, and credit transfer is also known as the bank giro system.

Bank draft

This is really a form of cheque, which instead of being drawn on a customer's account, is drawn on the bank. A bank draft is therefore considered to be less of a financial risk, than the acceptance of a cheque drawn on a customer's account where there is always the chance that it will not be honoured.

Credit cards

These are cards issued to credit worthy customers, by banks, enabling these customers to obtain goods or services on credit, up to a predetermined limit. The goods can either be paid for next month, in which case little or generally no interest is payable, or the payments can be spread over several months. Interest a little above that paid for a normal overdraft, is payable for this service.

Access, Barclaycard, American Express are examples of credit cards in wide use.

Bill of exchange

This can be defined as 'an unconditional order in writing, addressed by one person to another, signed by the person giving it, requiring the person to whom it is addressed to pay on demand or at a stated future date a sum of money to a certain person, or to the order of that person, or bearer.'

Bills of Exchange are used widely in international trade, and they would be used as follows.

A supplier would agree to accept payment for goods by a Bill of Exchange. He would then write out a bill, stating his address, the customer's name and address, the date, the amount in writing and in figures, and the date the bill becomes due. He would then sign it and send it to the customer. The customer would sign it as accepted, and would state the bank it would be payable at. The bill is then classed as an accepted bill, and the supplier has three alternative courses of action.

(a) He can hold the bill until it falls due for payment, and let the payment be made as directed on the bill.

(b) He can endorse the bill to be made over to someone else.

(c) He can discount the bill at a bank or more usually a discount house. This involves receiving a slightly lower value for the bill, but there is the advantage that he receives payment immediately. The discount house then holds the bill and receives payment when due.

Treasury bills are means used by government to finance the Public Sector Borrowing Requirement (PSBR). They are usually for three months, and are offered for tender each Friday, to the discount houses. They are payable in full (current values of bills offered are £5 000, £10 000, £25 000, £50 000, £100 000, and £250 000), therefore the tender figure offered would be lower than the face value.

Control of the money supply

Only about one-fifth of the so-called money supply is in the form of notes and coin, the rest is in the form of 'bank' money, or 'created' money, which is formed by the normal transactions of banking.

In the day-to-day running of a bank, it was soon discovered that not everyone who had deposited money with the bank wanted their money out at the same time. This meant that, providing the bank kept enough money in reserve for customer withdrawals in the form of cash, the rest could be loaned out at a favourable rate of interest. At present banks have to maintain 5 per cent of their eligible liabilities in the form of secured money with the discount market. The proportion held with the discount market must not fall below 2½ per cent on any one day. In very simple terms this means that if the bank receives a £1 000 deposit this can form the 5 per cent of secured money, and the bank can lend out £19 000 to another customer.

In Chapter 15, monetarism was discussed. The operation of this policy hinges on the ability to control the money supply, or more specifically the amount of money 'created' by banks. This is done in various ways.

1. By increasing the Bank Base Rates

This makes interest rates generally much higher, and people are reluctant to take out loans, therefore in theory the money supply shrinks. In practice, this may work with private individuals, but businesses are committed to try to continue in business, and during such periods when the government takes these actions, many businesses find that they require loans, often termed distress loans, to help them ride out the recession. Certain types of loans then are more likely to increase, rather than decrease during such periods, which makes the policy less effective.

2. Special deposits

In order to decrease a banks lending power, the Bank of England can insist on special deposits, calculated as a percentage of total eligible liabilities, being deposited with the Bank of England. This has the effect of reducing a bank's reserve assets, so that less money can now be loaned to customers, whilst still maintaining the 5 per cent reserve assets ratio. Special deposits bear an interest payable to the depositing bank, but at certain times, the Bank of England can insist on supplementary special deposits being lodged with it, which do not bear interest.

In the operation of a strict monetary policy, the Bank of England is likely to instigate other measures:

(a) It will give guidance to commercial banks on their method of lending, stating where preferences should be given when considering loans. Generally priorities are given to exporting, or depressed manufacturing industry first. Construction is not usually regarded as a top priority case.

(b) The amount of money in general circulation can be reduced somewhat, by the Bank of England selling off government stocks, more usually known as gilt edged stocks. As people buy these stocks, then the money in circulation declines, and hopefully results in a slowing down of inflation.

Because of the existence of many different kinds of so-called money today, in the UK, different definitions have been evolved as follows:

M_1

This consists of notes and coin, and current accounts at banks. This is known as the narrow definition of money, and is money in its most liquid form, which can be used to settle debts immediately.

M_2

This is a term not now used by official UK statistics, but nevertheless, this definition gives a slightly broader description of the money supply, as it consists of M_1 plus deposit accounts in banks.

M_3

This gives the broadest description of the money supply, for it includes M_2 plus all other deposits held in the UK in the form of foreign currency, national savings etc.

The Bank of England

This is the centre point of the whole British monetary system, and as such is often referred to as the Central Bank.

Although it does deal with a few private customers, the main activities of the bank are concerned with the carrying out of national policies and national and international banking transactions.

The main functions of the bank are described below.

Banker to the government

The bank looks after the income from taxation, and takes care of payments, it also manages the national debt. Loans are raised, mainly by the selling of short-term treasury bills, and by the issue of new long-term government stocks.

The accounts of many government departments are also held at the bank. Many activities are carried out as a service to government, by implementing various policies as described earlier. The bank also acts as Britain's link with international monetary bodies, as it helps to protect the value of the exchange rate, and also deals with the International Monetary Fund.

Banker to the commercial banks

A certain amount of reserves have to be deposited with the central bank, and this can be used to help regulate the monetary supply.

The daily workings of the banking system, means that by the paying and receiving of cheques, a bank may owe money to another bank, or *vice versa*, at the end of the days dealings. These transactions can be balanced by drawing on, or paying into the various banks' reserves at the central bank.

Controller of the issue of notes and coin

The bank is the sole supplier of notes in England, and new notes are issued either in return for old, or when backed by a new issue of securities.

The lender of last resort

Discount houses, as earlier mentioned, discount Bills of Exchange. In order to do this they borrow money, generally for very short periods, from commercial banks who may have a surplus of funds for a day or two, or from large companies in industry. The money which is borrowed is likely to be recalled at very short notice, and as the Bills of Exchange are not immediately cashable, except at a discount, the discount houses can find themselves temporarily short of funds at certain times. It is at these times, that the Bank of England acts as lender of last resort to the discount houses, by lending money to them at what used to be the minimum lending rate.

Questions

1 Discuss the role of the Bank of England:
   (a) In respect of implementing government policy.
   (b) In respect of daily banking activities.
2 Why is it so difficult to define the meaning of money.
3 Discuss with the aid of an example, how a fast flow of money in the economy can stimulate economic growth.

Chapter 18

International trade

When confronted with newspaper headlines containing such phrases as balance of payments, export drives, and import restrictions, many people ask the question, 'Why do we need to trade with other countries? Would it not be better to produce everything ourselves?'

This chapter discusses the factors affecting the operation of international trade, and hopefully by the end of this section, the answers to the above questions should be obvious.

The two main reasons why it is advantageous to practice international trade are set out below.

Inability to produce goods nationally

In all countries, there are certain commodities that cannot be home produced. This may be due to:
(a) Climatic reasons affecting the growth of crops, e.g. Britain cannot grow bananas or oranges, except in carefully controlled conditions.
(b) The total lack of certain minerals and other types of natural resources within the boundaries of a particular country, or the existence of these commodities in very limited quantities, e.g.
(i) The reliance of many nations on the Middle East countries for supplies of oil.
(ii) Japan has to import iron ore for its developing steel industry, from Australia.
(iii) As South Africa produces three-quarters of the world's gold supply, many countries have to obtain their quantities of gold from this source.

International division of labour

Earlier in the book, the advantages of division of labour within a business or industry were discussed.

The theory of division of labour can be extended internationally, so that it can be seen that particular countries become very expert and efficient at producing certain goods. For example, in Britain by expending 1 000 units of resources (a certain mix of the factors of production), either 400 units of pottery, or 50 cars could be produced. In Japan, the same 1 000 units of resources could produce 300 units of pottery, or 60 cars. If in each country, 10 000 units of resources were available for the manufacture of pottery and cars, and each country used 50 per cent of their resources for the production of each commodity. Table 18.1 would result.

If instead of the above situation, each country concentrated on producing the commodity which it could produce the most efficiently, then Table 18.2 would follow.

It can be seen from Table 18.2, that the totals jointly produced are better than before, so that if now an exchange can take place, so that Britain exports pottery to Japan, and Japan exports cars to Britain, then both countries will be better off.

Table 18.1

| | Production | | | |
| | Pottery | | Cars | |
	Resources used	Units made	Resources used	Units made
Britain	5 000	2 000	5 000	250
Japan	5 000	1 500	5 000	300
Totals	10 000	3 500	10 000	550

Table 18.2

| | Production | | | |
| | Pottery | | Cars | |
	Resources used	Units made	Resources used	Units made
Britain	10 000	4 000	—	—
Japan	—	—	10 000	600
Totals	10 000	4 000	10 000	600

216

Consider now another situation. For 1 000 units of resources in Britain, the same quantity of pottery, 400 units, can be produced, or 200 bicycles. In Japan, for 1 000 units of resources, 300 units of pottery, or 100 bicycles could be produced. In this situation Britain can produce both items more efficiently than Japan. Firstly however, consider Table 18.3, which shows the production of 10 000 units of resources in each country, again equally divided between the two products. This gives total production for the two countries of 3 500 units of pottery and 1 500 bicycles.

Even though Britain produces both items more efficiently, it has the greatest relative production advantage when making bicycles, where it is twice as efficient as Japan. In the production of pottery, it is only $1\frac{1}{3}$ times as efficient. Japan then could be said to be less inefficient in the production of pottery, and so it might concentrate all its resources on this commodity. This however would only produce 3 000 units. Britain would be best advised to concentrate the majority of its production on bicycles, just allowing say 20 per cent of its resources to be used to produce pottery, which will augment Japan's output. The result is Table 18.4, where it can be seen that when countries

Table 18.3

| | Production | | | |
| | Pottery | | Bicycles | |
	Resources used	Units made	Resources used	Units made
Britain	5 000	2 000	5 000	1 000
Japan	5 000	1 500	5 000	500
Totals	10 000	3 500	10 000	1 500

Table 18.4

| | Production | | | |
| | Pottery | | Bicycles | |
	Resources used	Units made	Resources used	Units made
Britain	2 000	800	8 000	1 600
Japan	10 000	3 000	—	—
Totals	12 000	3 800	8 000	1 600

concentrate their production on the commodities in which they have the greatest comparative advantage, then the overall production totals will be greater. This idea forms the basis of the law of comparative advantage.

By the operation of international trade it can be seen that the world as a whole gains more benefit if countries trade with one another. Also, by the action of trade, many countries are brought ino close negotiation with each other which in time leads to greater co-operation and less conflict.

The advantages of international trade, as detailed above, rely on certain assumptions, that do not occur in practice.

(a) It assumes that there is low unemployment in all the participating countries. Problems arise where a country has high unemployment, but still continues to buy many goods from abroad. The government must ask itself whether this is a good thing, or whether they should try to curtail imports, in the hope of stimulating home industries.

(b) International trade in its simplest and most advantageous form, does not cater for tariffs or quotas. These, when operated, restrict the operation of international trade.

(c) Broadly speaking, in order to trade with other countries, in the long term, trade has to be two ways, or better still, between many countries. If trade continued on a one way basis for a long period, then currency problems would arise (see later sections).

Disadvantages of international trade

It has been shown that in many ways international trade is advantageous. There are however certain situations where governments take steps to prevent trading taking place.

(a) In the past, in Britain, government has in times of war sought to make the country as self-sufficient as possible in terms of food.

(b) Where two countries have broken off diplomatic relations then the government of one or both countries may pass legislation to prevent trading between the countries, e.g. Rhodesia (Zimbabwe) in the late 1970s.

(c) When a developing new industry is struggling in a particular country by reason of overseas competition, then it is possible to build up a strong home market, by preventing the importing of the competing goods. Without this protection of new industries, they may not develop the scale of operations necessary to make them financially viable. This is particularly true of highly capital intensive industries.

(d) When a country has a high unemployment rate, and especially where certain industries are threatened by cheap imports, then the population may bring pressure to bear on the government, to impose restrictions.

Restrictions on international trade

These can be imposed in several ways.

1. Tariffs

This is simply the operation of a system of taxes, such as customs' duties on imported tobacco, wines and spirits.

The main function of a tariff, is to increase the price at which imported goods are sold, and so make home produced goods more attractive, from a cost point of view, to the consumers.

2. Quotas

With this method of restriction, the number of imported units of a particular commodity which are allowed to enter the country is regulated. Such a system is operated, for example, by a country limiting the number of cars being imported, to allow the domestic car industry to enjoy a larger home market. Quotas are sometimes operated on total value of goods, rather than number of items.

3. Embargoes

At certain times, the government may refuse to allow the importing of any units of a particular commodity, or it may ban the trading altogether, with certain countries.

Whilst trying to restrict imports into a country, government often tries to increase exports. In practice, the two are often not compatible Whatever type of restriction is imposed, it might ultimately lead to other countries, who can no longer export so much, imposing retaliatory restrictions on imports from the restricting country.

Balance of payments

A country has to operate its international trading activities like an ordinary business. As in an ordinary business, goods have to be bought in to be sold, and it is necessary to sell goods, in order to obtain money to buy more goods. Similarly, Britain has to export goods, in order to earn the foreign currency with which to buy goods from overseas. In a business, the transactions are noted down, and periodically a balance sheet is produced which will show the state of finances. Similarly, with a country, a balance sheet is produced annually, to show the state of the country's international financial dealings.

Consider Table 18.5, which is a simplified version of Britain's

Table 18.5 U.K. Balance of payments 1978 and 1984 in £ millions.

	1978	1984
Visible trade	−1 175	−4 384
Invisible trade	+2 207	+5 596
Current balance	+1 032	+1 212
Investment and other capital flows	−2 931	−1 026
Balancing item	+ 773	+5 124
Balance for official financing	−1 126	−7 362
Official financing		
IMF	−1 016	−
Foreign currency borrowing by government	+ 191	+ 613
Ditto by public bodies	− 378	+6 749
Drawings on official reserves		
Drawings on (+), additions to (−)	+2 329	−
Total official financing	+1 126	+7 362

Source: Annual Abstract 1980/1986

balance of payments for 1978 and 1984 which has been taken from the annual abstract of statistics.

Visible trade consists of balancing visible imports against visible exports. A negative figure indicates that import payments are greater than export receipts. Visible goods are those goods which are actually transported.

Invisible trade, is the value of work transacted in the services field, and includes such activities as shipping, insurance and money spent by tourists. A positive figure indicates greater exporting of these services than importing. Generally Britain has a positive balance on invisibles.

The visible and invisible trading balances make up the current account. The capital account shows the position with respect to the flow of money, other than that used in trading activities covered by the current account. Capital is moved from one country to another, for one of three reasons:

(a) As a loan or gift from one country to another. For instance, if Britain loaned £2 million to a foreign country, this would be shown as a debit, or negative figure on the balance sheet. Conversely if America loaned £10 million to Britain, this would be a credit or positive entry in the balance sheet.

(b) In order to invest money in businesses in foreign countries. For example, if a British company invested £2 million in a car assembly plant abroad, then this would be shown as a debit, for the money is going out of the country. The profits or interest gained on the overseas investment, providing it came back into Britain is a credit, under invisible trade. British banks often make international loans, a loan from a British bank to one overseas would be shown as a debit.

(c) When countries are threatened with war, or other major political problems, many people try to leave, together with as much wealth as they can legally, or illegally take with them. They invest their wealth in another trouble free country, in order to keep it safe.

It can be seen, that little can be deduced from looking at the final balance figure of the balance of payments. A good trading balance on the current account can be turned into a bad overall figure, by having a large debit balance on the capital account. This is in fact what happened in 1978.

The recording of so many transactions on the international trading and investment scene is a tremendous task, and very often precise figures cannot be obtained; for example it is difficult to know how much money is spent in Britain by foreign tourists. There are also time delays and sometimes disputes over payment of goods. These problems lead to the fact that the value of transactions recorded on paper, and the amount of money which eventually passes through the Bank of England in respect of these transactions, never tallies exactly. The difference is shown as the balancing item, and a positive figure (as in 1978) means that more money came in, than should have done.

The balance for official financing represents the final outcome of the country's accounts. A positive figure indicates that more money came into Britain than was paid out. A negative figure indicates that there was a net outflow of money.

As in all book keeping, it is necessary to balance the books, and in 1978 it was necessary to either borrow money, or draw on the country's capital reserves in order to get this balance. Table 18.6 details the way in which the balance for official financing has been dealt with in the years 1976–78.

Table 18.6 Sources of official financing

	1976	1977	1978
Balance for official financing	−3 629	+7 361	−1 126
Transactions with IMF and other monetary authorities	+ 984	+1 113	−1 016
Foreign currency borrowing	+1 792	+1 114	− 187
Official reserves (drawings on +), (additions to −)	+ 853	−9 588	+2 329
Total official financing	+3 629	−7 361	+1 126

Source: Annual Abstract 1980

Consider Table 18.6, in 1976 and 1978 there was a deficit on the balance which had to be made good. In 1976, money was borrowed from the International Monetary Fund (IMF), from foreign banks in the form of foreign currency, and by drawing on Britain's reserves of capital. In 1978, however previous debts to the IMF and foreign currency borrowing were being paid back, so this is shown as a debit. The total deficit still had to be made good, and this was done by drawing on the reserves.

In 1977 there was a positive balance for official financing, this indicates that Britain had an excess of funds. In the same year however it was still necessary to borrow heavily from the IMF and foreign currency markets, which meant that a massive total was put into the reserves, in order to balance.

Balancing the current account

From Table 18.5, the balance of the current account was positive. The actual balance of the visible trade however was negative; this means that a greater value of goods was imported than exported.

Why should there be this imbalance?

Quite simply, by the laws of supply and demand, there is less demand for British goods overseas than there is for foreign goods in Britain. This is usually due to price, although there are other factors such as reliability and delivery times for products. These last two factors are entirely in the hands of the manufacturers, but the price of goods can be affected by government action.

In order to improve the balance of visible trade of 1978 say, in Britain's favour it would be necessary either to reduce the costs of exports, or increase the costs of imports, or both. One method useful in achieving this solution is the imposition of tariffs or quotas as discussed in Chapter 16.

Two other methods of improvement are available.

1. Deflationary techniques

If inflation was to increase in Britain at a higher rate than in other countries, then eventually Britain's goods would become relatively more expensive than those in other countries, and so exports would fall. At the same time, foreign goods imported into Britain would become relatively cheaper than home produced goods. It can be seen that this would lead to a bad balance of visible trade. It should be remembered, that in this context the level of inflation is important, only when related to other countries. The fact that Britain might have 20 per cent inflation could be an advantage, at least to our balance of payments, if the rest of the world have 30 per cent.

Deflationary measures are carried out then, to try to bring inflation under control, and to improve trade. These measures generally involve cutting back on demand in home markets, either by fiscal or monetary methods, in order to cut home demand which will reduce imports, and also encourage manufacturers to export.

2. Devaluation and exchange rates

Up until 1972, the value of the £ was fixed or pegged, against other currencies at a fixed value. When a country has a fixed exchange rate, then it is possible to devalue its currency in terms of other currencies. For example, prior to 1967 the £ was valued at $2.8. In 1967 the £ was devalued, so that it was now valued at $2.4. Prior to 1967, a car valued at £10 000 in Britain would have cost $28 000 in America, after devaluation, it would have cost only $24 000. Thus devaluation tends to encourage exports as British goods now appear cheaper in America. By the same token, before devaluation, a car selling for $14 000 in America would cost £5 000 in Britain. After devaluation the same car would now cost £5 833. Devaluation, therefore also tends to discourage imports.

Floating exchange rates

There are many problems with the adoption of a fixed exchange rate. It means that there are often times when devaluation is thought necessary, due to imbalances of trade, and this not only causes sudden jumps in worldwide currency values and trading possibilities, but also problems of people speculating on possible devaluations, by hoarding vast sums of currency in the hope of making a profit when values change.

Since 1972, Britain 'floated' the £, and in 1973/74 all other major currencies did likewise. A floating currency is where the value is not fixed against others, but varies in response to the supply and demand conditions of the currency concerned. Consider Fig. 18.1, which shows the actual workings of international trade and payments. The problem of dealing internationally is that each country has its own currency. A British importer for example cannot pay an American exporter directly in pounds, for they would be useless in America. Each payment transaction therefore has to pass through the foreign exchange market, which in practice comprises the foreign exchange departments of banks in many countries. Consider the top trading transaction of Fig. 18.1. Goods are exported from Britain to America. The final consumers in America pass on their dollars eventually to the American importer who pays them into his bank. His bank then deals with the payment on paper, via the exchange market to the British exporter's bank. At this point the currency is changed from dollars to pounds, at the rate operating at that time. The payment then is credited to the British exporter's bank in pounds, the British exporter then paying the British manufacturer in pounds.

Consider now the bottom trading path (Fig. 18.1). Goods are exported from America to Britain and payment is made in a similar manner to that previously, but in reverse. At this point the workings of the foreign exchange market and the rates of exchange can now be studied in more depth.

The foreign exchange market gets the pounds to pay the British

223

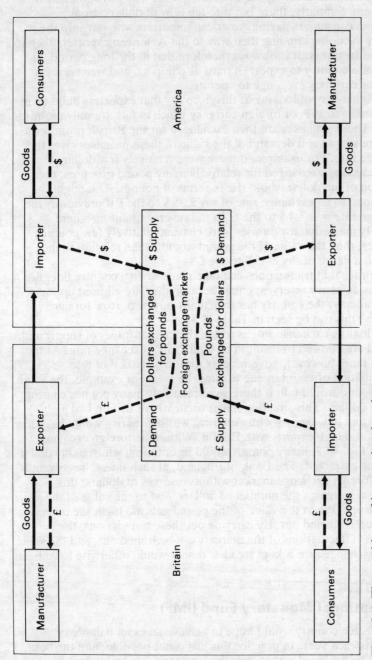

Fig. 18.1 The workings of international trade

exporter, in practice from the British importer who pays pounds into the system. Similarly, there is a through flow of dollars, from American consumers paying American importers who pay into the market, the dollars finding their way to the American exporters then to the manufacturers. It is obvious therefore that in the long period, in order for a country to export, it must also import, and *vice versa*, in order for currency exchange to operate.

Another way of looking at this, is to say that exporters build up at their banks reserves of foreign currency which in fact are only promises to pay. These promises are then exchanged for the British promises to pay. The supply and demand of the value of these promises gives the exchange rate. For example, if there were relatively few dollar promises being exchanged for relatively many pound promises, then the value of the dollar would rise in terms of pounds. This might correspond to an exchange rate of say 2.35 $ to the £ if previously the exchange rate was 2.4 $ to the £. In the reverse situation, where relatively many dollar promises were chasing relatively few pound promises, then the value of the pound would rise in relation to the dollar to a figure of say 2.45 $ to the £.

In order that transactions can take place when a country does not have any currency reserves, either because they are all used up, or it never had any, the country has to actually buy or borrow foreign currency; this can be seen in Table 18.5.

A floating exchange rate is where the market forces of supply and demand are allowed to result in an equilibrium exchange rate. At the present time, however, governments with this method of rate determination often intervene to alter the rate. For example, the value of the pound would fall, if there were relatively many pounds chasing too few dollars. This situation might occur where Britain had high imports and low exports with America, whilst America would have low imports and high exports with Britain. Within the foreign exchange 'box' of Fig. 18.1, many pounds would be entering, whilst many dollars would be extracted. The Bank of England, at such times, buys pounds on the foreign exchange market with its reserves of dollars; this operation increases the number of dollars, and so the value of the dollar drops. When the value of the pound gets too high, the reverse operation is carried out. By carrying out these transactions, the short-term fluctuations of the markets can be ironed out, and the value of the exchange rate is kept steadier than it would otherwise have been.

International Monetary Fund (IMF)

Ideally, each country would hope to achieve an exact balance of payments each year. In practice this just is not possible, and the best that can be achieved is that over the long term (several years), a balance could be obtained.

Inevitably there will be countries that have a net deficit on their balance of payments in certain years. One means of overcoming these short-term financial problems is to borrow money from other sources; one such source being the IMF.

The IMF came into being, as a result of the Bretton Woods Conference in 1944, which tried to put international finances on a stable basis, by fixing fairly rigidly the value of currencies in relation to one another. It was hoped that world trade would be encouraged by this action. When Britain devalued the pound in 1967 instabilities in other currencies ensued, with the result that by 1973/74 most currencies were no longer fixed, but were floating. This continues up to the present day, and so the IMF no longer has the rigid grasp on the control of international finance that it previously enjoyed.

The IMF's main function now is to act as a source of loans for member countries in financial difficulties, and in 1978 it had 128 member countries. Each member has to pay a certain quota into the fund, originally this was paid 25 per cent in gold, and 75 per cent in the currency of that particular country. Since 1976 however the payment in gold has not been necessary. Members are allowed to withdraw the first 25 per cent slice or 'tranche' as it is termed as of right. Each succeeding slice withdrawn, and this may take the withdrawals over the quota total, must be backed by strong assurances by the borrowing country. These usually take the form of adopting certain policies that will correct the particular financial problem. The quotas and withdrawals are valued in Special Drawing Rights (SDR), which in practice is a currency operated by the IMF and which can easily be compared and valued in terms of other currencies. Other facilities besides the SDR loans are operated; for example, the 'General Arrangements to Borrow' is a means whereby a country can arrange a private loan, from a group of ten powerful nations. 'Swap' arrangements can also be accommodated, where two countries agree to swap currencies to their mutual advantage.

The European Economic Community (EEC)

The EEC came into being as a result of the Treaty of Rome in 1957, and now consists of Belgium, Denmark, France, The Federal Republic of Germany, Italy, Greece, the Irish Republic, Luxembourg, the Netherlands, Portugal, Spain and Britain.

The true European Community comprises of three separate communities:

1. The European Atomic Energy Community
This was set up to develop jointly, policies concerning the research into and use of atomic energy, within the member countries.

2. The European Coal and Steel Community

This was formed in 1952 to co-ordinate operations concerning the mining of coal and iron ores, and the sales of the products concerned.

3. The European Economic Community

This was conceived in order to provide a 'common market' for the products of the member States, and to promote the abolition of trade restrictions on a regional basis, in order to provide an environment in which growth could progress.

It was seen earlier that the Law of Comparative Advantage showed a great benefit providing restrictions are not enforced. One of the main policies of the Community, is the existence of free trade between member countries. Certain countries other than members, have also negotiated preferential trade agreements, but the rest of the countries trading with the EEC are likely to have to pay import levies or taxes (the common customs taxes), on goods coming into the community.

The Community has active policies concerned with aid to under-developed countries.

It is envisaged that the Community will continue to expand, thus helping to stabilise and bring into closer communication previously distant nations. It is hoped that other countries will be persuaded to join in later years.

The Community has a common budget, which is mainly financed by a value added tax of less than 1 per cent on goods traded between nations. The distribution of these budget funds has lead to considerable political disagreement. Three-quarters of the fund allocation goes on maintaining the Common Agricultural Policy (CAP). The Community budget also finances regional development, social policy, industry, transport etc., and these have to share the remaining 25 per cent of the funds. The CAP aims at securing a decent standard of living for many small farmers, particularly those in France and certain areas of Germany. It is argued, particularly by some in Britain, that it is unwise to continue to support such inefficient farming methods with huge sums, while much of industry is crying out for capital for modernisation and development. The CAP broadly operates as follows. A high internal price is maintained for food. This is achieved by imposing taxes on imported foods in order to bring up the prices to those of home produced goods. Intervention prices are set on most produce, so that if for example during a good harvest the market price drops, it will drop only to the intervention price, for once it reaches this price, the government will buy all the surplus, at the guaranteed price. Two things can be done with this surplus:

(a) If possible it is put into storage; where cold storage is concerned, the actual storage costs are considerable, but if the intervention prices are realistic, over a period of time, the surpluses can be sold off during years of low production. In theory this could work quite well. In the past however, the situation seldom arose when the stocks could be sold off at a profit within the Common Market. This is because the intervention price is fixed too high, which encourages more farmers to produce food even though there is a glut. If there was no intervention system, then a glut would cause prices to fall etc so that an equilibrium would be reached.

(b) The alternative to stockpiling is to sell off the surplus to countries outside the Community. The problem here is that in many countries, food is cheaper than within the EEC, so that it invariably has to be sold off at a cost less than was initially paid by government.

At the present time, Britain is trying to alter, albeit gradually, the allocation of budget funds, and to drop or keep at the present level, the intervention prices. In the early 1980s Britain is the main net contributor to the fund, i.e., she receives in benefits nowhere near the monies paid in.

Many people are still asking, 'Why did we join, and what can possibly be the advantages for Britain?'

British industry during the 1960s and 1970s was suffering from ever-increasing competition from abroad. By joining the EEC, it was hoped that a suitable environment could be created which would encourage businessmen to take full advantage of any economies and growth prospects in their particular industry. The advantages can be summarised as follows:

(a) There is in the EEC a potential home market, five times the size of Britain's alone.

(b) Due to the larger market potential, greater use can be made in certain industries of economies of scale, particularly with reference to capital intensive industries. This may lead to products becoming more competitive, not only within the EEC but in the wider world market.

(c) By providing a stable market situation for industry, businessmen can plan further into the future without too many dramatic changes in policy. This situation will improve still further when common policies on industry, energy, transport etc. are finally agreed.

(d) Industry can take advantage of the grants and other forms of aid given via the European Regional Development Fund, which in time will replace aid given by the British government to the development areas.

Against these advantages, however have to be weighed the disadvantages of:

(a) The possibility of dearer food in Britain, than if we had not joined.

(b) The political and psychological effect on the population of losing a certain amount of its independence.

Questions

1 Discuss the advantages and disadvantages of international trade.
2 Newspaper headlines have suggested that North Sea oil will be Britain's saviour, in terms of balance of payments problems. Discuss this with relevance to the long and short term.
3 From the latest annual abstract of statistics, analyse the balance of payments over the last five years. Discuss possible causes which may be relevant to particular events.
4 Why does the foreign exchange rate fluctuate?

Chapter 19

Government effects on the construction industry

In the course of reading through the previous chapters, various isolated references have been made to the effects of government policies on the construction industry. This is inevitable, due to the overlapping nature of the various topics being discussed. As this point is of such fundamental importance to the levels of operation of the various sectors, it was thought best to devote a chapter purely to this topic. Where there has been previous discussion on a particular point, then only a summarised note will be made.

Government policies which are relevant here can be grouped under three headings: **Monetary;** **Fiscal**; and **Others**.

Monetary policies

The controlling of the money supply affects all sectors of the industry, for the operation of these policies is generally concerned with the level of interest rates, and the controlling of the bank's ability to lend. In times of monetary restraint, people are generally less inclined to borrow money, because of the high level of interest that will have to be paid. At the same time, high deposit account interest will encourage people to leave money in these accounts, rather than spend it.

Industrial and commercial expansion, or replacement of buildings may be cut, because to go ahead and pay excessive interest on projects may outweigh any profit or economies which might accrue, particularly when output from the business in question might have to be reduced due to a depression.

Private housing is hit especially hard by a period of high interest rates, and this is one of the main reasons for the erratic movement of the new private housing line in Fig. 7.2. A high B.R. inevitably leads to a high mortgage rate, for building societies find it necessary to increase their rates in order to offer attractive interest on their deposit accounts. High mortgage rates lead to a reduction in the demand for mortgages, for two reasons:

(a) The monthly repayments become too excessive for many people to cope with.

(b) The maximum that can be borrowed, based upon a person's income, is reduced, so that large advances can no longer be made.

This stagnation in house movement inevitably leads to less new homes being demanded.

Looking at house building from the supply side, speculative development necessarily involves the tying up of large sums of money, in the purchase of land, and in the erection of units ready for sale. A planned cash flow is essential, and if a phase of completed houses does not sell quickly, then much capital is tied up, on which high interest has to be paid. For this reason, speculative development of all types tends to be held back during high interest periods.

Monetary policy as such, does not have any direct effect on public sector works, although it may lead to an increasing of costs for the financing of contracts, which may result in certain jobs being shelved.

Fiscal policies

These do not often have a great direct effect on the industry, except possibly in two situations.

At present VAT is payable on maintenance and repair work, but not on new works. Although it is difficult to find proof of this, it would be fair to assume that a considerable amount of repair work is now being done on a d.i.y. basis in order not to pay the VAT on the labour used by a registered builder. It is also possible that when both maintenance, and new work are carried out on the same contract, some adjustments are made to include maintenance work as new work, in order to reduce the VAT payable by the client. This leads to the conclusion that maintenance work, as shown by the statistics, should be of a higher value than shown.

Prior to VAT, a tax existed on the number of employees that were employed by businesses. This was known as the Selective Employment Tax (SET), and lasted from 1966 to 1973. With this tax, manufacturing industry could claim back the tax, but service industries which included construction could not. This resulted in increased building costs, as the tax was passed on to the consumer.

Development Land Tax, 1976–1985 had the effect of making it less financially beneficial to sell land to developers. This lead to an increase in land prices, which eventually was passed on to the house buyer.

Taxation affects the industry indirectly, in that if tax rates are increased, then both private individuals and businesses have less to spend. Because the products of the industry are of a durable nature, then their replacement can always be shelved.

Other policies of government

The construction industry is very prone to what is known as the 'stop–go' policy. This is not really a single policy, but is the effect of many government and possible external actions on a particularly susceptible industry. The construction industry employs about 6 per cent of the country's labour force, which produces about 6 per cent of the GDP, which is the value of all domestic goods and services at their final market prices. In Chapter 7 it was also seen that the industry was responsible for 50 per cent of fixed capital formation. Because of the importance of the industry to the economy, the government often tries to regulate the economy by cutting back on construction activity which will inevitably lead to a slowing of the money cycle, as the multiplier takes effect. Both fiscal and monetary policies could act as a regulator, but often more direct policies affect the industry.

At certain times, government cuts back on public spending, which as was seen from Fig. 7.1, represented 50 per cent in 1978. Cutting back on spending, both on housing and service industries, has a devastating effect on the industry. These policies can come in many guises, from the reduction of budgets to certain sectors, such as major roadworks, local authorities, education, defence etc., to independent decisions on the refusal to allow the go-ahead of particular projects such as road schemes, town centre redevelopments, airports etc.

The construction industry is particularly susceptible to stop–go problems, for the following reasons:
(a) Products of this industry cannot be stockpiled, during periods of cutback, as can be done in some industries.
(b) Demand cannot be satisfied by distributing a limited number of products over the nation, due to the immobility of the product. This inevitably leads to greater problems in certain areas.
(c) A contractor often depends upon a few relatively large projects, a loss of only one or two contracts might lead to a dramatic reduction in turnover accompanied by cutback in staff.

There is often a time delay between the operation of government policies, and their effects upon the industry; this comes about for two reasons:
(a) There is a long lead time on contracts, often years, which is necessary for planning, design and tendering procedures to be completed.

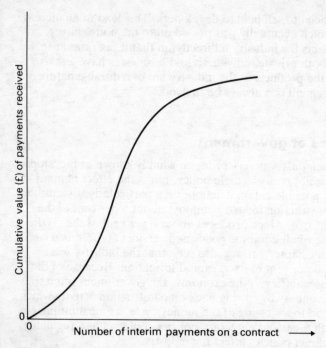

Fig. 19.1 Typical 'S' curve of cumulative contract payments

(b) The low level of activity at the start and finish of contracts,
    demonstrated by the 'S' curve of Fig. 19.1, means that as many
    contracts may only just have started when the 'brake' was applied
    by government, then these contracts will 'blossom', and hide the
    problem of depression for some months.

The above problems lead not only to a delay in the run-down of
the industry, but also to a delay in its stimulation, when this is thought
necessary.

Although the stop–go policies have been with us some time and
will probably exist for a long time to come, they do cause the industry
to be less efficient than if a steady workload could be depended upon,
for the following reasons:

(a) Not only construction companies are affected, but also materials
    manufacturers. Because they do not have a steady order level,
    they are less inclined to invest in new plant and equipment which
    might have to lie idle for much of the time. This leads to the
    situation where obsolete inefficient plant is being used, not only on
    site, but also in the factories producing the materials.

(b) There is little incentive for contractors to take on the responsibility
    of training new operatives, only to have to lay them off again.

(c) There is difficulty in encouraging workers to enter the industry,
    when there is such insecurity of employment.

(d) Specialist service functions to the industry, such as architects, surveyors, even local authority building control and planning departments may have to suffer fluctuations in staffing, as a result of these policies.

If some solution could be found whereby an even flow of work could be guaranteed, then the industry and the clients would benefit greatly. The two main political parties in Britain have differing views on the method of bringing this about.

The Labour Party would like to see a large proportion of the industry nationalised. By doing this, rationalisation would be possible, to avoid duplication of contracting establishments in a particular area. It would be possible then in theory, to control the flow of work to the government contracting departments, which could then plan, hopefully, over longer periods. The main fear that people have of this suggestion, is that because the element of competition has been destroyed, bureaucracy will prevail and cause costs to rise excessively, as is often the case with existing DLOs.

The Conservative Party has a much more subtle approach. Its idea is to lower the proportion of work which results directly from government. This party generally tries to reduce public sector budgets, and at the same time give incentives to industry, and to private individuals to encourage investment in capital projects.

In the areas of services, such as water, gas, electricity, even in some areas of further and higher education, by cutting back on central government support, the payment for these services falls more heavily on the final consumer. It can be said therefore that as these areas become more and more self-financing, then any construction work carried out for these authorities will be less and less dependent on central government.

In the area of public housing, greater home ownership is being encouraged with the permissible selling off of council houses, following the 1980 Housing Act, and again cash limits are being imposed on local authority spending in this area.

The seesaw effect which tends to occur as a result of the different parties alternating their terms of office, obviously affects the industry. Possible clients of the industry are reluctant to invest in capital projects, where unknown policies may be introduced affecting them. Again if there is uncertainty about the level of forthcoming interest rates, speculation will not occur.

This last chapter may seem somewhat pessimistic, but remember, there will always be a need for a construction industry. The choices open to it in the next few years are: Firstly, can it stabilise its workload to enable higher efficiencies and reductions of costs? Secondly, how will the industry cope with new technologies? Will the building of the future still be semi-traditional, or will construction go to the other

234

extreme, with all buildings being on a prefabricated modular basis, manufactured in one, or a few nationalised factories?

Questions

1 Discuss present government policies overall, in relation to their effects on the construction Industry.
2 Answer again question 5 from Chapter 1. Has your answer changed at all?

Glossary of economic terms

Acclerator principle: States that changes in the demand for consumer goods, cause greater changes in the demand for durable capital equipment used for their manufacture.

Agrarian Revolution: The second half of the eighteenth century, during which time a large increase took place in the efficiency of farming.

Balance of payments: This shows the summary of one country's payments to, and receipts from, other countries, during international trading, for all goods and services.

Balance of trade: Also known as the visible balance. A summary of one country's payments to, and receipts from, other countries, for dealings in actual goods.

Bilateral trade: International trading between two countries only, where each pair of countries balances its trading transactions.

Bill of Exchange: An unconditional order in writing addressed by one person to another, signed by the person giving it, requiring the person to whom it is addressed to pay on demand, or at a stated future date, a sum of money to a certain person, or to the order of that person, or to bearer.

Birth rate: The number of births, per thousand of population.

Budget: An estimate of the government's income and expenditure for the coming year, usually presented in early April.

Capital: In economic terms, means those goods used for the production of others. In financial terms it is the monetary value of real assets.

Capital gains tax: The tax payable on the realised increase in value of certain assets.

Capitalism: A political, economic system based on the making of profit by free enterprise activities.

Capital transfer tax: A tax on the transfer of wealth, both during one's lifetime, or at death. It replaces estate duty.

Clearing house: An institution where indebtedness between various organisations is settled.

Command economy: Otherwise known as a planned economy. A system where all planning is carried out by the State.

Common Market: Its formal title is the European Economic Community. Nine countries, France, West Germany, Belgium, Italy, The Netherlands, Luxembourg, Denmark, The Republic of Ireland and the United Kingdom, joined together for the elimination of obstacles to the free movement of goods, services, capital and labour.

Communism: A political and economic system, where the State formulates and implements all economic policies.

Corporation tax: A tax on company profits.

Cost benefit analysis: A technique for evaluating several alternative solutions, particularly taking into account social costs and benefits.

Cost push inflation: Inflation induced and sustained by rising production costs.

Death rate: The number of deaths per thousand of population.

Debentures: These are securities issued by companies for long-term loans, that carry fixed rates of interest.

Deflation: A reduction of the economic activity of a nation.

Demand: The amount of a commodity that will be purchased at a particular price.

Demand pull inflation: Inflation induced by higher incomes causing higher demand, i.e, too much money chasing too few goods.

Depreciation: An allowance for the reduction in the value of an asset, due to wear and tear.

Devaluation: Is the reducing of the value of one currency in terms of another.

Direct taxation: A tax that is levied on income, e.g., income tax.

Discount house: A financial institution that discounts Bills of Exchange.

Division of labour: Where workers in a production situation specialise on one particular task.

Dumping: The selling of goods abroad, cheaper than they are sold in the home market.

Durable goods: Goods which give utility over a fairly long period, e.g., furniture, motor cars, production machinery.

Elasticity: The measure of the change in either demand or supply, to a given change in price.

Entrepreneur: The organising factor in production. The risk-taking and decision-making function.

Equilibrium: A situation where economic forces are in balance.

Exchange rate: The rate at which one currency is exchanged for another.

External economies: Also known as 'economies of scale', economies of large-scale production of an industry.

Fiduciary issue: An issue of banknotes backed by government securities, rather than by gold.

Fixed costs: The costs of a firm which do not change with variation of output, in the short term.

Free economy: An economy where there is no interference by the State.

Free trade: Is international trade carried on without the imposition of any quotas or tariffs.

Gilt edged securities: Securities which carry very little risk, often restricted to government stocks.

Gross domestic product (*GDP*): The value of goods and services produced within a country, but excluding net income from abroad.

Gross national product (*GNP*): As GDP, including any net income from abroad, but excluding money earned by overseas investment in this country.

Hedging: Action taken to protect a business or asset against changes in price.

Homogeneous product: A product which is completely identical with all others.

Horizontal integration: The expansion of a firm to give it greater capacity to carry out a single activity.

Indirect taxation: Taxes on goods or services, e.g. VAT.

Industrial Revolution: The period of about 1760 to 1850 during which the factory system replaced the domestic system of manufacture.

Inflation: A situation where prices are rising:
    slowly – creeping inflation.
    fast – galloping or hyperinflation.

Infrastructure: Capital that is invested in the transportation, communication and services networks of a country.

Internal economies: Economies which a single firm can create by expanding output.

Investment: The actual production or acquisition of capital goods. In financial terms it means the purchase of shares or securities.

Issuing house: A financial institution which specialises in raising capital for companies by organising new issues of shares.

Jobbers: The actual dealers in securities, at the London stock exchange. They deal only with brokers and not with the general public.

Joint stock company: Also known as a limited company. A business organisation where the capital is divided into small parcels, known as shares, or blocks of stock. The shareholders enjoy the advantage of limited liability.

Laissez-faire: An economic political doctrine that believes State intervention in industry should be kept to a minimum.

Limited liability: Usually applied to shareholders of a limited company, where their liability is limited to the fully paid up value of the shares they hold.

Liquidity: The ease with which assets can be turned into money.

M_1: Is known as the narrow definition of money, in that it includes only the most liquid assets. It includes cash or money in bank current accounts or other assets or securities immediately convertible to cash without notice having to be given.

M_3: Is known as the wider definition of money. It includes M_1 plus all assets that are not immediately convertible to money, i.e. those that normally earn interest such as deposit accounts at banks and buildings societies.

Market price: The price determined by supply and demand forces, in the short term.

Minimum lending rate (MLR): Until 1972, known as the bank rate. It is the rate at which the Bank of England will act as lender of last resort to the discount market. In practice it is the rate at which it will discount eligible bills.

Mixed economy: An economy that is balanced between a free and planned economy.

Money: A commodity that is acceptable to all parties likely to use it as a medium of exchange.

Monopoly: A situation where a commodity, for which there is no substitute, can only be obtained from one supplier.

Multilateral trade: International trade between many countries, where individual pairs of trading nations do not have to balance payments.

Multiplier: A multiplying constant which indicates the level of output or income derived from the investment of a certain amount of capital.

Normal price: The long-term price, where supply is adjusted to demand.

Oligopoly: A situation where there are few suppliers of a commodity.

Oligopsony: A situation where there are few buyers of a commodity.

Opportunity cost: The cost, to the individual, firm, nation or whatever, of foregone alternatives that can not now be acquired, due to a decision to carry out a specific line of action.

Optimum population: The population that when combined with other factors of production, will result in the maximum output per worker.

Planned economy: See command economy.

Progressive tax: A system of taxation, where the rate of tax increases as the income, or whatever is to be taxed, increases.

Propensity to consume: The keenness with which a person or nation will consume goods.

Propensity to save: The keenness with which a person or nation will save.

Public sector borrowing requirement (*PSBR*): The expected difference between government expenditure, and government income.

Quota: Concerning international trade, it is the fixing of a maximum number of units, or maximum total value of a good, to be allowed into the country over a period of time.

Real income: The value of income based upon the goods and services it will buy.

Regressive tax: A tax which is not related to a person's ability to pay it. It is a tax which falls heavily on the lower paid.

Regulator: The term applied to changing of policies and taxes, to fit a given economic situation.

Shadow prices: Calculated prices or values that cannot be obtained from a market situation. Often used in cost benefit analysis.

Single use goods: These are non-durable goods such as food, fuel and tobacco.

Stock exchange: A market for dealing in stocks and shares, in which business can only be transacted by members.

Subsidy: A government grant to industry, or for any particular goods or service.

Substitute: Two goods could be said to be substitutes, if a rise in price of one, followed by a fall in demand directly causes a rise in demand for the other.

Supply: The quantity of a commodity that will come onto the market at a particular price, at a particular time.

Tariff: A duty or tax, imposed on imports.

Trade cycle: The regular fluctuations of business activity.

Treasury bills: These are issued by the government and are a means of obtaining short-term finance, usually three months, for the government.

Utility: The utility of a good can be said to be the degree of satisfaction a person can obtain from owning it.

Value: A good's ability to be changed for other goods.

Value added tax (*VAT*): A general tax added at each stage of production or exchange, on goods and services, as defined by the tax, from primary industry right through to consumption.

Variable cost: Costs which vary directly with output.

Vertical integration: Combination of firms, so that they carry out all stages of production of a commodity, from primary, through secondary processes.

Wants: Desires for commodities or services.

Weighting: A system of giving greater emphasis to certain items in a list used for compiling an index.

Yield: The relationship between the current return and current value of an investment or security.

Index